Jesus: His Story

The Four Gospels as One Story by

David Brooke Fenwick

Port Hole Publishing

Florence, Oregon and Polson, Montana

Cover and Book Layout and Design by Port Hole Publishing
Cover Image: iStock.com/eyecrave

ISBN-13: 978-1-943119-10-3
ISBN-10: 1-943119-10-4

Published by:
Port Hole Publishing
179 Laurel St. - Suite D
Florence, Oregon 97439
Ph: 541-999-5725

Foreword

By Michael MacIntosh
Founder Horizon Christian Fellowship, San Diego, CA

The Rev. David Fenwick has created a work which I commend to people everywhere.

Jesus: His Story is capable of changing your life and the lives of those whom you love.

Most people (and strangely enough that includes some Christians) need to know Jesus personally. He is a joy to walk with and talk with every day of our lives. Jesus becomes very close and comfortable as we read from the beginning to the end of His life here on earth.

Rev. Fenwick has given us a jewel to follow Jesus through the eyes of the four men who stood "afar off at the Cross," went through storms with him, saw boys and girls loved and the elderly provided for and healed. Jesus took time for everyone, everywhere and every time. These men - Matthew, Mark, Luke and John - wept with Jesus, laughed with Jesus, prayed with Jesus.

In reading their accounts as Rev. Fenwick has meticulously woven the "Gospels" into one seamless lifespan of Jesus, we experience our Lord in a new way.

Mike MacIntosh

Publisher's Foreword
How this Book Came to Be Written

Jesus: His Story is a paraphrase of the complete biblical account of the life and teachings of Jesus, compiled by the Rev. David Brooke Fenwick. He graduated with a B.A. and M.Ed. from Seattle Pacific University and served as a pastor and teacher for over 45 years. During about 40 of those years, he devoted considerable time to a careful study and integration of the Four Gospels: Matthew, Mark, Luke and John, along with a few brief quotes from other books of the Bible. [Notes in brackets offer additional related information.]

The chief sources that contributed to the paraphrase are: *The New Living Translation* (NLT), *The New International Version* (NIV) and *The New Englishman's Greek Concordance.*

Jesus: His Story is not extensively copied word for word from any of those sources, but it does express the clear meaning of the whole scriptural account of the life and teachings of Jesus. It is written in the everyday English commonly spoken in the United States.

After serving four years as a pastor and Christian college teacher in the Portland, Oregon area, Rev. Fenwick moved to Southern California where he invested nearly 40 years of his ministry in the Los Angeles Mexican American districts of Boyle Heights and East Los Angeles. While ministering in L. A., he served over 40 years as the principal and a middle school teacher in the *East L. A. Light and Life Christian School.* During that time, he also founded an English-speaking Free Methodist Church serving Latinos, known as *Light and Life Chapel.* Since he was fluent in Spanish, the General Missionary Board of the Free Methodist Church of North America appointed him to serve as Mission Superintendent over the Latino churches in Southern California, Southern Arizona, and three states in Northern Mexico.

Jesus: His Story is Rev. Fenwick's *magnum opus*, a life's work of amazing dedication and perseverance. The scholarship and insights brought to this work make it a useful tool for students of the Bible of every level of expertise and background.

It is our honor to publish this important work, and we trust that readers everywhere will be blessed by the author's diligent commitment to the Word of God.

Ellen Traylor

Publisher - Port Hole Publishing

Dedication

To my grandchildren,
Eden Grace Fenwick and Zion David Fenwick,
together with all who have attended my Bible studies.
May they always be guided by the
One who is the *Light of the World*.

Compiler's Preface

Jesus is a real person who lived in Earth's history, yet he is also alive forevermore. He is now represented on earth by means of the Holy Spirit. Four authors (Matthew, Mark, Luke and John) left careful accounts of Jesus that became part of the New Testament. Matthew and John were personal witnesses and followers of Jesus. It is very likely that Mark received much of his information from association with Peter, a disciple of Jesus. Luke, a physician, made his own careful investigation. The purpose of this paraphrased account, *Jesus: His Story*, is to present the whole story of the life and teachings of Jesus, *one time through, in everyday contemporary English, with no omissions or needless repetitions.*

Matthew, a tax collector and one of Jesus' followers, recorded Jesus' ancestry from Abraham to Joseph, Jesus' legal father. (Matt 1:1-17) Mark, author of the second Gospel and a part-time fellow traveler with the Apostle Paul. (Acts 12:25), lived in Rome, where he was likely able to record Peter's memories as a follower of Jesus. Luke was a physician near the time of Christ's earthly life. He interviewed many who knew Jesus and traveled with him. This included Mary, the mother of Jesus. (Luke 1:3) She likely told Luke about the amazing birth of Jesus. Luke also recorded Mary's ancestors back to Adam, the first man created by God. (Luke 3:23-38) Peter, James, and his brother John, were three followers who stayed consistently close to Jesus. It seems Jesus called these three to come apart with him more often than any of his other followers. It is not surprising, then, that John has given us the most intimate record of the life and teachings of Jesus Christ.

Altogether, there were twelve followers known as disciples (or students) of Jesus. Most of these went on to be founders and Apostles of the early Christian Church.

I hope that this integration of the four gospels into one continuous story will help you appreciate the scope of Jesus' life and ministry, and that it may clarify areas of the Scriptures that you have wondered about.

God Bless You!

David Fenwick

My love and prayers for Paul and Delia (My friends!)

David Brooke Fenwick

Note: There is a numbered Index of Section Titles at the end of this book for easy reference. The author's notes will be bracketed throughout the text.

Jesus: His Story

1. Luke Verifies the Careful Investigation behind His Account - Luke 1:1-4

Luke begins his account by informing us that several different writers have provided a record of the events relating to the life and teachings of Jesus, who is also called the *Messiah* in Hebrew, or the *Christ* in Greek. "With this in mind, I, Luke, carefully made my own investigation. With the information that I uncovered, I am able to provide an orderly report to Theophilus [Friend of God]. He is a scholar and my personal friend. I desire to help him become absolutely certain that the accounts of Jesus that were passed on to me (Luke) by word of mouth are indeed true."

2. John Introduces Jesus as the Living Word - John 1:1-18

From the very beginning God has spoken his Living Word. That Word is God's eternal Messenger. He came into our world in the form of the Person we know as the Lord Jesus Christ. He was with God from the very beginning and he made everything that exists. He is the source of all life and is the light of the whole human race. All the darkness of our world could never shut out that light.

A man named John came to tell about that light so that everyone who heard about it could believe that the true light is actually a Person who came into our world from above. In fact, from the very beginning he was in the world that he had made. However, no one recognized who he really was. Most of his own people didn't even welcome him. But those who did receive him and believe in him were given the right to become God's very own children. God decided to make them his own sons and daughters by means of their spiritual rebirth.

The Living Word became human flesh and blood, and he actually lived among us. Because of this, we are now able to see the light of God's justice, truth and love shining out from the Son, who came from God. Yes, God really is his Father!

From the abundance of God's revelation in the Word, we are all able to receive his loving presence. No one has actually seen God. However, his only son, Jesus, lives in the very closest imaginable relationship with God, the Father. Therefore, Jesus is qualified to make God known to the whole world.

3. Matthew Reports the Genealogy of Jesus through Joseph – Source: Matthew 1:1-17

4. Luke Gives the Human Lineage of Jesus Starting at Abraham – Source: Luke 3:23-38

Luke may have written the genealogy of Mary, the mother of Jesus. Since Joseph and Mary were both of Hebrew linage, there certainly would be both likenesses and differences in their family ancestry.

5. An Angel Tells Zechariah that He Will Have an Important Son – Luke 1:5-25

Zechariah was a priest in Israel during a time when the Roman Empire controlled much of the civilized world. However, the Romans had allowed King Herod to rule over Judea, Samaria, Galilee, and much of Syria, as well as Perea. The ancient Hebrew people were ancestors of the Jewish people who now live in modern Israel. Zechariah and his wife, Elizabeth, were both descendants of Aaron who had been the first Jewish priest. Zechariah and Elizabeth were righteous in God's sight. They were blameless when it came to faithfully keeping all the laws God gave to Moses. However, Elizabeth was not able to become pregnant because she was too old to have a child. Due to the culture of that time, Elizabeth felt ashamed and cursed because of her inability to produce offspring.

During a time when Zechariah's priestly group was on duty in the Temple at Jerusalem, it was his turn to go in and burn incense. All the worshipers were praying outside of the Temple area that was reserved for the priests.

Zechariah was standing at the right side of the altar of incense when an angel of the Lord suddenly appeared. Zechariah became terribly frightened. However, the angel said, "You don't need to be afraid, because God has heard your prayer. Elizabeth is finally going to have a son. You are to name him John. Your shame will be changed into great joy. Many others will also join in celebrating his birth. He will be great in the Lord's eyes. But you must vow never to give him wine or any other drink that is fermented. Even before he is born he will be filled with the Holy Spirit, who will help him carry out the work God has given him to do. He will be able to lead many people in Israel to dedicate themselves to the Lord, their God. He will also walk with the Lord in the same kind of spirit that was upon the prophet Elijah. He will have special ability to make peace between parents and children. God will help him lead disobedient people to receive the kind of wisdom that produces righteous living. Then people will be prepared to welcome the Lord's arrival."

After hearing the angel's message, Zechariah asked, "How can I be sure that all these things will really happen? After all, I'm an old man and my wife is also up in years."

The angel responded, "Don't you realize who I am? I'm Gabriel, the angel who stands in the very presence of God. I was ordered to give you this good news that I have just delivered. Now because you didn't believe me, you will be unable to speak until the right time, when everything I have told you comes true."

While all this was happening in the Temple, those outside were wondering why Zechariah had stayed inside for so long. Finally, Zechariah came out, but when he did, he was making signs with his hands because he was unable to speak to them. The people understood that he must have seen a vision.

After Zechariah completed his time of service in the Temple, he returned home. And soon after her husband came home, Elizabeth became pregnant. Of course, she was filled with great joy because of the miracle of birth she was experiencing. However, she stayed out of the public eye for five months. But she kept on praising the Lord for his mercy that allowed her to experience the miracle of birth, even in her old age. She said, "All this has happened only because, in his mercy, the Lord has done it for me. Even now that I'm old, the Lord has removed my disgrace among all those who knew that I was unable to have any children."

6. Gabriel Tells Mary that She Will Give Birth to the Messiah - Luke 1:26-38

When Elizabeth was six months pregnant, God sent the Angel Gabriel to the town of Nazareth located in Galilee in northern Israel. And there Gabriel appeared to a young virgin named Mary who was already promised to a carpenter named Joseph. He was a descendant of David who had ruled as king over Israel nearly a thousand years earlier. Some of God's prophets had already predicted that the Messiah would be a descendant of King David. [He would also be known as the *Anointed One*.]

When Gabriel came to Mary, he said, "I bring you greetings and I assure you that the Lord is with you and he has highly favored you."

Mary was shocked! She wondered, *What does all this mean? What am I about to experience? What is happening to me?*

However, Gabriel reassured her, "Do not be afraid, Mary. God plans to greatly honor you. You're going to conceive a child in your womb. You'll give birth to a son, and you will name him Jesus." [Jehovah is Savior. Translated from the Hebrew language, this means The Lord Yahweh, or "The One known as 'I AM' is Savior."] The angel then added this: "He will be great and will, in fact, be the Son of the Most High God. He will be your son, Mary, but He will also be the One and only Son of God. He will inherit the throne of his ancestor, David, and will rule over Jacob's offspring forever."

"How can this come about, since I am a virgin?" Mary asked.

The angel answered, "The Holy Spirit will be upon you, and the power of the Most High God will hover over you. You will give birth to a child who is holy and he will even be called the Son of God. At this time, your relative Elizabeth is also experiencing a miracle. In her old age, she who couldn't conceive is already six months pregnant. You can be absolutely sure of this: God never fails to keep every promise he makes!"

Mary responded, "I am dedicated to serve the Lord with my whole heart! May everything you have declared really happen, just as you have announced." Then the angel departed.

7. Mary Goes to Visit Elizabeth before Their Sons Are Born - Luke 1:39-45

Then Mary prepared herself and quickly traveled south toward a town in the hills of Judea. There she was welcomed into the home of Zechariah and Elizabeth. The baby in Elizabeth's womb jumped just as Mary was greeting them. Immediately, Elizabeth was filled with the Holy Spirit and loudly shouted, "Mary, you are truly blessed among all women, and the child you are about to bear will also be greatly blessed! But why am I so privileged? And why should my Lord's mother come to visit me? Just when your greeting reached my ears, my baby jumped for joy in my womb! Happy is the woman who has trusted that the Lord will surely fulfill every promise he gave to her!"

8. Mary Rejoices and Glorifies the Lord - Luke 1:46-56

Then Mary praised and honored the Lord with these words:

> *With my whole being I praise and honor the Lord*
> *and my spirit is full of joy, when I think of*
> *what my God and Savior has promised.*
> *He has paid attention to his humble servant.*
> *Now people in all coming generations*
> *will call me blessed,*
> *For God Almighty has done*
> *great and amazing things for me.*
> *Holy is the name of the Lord!*
> *His undeserved kindness reaches everyone*
> *who reverences him,*
> *from one generation to the next.*
> *He has accomplished great things*
> *with his powerful arm;*
> *He has sent away all who have*
> *proudly depended entirely on*
> *their own wisdom and strength.*
> *He has dethroned proud rulers,*
> *but exalted those who are humble.*
> *He has satisfied the hungry with good things,*
> *but left the self-sufficient empty-handed.*
> *He has faithfully provided for his servant, Israel,*
> *by often giving His descendants*
> *better than they deserved.*
> *Through all ages He has remembered*
> *Abraham's descendants, exactly as*
> *He promised to Israel's ancestors.*

Mary visited with Elizabeth for nearly three months before she returned home.

9. John the Baptizer is born - Luke 1:57-66

When the time arrived for Elizabeth to have her baby, it was a boy. Her relatives and neighbors all realized that the Lord had shown mercy to her in her old age. Everyone celebrated with her and shared her joy.

As required by the laws of Moses, when he was eight days old, they went to have him circumcised. At that time, they planned to name him Zechariah after his father. However, Elizabeth spoke up and objected. "No!" she said. "His name will be John."

But those present said to her, "You don't have any relatives with that name, do you?"

So, they used signs to talk to Zechariah, who still could not speak, nor hear. They wanted to know what name he would like to give to the boy. Then he asked for a tablet to write down the name. Everyone present was amazed when he wrote down, "He will be called John."

Just as soon as he did this, his ability to speak was immediately restored and he started praising God. His neighbors and many people all around the Judean hill country were amazed at the unusual news about baby John's birth. It was the talk of the whole area. Everyone was speculating, "What will this child become? Certainly, the Lord has a hand in this!"

10. Zechariah Offers Words of Prophetic Praise - Luke 1:67-79

Then little John's father was filled with the Holy Spirit. And Zechariah spoke the following words of prophecy:

Praise the Lord God of Israel
for coming to his people to redeem them.
Salvation more powerful than a bull's horn
has arrived in the house of God's servant David.
Even as he promised through the holy seers of long
ago, we will surely be saved from our enemies and
from all who hate us.
God will remember his holy promise and
will show mercy to our ancestors.
He made a covenant with Abraham
to deliver us from our enemies.

14

God will help us to boldly
and fearlessly serve him,
In godliness and purity,
through all our lifetime.
And John, my little boy, you'll be called a prophet
of God Most High.
You will go before the Lord
to pave the way for him.
You will tell the people that
they can be forgiven of their sins,
and they will experience salvation.
The tender forgiving-kindness of God
will shine upon us like
the rising sun from heaven.
It will shine upon people living in spiritual darkness
and in death's shadow,
Guiding us into the path of God's peace.

11. John the Baptizer Grows Strong in Spirit - Luke 1:80

When John was growing up as a child, his spirit grew strong and he withdrew into a wilderness area. He lived there in the desert until he was ready to carry out his public ministry to the people of Israel.

12. An Angel Explains the Child's Conception to Joseph - Matthew 1:18-25

In harmony with the customs of their time, Joseph and Mary had formally pledged to get married. However, they remained faithful to God and did not enter into marital relationships. But when Joseph discovered that Mary was pregnant, of course he was certain that he was not the father. So, he planned to do what was proper under Mosaic Law. He was about to privately cancel their marriage agreement.

But even as he was considering this, he had a dream in which an angel appeared to him and said, "Joseph, son of David, you don't need to fear to live with Mary as your wife. The Holy Spirit is the One who conceived the child developing in her. When her son is born, you must name him Jesus. He will save from their sins, everyone who belongs to him by faith." [Jesus means the Lord saves.]

All these events are a fulfillment of what God said more than 600 years previously through the prophet Isaiah: "The Lord himself will give you the sign you want. Just imagine this! A single, young woman will become pregnant, while remaining sexually pure. She will have a son who will reveal God to the world. People with faith will understand that God is near. In fact, one of his names will be Immanuel." [Immanuel means God is with us.]

After Joseph woke up, he followed the angel's instructions. He took Mary home to be his wife. He also abstained from sexual relations until after her son was born.

13. Mary Gives Birth to Jesus and Places Him in a Manger - Luke 2:1-7

At that time, Caesar Augustus served as emperor of the Roman Empire. He issued a decree that everyone must register for tax purposes. Quirinius was governor over Syria, including the land of Israel. Therefore, all the people traveled to their birth-town. [That is, they went to their inherited ancestral town to be registered.]

Joseph was a descendant of King David. Nearly a thousand years earlier, Bethlehem had been King David's birth town. Due to the decree from Rome, Joseph decided he must take Mary with him from his home in Nazareth—in the region of Galilee—and travel south to Bethlehem. As a result, Bethlehem was completely flooded with all the families who were descendants of King David. That was why Joseph couldn't find a single available room anywhere in Bethlehem. Finally, Joseph and Mary had to make do with a place given to farm animals. So it was, that while they were there, Mary gave birth to her first baby. And Joseph named him Jesus, just as the angel had earlier instructed him to do in his dream.

14. Angels Announce the Birth of the Savior to Shepherds - Luke 2:8-20

In the area near Bethlehem, some shepherds were staying in the nearby fields. Even at nighttime they were watching over their flocks. Suddenly, an angel of the Lord appeared to them. The angel was surrounded by the shining presence of the Lord. The shepherds were completely terrified! But the angel assured them, "Don't be afraid! I'm bringing you amazing news. When all the people hear about it, they'll be overwhelmed with joy. Here's that good news: Just now, in David's town of Bethlehem, the Lord your Savior has been born. He is the long-promised Messiah—God's Anointed One. Here's how you will know you have found the right place: Look for a baby wrapped up tightly and lying in a manger."

Immediately, a huge choir of heavenly beings appeared to the shepherds. They were praising God with these words:

> *Give praise and honor to God,*
> *who dwells in the highest heaven,*
> *and let peace rest on all God's favored people*
> *who dwell on earth.*

As soon as the angels had gone back into heaven, the shepherds said excitedly to each other, "Let's go right now to Bethlehem and see for ourselves this amazing thing that the Lord has told us."

They hurried away and sure enough, they did find the manger with the baby lying in it, just as the angel had said. Joseph and Mary were right there with the baby. After they had witnessed all of this, of course they couldn't keep it to themselves. They told everybody they could find all about the angels who announced the birth of the Messiah and about the amazing little baby they found lying in a manger. It was exactly as they had been told. Everyone was impressed by the story and the excitement of the shepherds. They had obviously experienced an unforgettable miracle.

Mary kept replaying over and over in her mind and heart the amazing sequence of events that had happened to her. She knew God had given her an unforgettable treasure. And the more she thought about it, the more meaningful it all became.

15. Jesus Is Circumcised - Luke 2:21

Eight days after the birth of Jesus, according to the Laws of Moses, it was the proper time to circumcise him. Then Joseph named him Jesus, the name given by the angel before he was even conceived.

16. At His Presentation, Simeon and Anna Praise God for Jesus - Luke 2:22-38

When Jesus was eight days old, according to the Law of Moses, it was the correct time for Joseph and Mary to present him to the Lord at the Temple in Jerusalem:

Every firstborn male is to be consecrated to the Lord. (Exodus 13:2, 12) They must also offer a pair of doves or two young pigeons. (Leviticus 12:8)

When Joseph and Mary brought Jesus into the Temple, there was a dedicated righteous man there named Simeon, who believed the prophecies about the coming Messiah. In fact, the Holy Spirit had revealed to him that he would actually see the Messiah with his own eyes before he died. The Holy Spirit led him into the temple courts, just as Joseph and Mary were bringing Baby Jesus to dedicate him, as the Law required. When Simeon saw Jesus, he put him in his arms and spoke these words of praise to God:

Sovereign Lord, you may now dismiss your servant in peace,
for in fulfillment of your promise to me
my eyes have seen the One you have chosen
to bring salvation to all nations,
and the light of truth to the whole world,
while also honoring your people Israel.

Joseph and Mary were amazed at what Simeon said about their child. Then Simeon blessed them both and added these words to Mary: "Your child will become a reason why many in Israel will either be praised or dishonored. Some will actually believe they have found a good reason for rejecting him. However, what they think about him will often show more about their own hearts. Mary, your own soul will also be pierced because of your great love for him."

At the same time, there was also a prophetess at the Temple. Her name was Anna. She was the daughter of Penuel from the tribe of Asher. She had been married for seven years, after which she became a widow until she was eighty-four. She was constantly in the temple fasting and praying, both day and night. Coming up to Mary and Joseph and little Jesus, she praised God and talked about their child to all those who were waiting for the Messiah to redeem Jerusalem.

17. The Wise Men (Magi) Travel to Worship the Newborn King - Matt 2:1-12

Some time had passed after Jesus was born in Bethlehem in the region of Judea when Magi, who were also known as Wise Men, came to Jerusalem from the East. They asked around, "Where can we find the newborn king of the Jews? We identified his star when it appeared in the sky, so we have come to worship him."

King Herod was greatly disturbed when he heard that a competitor to his throne might have been born. So, he called together the well-known priests and teachers of the Law. He believed they would surely be able to interpret the prophecies about the promised Messiah. They told him, "He is to be born in Bethlehem, in the region of Judea. Here's what the prophets have written:

O Bethlehem, you may be a little village in Judah, but you are certainly not the least place among all the rulers of Judah; because from you will come a ruler. He will be like a shepherd to my people Israel. (Micah 5:2,4)

After King Herod had heard this prophecy, he met privately with the Wise Men. They told him the exact time when they first saw the star. Then he told them, "You must go to Bethlehem and carefully search for this child. As soon as you find him, report back to me so I can also worship him."

As soon as they heard from the king, they started on toward Bethlehem. The same star they had seen when it first appeared moved ahead of them until it stopped right over the place where the child now was. When they saw this, they became excited and filled with joy.

When they entered the house where Baby Jesus and his mother had been staying, they bowed down and worshiped him. Then they presented him with gifts—proper and expensive gifts fit for a king:

Gold, frankincense [burning incense was an appropriate way to worship God], and myrrh [which was used for embalming, as this child would offer his life for the sins of the world. The number of gifts may suggest there were three Wise Men. However, there may have been more than three.]

In order to avoid King Herod's plot, the Magi were warned in a dream not to go back to Herod, so they returned home by a different route.

18. Mary and Joseph Escape with Jesus to Egypt - Matt 2:13-18

After the Wise Men left, Joseph had a dream in which an angel of the Lord appeared to him. The angel told him, "Take Mary and the child and quickly escape to Egypt. Stay there until I tell you it is safe to come back. King Herod will try to find the child, Jesus. He wants to kill him in order to defend his own position as King.

So, Joseph, Mary and little Jesus all left at night to travel toward Egypt, and they stayed there until King Herod died. This fulfilled what the Holy Spirit had inspired the prophet Hosea to say:

I called my son from Egypt. (Hosea 11:1)

When Herod discovered that the Wise Men had gone behind his back, he became violently angry and gave the order to kill all the little boys two years old and younger who lived in the vicinity of Bethlehem. This fulfilled the prophecy of Jeremiah:

> *A cry will be heard in Ramah—*
> *deep distress and bitter sobbing,*
> *Rachel cries for her children,*
> *refusing to be consoled—*
> *for they have been slaughtered.*
> *(Jeremiah 31:15)*

19. Mary and Joseph Return to Establish a Home in Nazareth - Matt 2:19-23 and Luke 2:39

When King Herod died, and while Joseph's family was still in Egypt, an angel of the Lord appeared to Joseph in a dream saying, "Arise now. Take Mary and the child, Jesus, back to Israel. It is now safe because Herod is dead."

After having fulfilled all the rituals required by the Law, Joseph obeyed the angel and took his family back toward Israel. But he found out that Herod's son, Archelaus, had replaced his father as king in Judea. And when he was warned in another dream, Joseph took his family farther north to the area of Galilee. They decided to settle there in Nazareth—their own hometown.

That is how Isaiah's prophecy came to be fulfilled:

He will be called a Nazarene. (Isaiah 11:1)

20. Jesus Develops as a Well-Rounded Child - Luke 2:40

The boy, Jesus, was growing up as a healthy, strong young man filled with wisdom, and God's just and loving power was upon him.

21. Young Jesus Attends a Passover Celebration in Jerusalem - Luke 2:41-50

Each year Joseph and Mary carried out the Jewish tradition of going to Jerusalem to take part in the Passover Festival. When Jesus reached the age of twelve—as was the custom—they took Jesus with them on this pilgrimage. When it was all over, they joined the caravan of people heading home, but unknown to them, Jesus had stayed behind in Jerusalem.

Meanwhile, Mary and Joseph had traveled a full day before they discovered he was not with their friends and relatives. Of course, they immediately went back to look for Jesus. And after three days of searching, they found him in the courts of the Temple where he was sitting with the respected Jewish teachers. He was listening to them and asking them questions. Often, the highly respected Jewish teachers used that method when they wanted to bring out a better understanding of inspired truth. Everyone who took part or looked on was amazed.

Mary interrupted and asked him, "Son, how could you treat us this way? Your father and I were terribly worried. We have been looking everywhere for you."

Then Jesus asked her, "Why did you need to do that, Mother? Didn't you realize I would be in my Father's house?" Yet they couldn't understand all the implications of what Jesus had just said to them.

22. Jesus Submits to His Parents as He Grows into Manhood - Luke 2:5

Then Jesus went home to Nazareth with Joseph and Mary, and remained obedient to them. But to Mary, these memories were an unforgettable treasure. Meanwhile Jesus continued to grow mentally, physically, spiritually, and socially.

23. John Begins His Ministry of Repentance and Baptism - Matt 3:1-12; Mark 1:1-8; Luke 3:1-18

The following provides background to the story about Jesus, the Messiah and Son of God. It was the fifteenth year in the reign of the Roman Emperor, Tiberius Caesar, the same time Pontius Pilate served as governor of Judea. Meanwhile, Herod and his brother, Philip, shared subordinate rule over Iturea and Traconitis, while Lysanias held a similar position over Abilene. During that same period, the high priests were Annas and Caiaphas. It was then, while living in the desert, that John, the son of Zechariah, began to hear from God.

About that time, John the Baptizer began preaching out in the wilderness of Judea. His message stressed the need for everyone to be baptized as a sign of repentance and forgiveness of sins. Here is what John commanded: "All of you must repent. And you must ask God to forgive your sins, because the kingdom of heaven is about to be revealed. I, John, am the one Isaiah was talking about when he said:

I will prepare your way
by sending my messenger ahead of you.
A voice out in the wilderness will shout,
'Prepare the way for the Lord.
Straighten out the path for him.

All valleys will be filled up,
all the hills and mountains will become plains.
The crooked roads will be straightened,
and the bumpy roads will be smoothed.
And everyone will witness God's great salvation.
(Isaiah 40:3-5)

Everyone in and around Jerusalem and in the province of Judea went out into the wilderness to hear John's message. They confessed their sins and were baptized by John in the Jordan River. He wore the kind of clothing that was customary among the prophets of old. He dressed in camel skins with a leather belt around his waist. He lived off the desert land by eating locusts and wild honey.

However, John noticed that among those coming to hear him, there were many well knows religious leaders who represented the religious elite. Some were legalists, known as Pharisees. Others were worldly-wise, liberal Sadducees. When they came to where he was baptizing, he rebuked them saying, "You brood of snakes, who told you to hurry out here to escape the wrath of God that will soon come? If you're so serious about finding God, then turn from your proud self-sufficiency. Trust God to change you. Don't be so foolish as to think that just because you're all descendants of Abraham, you have it made. Why, God could even turn these desert stones into children of Abraham! God's ax is ready to strike at the very roots of the tree that represents your life. And every single tree that does not produce good fruit will be cut down and destroyed by fire."

"Then what should we do?" the crowd asked.

"Anybody who has two shirts," John answered, "should share a shirt with somebody who doesn't have even one shirt. And in the same way, if you have some food, you should share it with those who are hungry."

Even cheating tax collectors also came to be baptized. "What should we do, teacher?" They asked.

John told them, "Don't try to collect more than is required, in order to keep more for yourselves."

Then some soldiers also came and asked John, "What should we do?"

"Don't make people bribe you, so you'll go easy on them. And be satisfied with what you're paid."

All the crowds coming to hear John were excited about the possibility that he might actually be the long-awaited Messiah. However, John told them plainly, "Someone else is about to come. My ministry will soon be over. He is so much greater than me, that I'm not even worthy to carry his sandals. I'm merely baptizing you with water, but he will baptize you with the Holy Spirit and fire. He carries a tool that workers use to separate the valuable wheat from the useless plant scraps. He will clear the useless stuff from the floor of the barn, then burn it in a fire that can never be put out."

John also said many other things as he preached to the crowds about the good news that the Messiah's coming was at hand.

24. John Baptizes Jesus - Matt 3:14-16; Mark 1:9-10; Luke 3:21-23; John 1:15

Multitudes were coming to John to be baptized. Then Jesus also came to John from his hometown of Nazareth in Galilee. He came to be baptized by John in the Jordan River.

However, John tried to get Jesus to reconsider by replying, "I'm the one who should be baptized by you, so why are you coming to me?"

Jesus told him, "We must do everything the Law requires. So why should we wait? Let us go ahead and do it right now." John agreed it was the right thing to do.

During his baptism, Jesus was praying as he came up out of the water. At that moment, he saw heaven open up like a curtain. Then the Holy Spirit descended on him in a bodily form—as a dove—settling on him. A voice from heaven spoke: "You are my greatly loved Son and I am very pleased with you."

25. Jesus Is Led to the Desert to Be Tempted - Matt 4:1-11, Mark 1:12-13, Luke 4:1-13

When Jesus was ready to begin his public ministry, he was about thirty years old. Filled with the Holy Spirit, he left the area by the Jordan River and immediately the Spirit led him out into the wilderness where he was tempted by the Devil.

Jesus was out there with the wild animals, and after he had been fasting forty days and nights, he became very hungry. Then the Devil tried every way he could to tempt Jesus. First, he said, "If you really are the Son of God, prove your power and make these desert stones turn into bread, so you won't starve."

But Jesus answered, "The Scripture says: 'It takes more than bread in order to really live. Spiritual life is nourished by every word that God speaks.'" (Deuteronomy 8:3)

Then the Devil took Jesus into the holy city of Jerusalem and had him stand high up on the Temple. "If you're really God's Son, then jump off," he said. "After all, doesn't the Bible say, 'God will order his angels to protect you by holding you up in their hands, so you won't even hurt your foot on a single stone?'" (Psalm 91:11-12)

Again, Jesus answered back, "It is also written, 'You must not test the Lord your God.'" (Deuteronomy 6:16)

Finally, the Devil took Jesus to the top of a very high mountain where he was able to instantly show him all the rulers of the world along with their kingdoms. "Let's make a deal," the Devil said, "if you'll just bow down once and worship me, everything you see will be yours."

But Jesus rebuked the Devil, "Get out of my sight, Satan! For God's Word says, 'You must worship the Lord your God and serve only him.'" (Deuteronomy 6:13)

That brought an end to these temptations from the Devil until his next opportunity. Then heavenly angels came to Jesus. They served him and provided for his earthly needs.

26. John the Baptizer Tells the Jewish Leaders Who He Is
- John 1:19-28

Some of the Jewish leaders in Jerusalem sent priests and experts in God's Law to ask John who he really was. John told them clearly, "I am not the promised Messiah."

They replied, "Then who are you? Could you possibly be Elijah, the prophet, returned from the dead?"

John answered, "Of course I'm not!"

Finally, they asked, "Tell us then, who are you? What do you have to say for yourself?"

Then John told them using the prophet Isaiah's words. "I am a messenger calling from the desert, 'Open up a clear passageway for the Lord to come through.'" (Isaiah 40:3)

However, some Pharisees who strictly kept the Law of Moses had been sent to question John. So, they asked, "If you're not the Messiah, nor Elijah, nor the promised Prophet, who then gives you authority to baptize?"

John answered, "I'm baptizing only with water, but you don't realize there is One standing here among you that you haven't yet recognized. He will come after I've completed my ministry. And I am not even worthy to untie his sandal straps."

All this happened on the other side of the Jordan River where John was baptizing near Bethany.

27. John Says, "Jesus Is God's Son Who Cleanses from Sin" - John 1:29-34

The day after the Jewish leaders questioned John, he saw Jesus approaching and declared, "Look! There is the Lamb of God, who will take away the world's sin. This is the One I was talking about when I said, 'The man who is to follow me has already passed me up, because he was here before I was.' I actually didn't know him. However, the reason I started baptizing with water was to introduce him to the people of Israel."

Then John told what he had actually witnessed: "I saw the Spirit of God descending from the sky. It seemed exactly like a dove coming down and resting on him. I actually did not know who he was, but the One who sent me to baptize in water informed me, 'When you see the Spirit of God come down and stay there, that's the man who is qualified to baptize with the Holy Spirit.' I saw this with my own eyes and I'm positive this was God's Son—his Chosen Messiah!"

28. Jesus Calls His First Followers - Matt 4:18-21, Mark 1:20, John 1:35-51

The next day, John was there again with two of his followers. As Jesus passed by, he told them, "Look, there's the Lamb of God!"

When his disciples heard what he said, they immediately began to follow Jesus. Then Jesus turned around and saw them following him and asked them, "What is it that you want?"

They answered, "Where are your staying, Teacher?"

"Come with me," Jesus said, "and I'll show you."

It was around four o'clock in the afternoon, and they went with him to see where he was staying.. Then they spent the rest of the day with him.

Simon Peter's brother, Andrew, was one of the two who heard what John had said about Jesus, and he followed him. Andrew quickly found his brother, Simon, and told him, "We've found Christ, the Messiah." Then he took him to see Jesus. Jesus looked right at him and declared, "You are Simon, the son of John. But from now on I am going to call you Peter. [*Peter* means rock in Greek, and in Aramaic, *Cephas* means rock.]

The following day, Jesus planned to leave for Galilee, but first he found Philip and said, "Follow me."

Philip, Andrew, and Peter were all from the town of Bethsaida. Philip went to find Nathanael and told him, "We have found the Messiah that Moses and the prophets wrote about in the Law. His name is Jesus, the son of Joseph, from the town of Nazareth."

"Nazareth?" Nathanael asked. "How could anything good come from that place?"

"Come and see for yourself," Philip answered.

When Jesus saw Nathanael coming toward him, he announced, "Here comes an absolutely honest man of Israel!"

Surprised, Nathanael asked, "How do you know me?"

Jesus responded, "I saw you while you were under that fig tree, even before Philip called you."

Then Nathanael exclaimed, "Teacher, you really are the Son of God and the only One who is worthy to be the King of Israel!"

Jesus asked, "Do you believe just because I told you that I saw you under the fig tree? You'll surely see much greater things than that." Then Jesus added, "I promise that all of you will actually see heaven open up with angels rising up and also descending upon God's Son. He is like a passageway between heaven and earth."

Another day as Jesus walked along the shore of the Sea of Galilee, he saw Andrew and Peter as they were casting their net into the lake. Jesus invited, "Come right now to be my disciples and follow me. I will teach you how to fish for people."

Without hesitation both Peter and Andrew left their fishing nets and followed Jesus.

As they went on, Jesus saw two other brothers named James and John, sons of Zebedee. They were both getting their nets ready while in a boat with their father. At once Jesus called them and they immediately followed Jesus, leaving their father in the boat with the hired men. (Luke 5:10)

29. At a Wedding Reception Jesus Performs His First Miracle - John 2:1-11

The following day there was a wedding at the town of Cana in the area of Galilee. Jesus' mother, Mary, was there and his disciples were also invited to attend. When the wine ran out, Mary told Jesus, "The wine is all gone."

"Mother," Jesus replied, "This is not yet the right time to reveal to the people what I have been called to do."

So his mother told the servants, "Just do whatever he says to do."

Standing nearby were six big stone jugs for holding water. They were the kind of jars that the Jews used for their cleansing ceremonies. Each one held around twenty or thirty gallons.

Jesus told the servants, "Go and fill up the jars with water." So, they did. They filled them to the brim.

Next, he told them, "Now go dip some out and take it to the person in charge of this banquet."

When they had done it, the one in charge of the banquet tasted the water that had suddenly become wine. But he didn't know the source. However, the servants certainly knew. Then the head of the banquet called the bridegroom over and asked, "Why have you saved the best wine until now? Usually everyone serves the best wine first. Then after the guests have had too much to drink, they serve the cheap wine."

It was there in Cana of Galilee that Jesus performed the first miraculous sign that showed the presence of God shining through him. As a result, his disciples began to see evidence that he really was the Messiah.

30. Jesus Visits Capernaum with His Disciples - John 2:12

After the miracle in Cana of Galilee, Jesus traveled to Capernaum, along with his mother, brothers, and disciples. And they stayed there a few days.

31. Many See His Miracles and Believe, but Jesus Shows No Confidence in the Human Heart - John 2:23

While Jesus was there in Jerusalem, during the Passover Festival, people saw the miraculous signs he was performing. As a result, many believed in him. However, Jesus was not fooled by his popularity with the crowds. He wasn't depending on what people thought of him. He knew all about human nature and what was in each person's heart.

32. Nicodemus Meets Jesus Secretly and Learns of the New Birth - John 3:1-21

There was a certain member of the Pharisee party named Nicodemus. He was also a member of the ruling Jewish council. [Pharisees believed that people should keep the whole Law of God, along with all the rules they had added to interpret the Law.]

Nicodemus visited Jesus after nightfall. [He may have come at night to avoid criticism from his fellow Pharisees.]

Here's how he approached Jesus: "Rabbi, we can't help but see that your teachings come from God. It is obvious to us that no one could do the miracles you are doing unless God is with you and helping you." [Rabbi was the customary and respectful way to address one who was recognized as a well-trained teacher.]

Then Jesus replied, "I assure you that no one can begin to understand God's kingdom until that person is born once more, this time from above."

"How is that possible?" Nicodemus asked. "You surely don't mean they must return to their mother and be born all over again!"

Jesus explained, "I assure you, only those who experience both physical birth and spiritual birth with water baptism can begin to understand God's kingdom. Physical birth produces new physical life. But the Holy Spirit gives birth to new spiritual life. So, don't be surprised when I say, 'You must be born again.' The wind also illustrates this. It blows wherever it chooses. You can hear it, but you have no idea where it came from or where it is going next. This illustrates well a person who has received new spiritual life."

"How could this be? How can it happen?" Nicodemus asked.

Jesus answered, "You are a highly recognized teacher in Israel. Don't you understand these things? I assure you, I'm talking about things I do understand. I'm talking to you about things I have actually seen, but you Jewish teachers won't accept my testimony. I have been talking about common and ordinary earthly things. So how will you ever believe it when I tell you about heavenly things? There is only one person who has come down from heaven and will soon return. It is I, the Son of Man. Even as Moses lifted up the statue of a snake in the wilderness, so the Son of Man must also be lifted up. Then everyone who believes who he really is, and accepts what he has done, will certainly have eternal life through him.

"For God loved the world so much, that he sacrificed his One and only Son. He did this so that everyone who believes in who Jesus really is, and what he actually accomplished, might have eternal life through him. God certainly didn't send Jesus into our world in order to condemn us, but in order to save the world through his Son. All who place their trust in him will not be condemned.

"But all who choose not to believe are already condemned, because they refused to trust in the name of God's one and only Son. Here is the verdict: God's truth and love are like a great Light shining into our world. And this is the situation: People are evil. They love darkness more than light. Those who do evil actually hate the light. They won't come near to it. They fear having their evil deeds revealed for what they are. However, everyone who lives in harmony with God's truth chooses to come to the light. Then it will be obvious that God has seen and approved their actions."

33. John the Baptist's Ministry Fades as the Fame of Jesus Rises - John 3:22-30

After meeting with Nicodemus, Jesus left for the Judean countryside where he took time to be with his disciples. While there, he was baptizing those who were embracing his teaching. And John was also baptizing at Aenon near Salim, in a desert area that was likely near where the Jordan River empties into the Dead Sea. People came there to be baptized because there was plenty of water in that area. This happened before John was sent to prison.

Then some of John's disciples got into a discussion with a certain Jew. They were arguing over the proper way to observe customs of ceremonial washing. They came to John seeking a solution.

"Rabbi," they said, "that man that was with you across the Jordan— the one you pointed out to us—he is now baptizing over there. Everyone is following him.

Here is how John responded. "Each person can carry out only the kind of ministry that is inspired from heaven. You yourselves are witnesses that I said, 'I am not the promised Messiah. However, I was called by God to pave the way for him.' For example, a bride belongs to the bridegroom. However, the best man who serves the bridegroom waits to hear from him, and when he hears the bridegroom's voice, he becomes excited and filled with joy. And right now, that's exactly the kind of satisfying joy that I have! It is God's will for him to become greater, but I must fade away.

34. The One Who Comes from Heaven Is Above All - John 3:31-36

"The One who comes from heaven is above all. I, John, am from the earth. The person, who belongs to the earth, speaks from an earthly perspective. However, the One from heaven speaks with heavenly authority, but few accept his witness. Only those who believe everything he teaches are qualified to confirm that what God declares to be true is certainly true. Therefore, the One sent by God speaks God's message, and that message is absolutely true. He speaks God's words, and God pours out the Holy Spirit in limitless abundance. The Father loves the Son and trusts him with everything. Whoever believes in the Son of God has eternal life. Anyone who rejects God's Son will never experience real life, for God's righteous anger rests upon him."

35. Jesus Goes from Judea through Samaria to Galilee after John is Put in Prison - Mark 1:14, Luke 3:19-20, John 4:1-4

The Pharisees found out that Jesus was winning over and baptizing more disciples than John the Baptist. But in fact, it was not Jesus doing the baptizing. It was his disciples. So, he left Judea and immediately returned again to Galilee.

Meanwhile, John rebuked Herod, the assistant governor, for all the evil things he had done. In fact, he had married his brother's wife, Herodias. On top of that, he locked up John in prison. About that same time, Jesus went back to Galilee. He knew he must travel through Samaria on the way, even though Jews usually tried to avoid the route through Samaria. [There was a great deal of prejudice between Jews and Samaritans.]

36. Jesus Has a Talk by a Well with a Samaritan Woman - John 4:5-26

It was almost noon when Jesus arrived at a Samaritan town called Sychar. Jacob had deeded the plot of ground in that same area to his favorite son, Joseph. In fact, Jacob's well was right there.

Jesus' disciples went into town to buy food while Jesus waited by the well. Just then, a Samaritan woman came to draw water from the well. Jesus asked her, "Will you give me a drink?"

Knowing that Jews were prejudiced against Samaritans, the woman was surprised and asked him, "You're a Jew and I'm a Samaritan. How can you ask me for a drink?"

Jesus answered, "If you only knew what God wants to give you and who is asking you for a drink, you would have asked me for a drink. Then I would have given you the water of life."

Then the woman said, "Sir, this well is very deep and you don't have anything for drawing up the water. So where can you get this water of life? Could you be greater than our ancestor, Jacob, who dug this well and drank from it himself along with his sons and his livestock?"

Jesus answered her, "All those who drink from this well get thirsty again. Here's the truth. Anyone who drinks the water I have to give will never be thirsty again. In fact, the water I'm able to give keeps flowing on and on and producing eternal life."

"Sir," the woman said, "please give me this kind of water. Then I won't get thirsty and have to keep coming back here to get water."

Then he told her, "Now, go and call your husband and come right back."

"I don't have a husband," she replied.

"Yes," Jesus said, "I know you've confessed the truth when you said you don't have a husband. You've really had five, and the man you're living with right now is not your husband."

"Sir, I can see that you're a prophet," she said. "We Samaritans know that our ancestors worshiped right here on this mountain, but you Jews believe we ought to worship God in Jerusalem."

"Precious woman," Jesus said, "believe me, a time will come when you won't worship your Heavenly Father, here or in Jerusalem. You Samaritans aren't sure about the one you are worshiping. But we Jews do know the source of our hope because God has chosen to offer salvation through the Jews. However, a time is near. Yes, it has arrived when all true worshipers will worship God the Father in the Spirit of truth. Those are the kind of worshipers the Father is looking for. God is Spirit, and the kind of worshipers that are acceptable to him must truly worship him in all sincerity."

Then the woman said, "I have heard that the one they call the Messiah (or Christ) is supposed to come. And when he does come, he will have the answers to all of our questions."

Then Jesus told her the truth, "I, the very one who has been talking to you—I am the Anointed One—I'm the Messiah—the Christ!"

37. Jesus Finds Fulfillment Ministering to the Samaritan Woman - John 4:27-38

Right at that moment, his disciples came back and were shocked to find Jesus talking with a Samaritan woman. However, no one dared to ask him why he was conversing with her.

The woman was so excited that she left her water jar behind and hurried back into town to invite the town-people. "Come and see for yourselves a man who knew all about my life and could tell me what kind of life I've been living. Could this possibly be the Messiah?" Then the town people became curious and went to find him.

Meanwhile, the disciples knew he hadn't eaten for a long time, so they urged him, "Rabbi, you must eat something."

But Jesus said, "You have never experienced the completely satisfying kind of food I have been tasting."

Then his disciples were puzzled and said to one another, "Who could have brought him food?"

"My food," Jesus answered, "is to be able to finish the work assigned to me by the One who commissioned me. Sometimes people say, 'There are still four months until the harvest is ready.' Now open your eyes. Take a good look at the fields. Needy people are like a ripe harvest. You can be a reaper right now. Quickly get at the task. You will surely be rewarded for your labor. Those you bring in will be rewarded right along with those of you who do the harvesting. Of course, it is true when they say, 'One person sows while another reaps.' Now I have sent you to reap a harvest where you have not done the work of sowing. Others have already done the hard work and you have benefited from their labor."

38. Many Samaritans in Sychar Come to Faith in Jesus - John 4:39-42

Many of the Samaritans from Sychar believed that he was the Messiah as a result of the woman's testimony: "He told me all about the kind of life I have been living." Therefore, the Samaritans urged him to stay longer with them, so he stayed another two days. And his words convinced many more people to believe in him.

They said to the woman, "We don't believe just because of what you told us. Now we have seen and heard him for ourselves, and we are sure this man really is the Savior of the whole world."

39. Jesus Arrives to Minister in Galilee - Luke 4:14-15; John 4:43-45

Two days later, Jesus left for Galilee in the power of the Holy Spirit. The news about him was spreading to the whole surrounding area. However, Jesus himself had explained that it is highly unusual for a prophet to receive honor in his hometown, among his own people. But when he came home to Galilee, they welcomed him. Everyone who had gone to Jerusalem for the Passover had seen everything he had done there. As he was teaching in their places of worship, the people were all praising him.

40. Jesus Preaches the Message of the Kingdom of God - Matt 4:17; Mark 1:15

Then Jesus began proclaiming this message as he preached: "The time has arrived for the Kingdom of God to come near. Turn now from your sins and place your trust in the Good News!"

41. Jesus Heals a Child from Capernaum - John 4:46-54

Once again, Jesus visited Cana in Galilee. That's where he had turned water into wine. There was a royal official from Cana whose son was sick in bed at Capernaum. When he found out that Jesus had come back to Galilee from Judea, he found him and begged him to come and heal his son who was about to die.

Jesus told him, "You people just can't believe unless you see signs and miracles." But the royal officer responded, "Please, come over to Cana right away and heal my child because he is about to die."

Jesus answered, "You can go home now, because your son will live."

The man accepted what Jesus said, and left to go home. But while he was still on the way, his servants met him with good news—his boy was alive and well. When he asked when it was that his son started to recover, they said, "It was yesterday at one o'clock in the afternoon that the fever left him."

The father was amazed, because that was the exact time when Jesus told him, "Your son will live." Then everyone living in his house believed in Jesus.

This was the second miraculous sign that Jesus performed after he came back from Judea to Galilee.

42. The Ministry of Jesus Is Rejected in Nazareth, His Hometown - Luke 4:16-30

Then he went back to the area where he had grown up, and on the Sabbath day, he entered the synagogue as was his custom. As the Rabbis customarily did, he stood up to read. Then they gave him the scroll of the prophet Isaiah. Jesus unrolled it and found where Isaiah had written the following:

> *The Spirit of the Lord is upon me,*
> *because he chose me and anointed me*
> *to bring good news to those who are poor.*
> *He has commissioned me to announce freedom*
> *for those who are locked up,*
> *and new sight for those who are blind,*
> *in order to liberate those who are oppressed,*
> *and to announce the year of the Lord's favor.*
> *(Isaiah 61:1-2 and Isaiah 58:6, Septuagint version)*

After reading this, he rolled up the scroll, returned it to the assistant, and sat down. Then all those in the synagogue focused their eyes on him. He began to speak. "Today you have witnessed the fulfillment of the Scripture that was just read."

Everyone present complimented him. They were all amazed at the inspired words they heard from his lips. "Isn't this Joseph's son who grew up right here in Nazareth?" they asked.

Then Jesus said this to them: "No doubt you will quote this familiar saying to me, 'Physician, heal yourself!' Probably you will also tell me, 'Why don't you do here in your own town, those things they claim you did over there in Capernaum?'

"I tell you the truth," he went on, "no prophet is welcomed in his own hometown. There were certainly many needy widows in Israel in the time of Elijah, when the sky was shut for three and a half years. It was a time of severe famine all over the land. But Elijah was not sent to any others, except a widow living in Zarephath, in the area of Sidon. Also, there were many in Israel suffering with leprosy during the time of the prophet Elisha, yet none of them were cleansed except Naaman from Syria." [It seems that the Prophets were not welcome among their own people, so they performed their miracles among the Gentiles.]

When they heard this, the whole crowd that was in the synagogue was furious. They grabbed him and pushed him out to the edge of the cliff by the hill where the town had been built. They were about to push him off the cliff, but he walked right through the crowd and went on his way. [His escape was the only miracle he could do in his hometown.]

43. When Jesus Is Opposed at Nazareth, He Makes Capernaum His Headquarters - Matt 4:13-16; Luke 4:31

Upon leaving Nazareth, Jesus went over to live in the town of Capernaum. It was by the Sea of Galilee in the area of Zebulun and Naphtali. His presence there fulfilled the prophecy spoken by Isaiah:

> *There in the land of Zebulun and in the land of Naphtali,*
> *on the way to the sea, beyond the Jordan River,*
> *in Galilee where many gentiles live --*
> *The people who live in spiritual darkness*
> *have seen a great light;*
> *That light has dawned*
> *upon those living in the land*
> *of the shadow of death. (Isaiah 9:1-2)*

44. As a Sign of His Authority to Teach, Jesus Heals a Demon-possessed Man - Mark 1:21-28

Then Jesus and his disciples were in Capernaum on a Sabbath day. He entered the synagogue and began teaching, and they were all amazed at how he taught. He spoke with authority, not like their teachers of Jewish law. And right then a demon possessed man yelled, "What are you going to do? Are you here to wipe us out? I know exactly who you are. You're the Holy One who has come from God!"

Jesus spoke sternly, "Come out of him!" And immediately the impure spirit violently shook the man and he gave a shriek as the spirit was coming out.

The crowd was so amazed, they asked each other, "What is this all about? It seems to be some new kind of teaching that demonstrates powerful authority! He even commands the evil spirits and they must obey him." As a result, reports about Jesus quickly spread all over the whole area of Galilee.

45. Jesus Heals Peter's Mother-in-law and Others - Matt 8:14-17; Mark 1:29-33; Luke 4:40-41

When they left the synagogue, they went right away to the home of Simon Peter and his brother, Andrew. Then Jesus saw that Peter's mother-in-law was in bed with a fever. And when Jesus touched her hand, the fever immediately left her, and she got right up and began to serve them.

At sunset that same evening, the whole town gathered outside the door. The townspeople brought to Jesus those with all kinds of sickness. He laid his hands on each sick person and healed them all. In addition to all that, demons were coming out of many who were possessed. As they came out they shouted, "You are the Son of God!"

But Jesus rebuked them and wouldn't let them speak because they knew he was the promised Christ—the Messiah. With just a word, he could drive out spirits or heal the sick. This fulfilled what Isaiah the prophet had said: "He carried our disabilities and our diseases." (Isaiah 53:4)

46. Jesus Tours Galilee and Judea with Simon Peter and Others - Matt 4:23-24; Mark 1:35-39; Luke 4:42-44

Very early one morning while it was still dark, Jesus got up and left the house to go to a place where he could be alone and pray. People were trying to find him. Simon Peter and his friends also went to look for him. When they did find him, they exclaimed, "Everybody is looking for you!" And they urged him to stay there.

But Jesus said, "Let's go somewhere else. I must tell the Good News about God's kingdom, drive out demons, and heal all kinds of disabilities and sicknesses that are causing people to suffer."

And the news about Jesus spread all over the area of Syria. People kept bringing to him everyone who was sick with all kinds of diseases—those suffering awful pain, those who were demon-possessed, those experiencing seizures, and those who were paralyzed—and Jesus healed every one of them.

47. Jesus Calls Some Fishermen to Fish for People - Luke 5:1-11

Once, when Jesus was standing by the Sea of Galilee, [this sea is also known as the Lake of Gennesaret] people were crowding around and listening to God's word. Jesus looked up and saw two boats at the water's edge. He got into one of the boats that belonged to Simon Peter, and asked him to shove it off a little way from the shore. Then, he sat down there in the boat and addressed the people.

After he finished, he told Simon Peter, "Push out into deeper water, and let down your net to catch some fish."

But Peter answered, "Master, we've worked hard at fishing all night long and we haven't caught a thing. But since you say so, I'll let the nets down."

When they had done this, they caught so many fish that their nets started breaking apart. They signaled those in the other boat to help them out, and they came and filled up both boats so full of fish that they began to sink. When Peter saw what had happened, he fell at the knees of Jesus and cried out, "Lord, I'm a sinful man. I don't deserve to have you near to me." He said this because he was shocked at the huge catch they had taken in. His partners, James and John who were Zebedee's sons, were just as amazed as Peter was.

Then Jesus said to Simon Peter, "Don't worry, because from now on you'll learn how to fish for people." So, they pulled the boats up on the shore. After that they left their former life and began to follow Jesus as his disciples.

48. Jesus Cleanses a Leper and Much Publicity Follows - Matt 8:3-4; Luke 5:12-15; Mark 1:40-41

When Jesus was in a certain town, a man came along whose body was completely covered with a skin disease. [This was likely leprosy.] When he saw Jesus, he fell on his knees with his face to the ground and pleaded, "Lord, I'm sure you can make me clean if you're just willing."

Jesus was filled with compassion, but at the same time he was also indignant that the man had been suffering for so long. Jesus reached out his hand and touched him. "I'm willing," he said. "Be clean right now!" Immediately, all the spots of his disease were cleansed away. Then Jesus told him, "Please don't tell anyone how this happened. You must go and show the priest what has taken place, then offer the gift Moses commanded as a testimony to them." [Refer to Leviticus 4:13-21.]

Instead of keeping quiet, the man went out and spread the wonderful news about how he had been healed from the disgrace of his terrible disease. As a result, Jesus became so popular that he couldn't openly enter a single town. He had to stay away in lonely places. Even then, the people kept coming from everywhere to listen to him, and to be healed from every kind of sickness. Still, Jesus often found lonely places where he could go and pray.

49. Jesus Forgives and Heals a Paralyzed Man ~ Matt 9:1; Luke 5:17-26

Then Jesus got into a boat and crossed over to the town of Capernaum where he had been based. One day, he was teaching the Pharisees and other teachers of the Scriptures who were sitting there. They had come from every little town in the areas of Galilee, Judea, and Jerusalem. [The Pharisees were experts in Jewish Law.]

Just then the Lord's power to heal the sick was on Jesus in a special way. Some men came carrying a paralyzed man on a mat. They tried to get him into the house so they could lay him down in front of Jesus. But they couldn't find a way to get in because the crowd was jammed tightly together. Instead, they climbed up on the tiled roof and removed enough tiles to let him down into the midst of the crowd right in front of Jesus.

When Jesus saw their strong faith, he said to the paralyzed man, "My friend, your sins are all forgiven."

The Pharisees and teachers of the Law were indignant and thought, *Who does this fellow think he is, that he tries to get by with such blasphemy? Who has the right to forgive sins? Only God can do that!*

Jesus knew what they were thinking and asked, "Why are you thinking such things in your hearts? After all, which is easier, to say, 'Your sins are forgiven,' or to say, 'Stand up and walk?' However, I want you to realize that the Son of Man has complete authority on earth to forgive sins." He then said to the paralyzed man, "I tell you right now, you are healed! Get up and pick up your mat and walk home."

Immediately, the man stood up in front of them all. Then he took his mat, used for a ground covering, and walked home joyfully, praising God. The whole crowd was amazed and gave praise and honor to God. They were full of wonder and exclaimed, "What unusual, remarkable things we have seen today!"

50. Jesus Calls Matthew (also known as Levi) to Follow Him - Matt 9:9; Mark 2:13-14; Luke 5:27-28

Jesus went out by the lake, as he often did. A large crowd followed him. He began to teach them right there.

After he left, Jesus found a man named Matthew (also called Levi, the son of Alphaeus) sitting at a Roman tax collector's booth. [The Jews resented the fact that the Romans were ruling over their country. In fact, Matthew was a Jew collecting money from Jews to pay the Romans.]

Speaking to him, Jesus said, "Follow me." Right away, Matthew got up and left everything in order to follow Jesus.

51. Jesus Attends a Banquet at Matthew's House - Matt 9:11-13; Mark 2:15; Luke 5:29-32

Then Levi (also known as Matthew) invited a big crowd to his home for a large celebration in honor of Jesus. While Jesus was having dinner, many greedy tax collectors and other sinners were there as guests. They were eating with Jesus and his disciples because all kinds of people followed Jesus. However, the legalistic Pharisees and teachers of the Jewish Law who also supported the Pharisees, complained to the Lord's disciples. "How can your teacher eat, or even associate with tax collectors and such awful sinners?"

When he heard what they said, Jesus gave them this to think about: "It isn't the healthy people who need a doctor, but the doctor is there for those who are sick. I didn't come to call godly people, but sinners to turn away from their sins and to start following the Lord. Now go and find out why God said this, 'I desire mercy, not sacrifice.'" (Micah 6:6-8)

40

52. Jesus Illustrates How Things Have Been Changed by the Arrival of the Messiah and His Kingdom ~ Mark 2:18-21; Luke 5:33-39

Some people who came to Jesus complained, "John the Baptist's disciples often fast by abstaining from food during their times of prayer. The disciples of the legalistic Pharisees do the same thing. However, your disciples go right on eating and drinking."

Then Jesus answered them this way. "Can you ask the bridegroom's friends to fast while the bridegroom is there with them? But the time will come when, like a bridegroom, I will be taken away from them. At that time fasting will be appropriate.

"What sensible person would put a brand new piece of cloth that hasn't been shrunk on an old garment? If they did that, the new piece of cloth would pull away from the old piece and make the tear worse. In the same way, nobody pours new wine into old wineskins. If they did that, the new wine would burst the skins while it is aging. Then the wine would ruin the wineskins as it is leaking out. No, that's not how it should be done. The new wine has to be poured into new wineskins. But those who drink the old wine don't want to drink the new, because they say, 'The old is better.'"

53. Jesus Heals a Lame Man on the Sabbath Day ~ John 5:1-9

At the appropriate time, Jesus left for Jerusalem to attend one of the Jewish festivals. Near the Sheep Gate was a pool called *Bethesda* in the Aramaic language. [Some people called it *Bethzatha*. There were five covered colonnades surrounding the pool. A large number of disabled people, including the blind, lame and paralyzed people were accustomed to gathering there. Some accounts mention that they waited there because they believed that occasionally an angel of the Lord would come unannounced and stir up the water in the pool. The people believed that whoever got into the pool first after the angel's visit would be cured of whatever disease the person had.]

When Jesus came to visit that pool, he saw a paralyzed man lying there who had been unable to walk for thirty-eight years. Then Jesus asked him, "Would you like to get well?"

41

The man replied, "Sir, I have no one to help me get into the pool when the angel stirs up the water. When I try to get in, someone always gets in ahead of me."

Jesus answered, "Get up right now! Pick up your mat and carry it home." Instantly, the man was completely cured. This healing took place on a Sabbath day.

54. The Jews Seek to Kill Jesus for Healing on the Sabbath and Claiming God as His Father - John 5:10-18

When the Jewish leaders saw him carrying his mat, they said, "Don't you realize that today is Sabbath? Moses informed our nation that God does not allow us to work on the Sabbath day. Certainly, you are aware that you are working on the Sabbath when you carry your mat."

The man replied, "The man who made me well said to me, 'Pick up your mat and walk with it.'"

Then the leaders asked him, "Who is this fellow who told you to pick it up and walk?"

But he had no idea who had healed him and told him to carry his mat because Jesus had slipped through the crowd.

Later, Jesus found the man at the temple and told him, "You have been completely restored, so don't deliberately sin anymore. If you do, something even worse could happen to you." Then the man left and told the Jewish leaders that it was Jesus who had made him well.

Because of this, the Jewish leaders began to persecute Jesus as he continued to heal on the Sabbath. Yet, Jesus defended himself with these words, "My Father constantly keeps on working right up to this very day, and I'm working, too."

They believed his words gave them a good excuse for trying all the more to kill him; not just because he was breaking the Sabbath, but because he made himself equal with God by calling him his own Father.

55. Jesus Presents Evidence of His Equality with the Father - John 5:19-47

Jesus answered their criticism in these words: "I'm telling you the absolute truth when I assure you that the Son cannot do anything apart from the Father. He does exactly what he sees the Father doing. In fact, whatever the Father is doing, the Son is also doing. Since the

Father loves the Son, he reveals to him everything he does. You can be sure that he will show him even greater works than what you have seen already. Then you will be amazed. The Father is able to raise the dead and give them life. So, you can also trust the Son to give life to anyone he chooses. The Father is not really the one who judges. Rather, he has entrusted all judgment to the Son. Therefore, everyone will honor the Son, even as they honor the Father. Anyone who does not honor the Son is not able to honor the Father who sent him.

"I assure you truthfully, that anyone who receives what I am saying and trusts the One who sent me, already has eternal life. That person will not be judged, but has passed from death into life. I tell you truthfully, the promised time has arrived when those who are spiritually dead will be able to hear the voice of the Son of God, and those who do hear, will be given real life. Since the Father has life within, he has also allowed the Son to have life within himself. The Father has also given the Son authority to judge humanity because he is the Son of Man.

"Don't let this amaze you, because a time will actually come when all who are in their graves will hear the Son's voice. Then those who have made the right choice, based upon faith, will rise and live. But those who have chosen evil will rise to be condemned. Acting alone, I can't do anything. My judgment is based completely on what I hear. And my judgment is absolutely fair because I'm not trying to please myself. Instead, I'm seeking the pleasure of the One who sent me.

"If my witness is just about me, then my testimony is not really true. However, there is someone else who testifies in my favor. And I'm sure that his testimony about me is absolutely true.

"There was a time when you listened to John (the Baptist), and he told you the truth. I am not using human testimony to prove what is true, but it can point toward salvation. John was like a lamp burning and providing light for you to enjoy for a short time.

"However, I have a witness that is even more convincing than John's witness. What the Father has given me to complete—I mean the very works I am doing—they prove that the Father has sent me. Even the Father who sent me has served as a witness on my behalf. You have never heard him nor seen him, and his message does not dwell in you. That is because you don't believe the One he sent into the world. You diligently search the Scriptures looking for the way to find eternal life. And they are the very same Scriptures that speak about me. But you refuse to come to me and receive the gift of life.

"I'm not looking for human compliments. But I know what you are like. I'm well aware that your hearts are not filled with love for God. I have come in my Father's name, and you don't accept me. However, if someone else comes honoring himself, you'll accept him. How are you going to believe real truth, as long as you are seeking honor from each other, while you refuse to seek the honor that the One and only God can give?

"On the other hand, do you suppose that I will be the one to accuse you before the Father? Actually, you have set your hopes on Moses, but in fact, he is your accuser. You would be able to believe in me, if you would truly believe Moses. After all, he wrote about me. Of course, when you don't really believe what he wrote, how will you be able to believe what I say to you?"

56. Jesus Answers the Criticism against His Disciples for Picking Grain on the Sabbath - Matt 12:1-8; Mark 2:26; Luke 6:1

One Sabbath day, Jesus was walking with his disciples through the fields of grain. His disciples were hungry, so they picked some heads of grain, rubbed the husks off in their hands, and ate the kernels. But the legalistic Pharisees saw this and said to Jesus, "Did you see that? They're doing the work of harvesting on the Sabbath. They're breaking the Law given to us through Moses!"

Then Jesus answered, "Haven't you read in the Scriptures what David did when he and his companions were hungry? At that time Abiathar was the high priest. Then David entered the house of God. He and his companions ate some of the consecrated bread, that according to the Mosaic Law, only the priests were allowed to eat. Haven't you also read that according to the Law, the priests are innocent when they carry out their duties on the Sabbath, while they are working in the temple? Let me inform you, right now, something greater than the temple is here! You wouldn't have condemned the innocent if you had only understood what these words mean, 'I desire mercy, not sacrifice.' (Hosea 6:6) Then you would not have condemned the One who is innocent. The fact is that the Son of Man is even Lord of the Sabbath."

57. Jesus Heals a Man's Shriveled Hand on the Sabbath - Matt 12:11-12; Mark 3:1-6

Once, when Jesus entered the synagogue, there was a man there whose hand was shriveled. Some were watching Jesus closely because they were looking for evidence that could be used to condemn him. Would he break the Sabbath day Law as interpreted and promoted by the legalistic Pharisees? They believed that healing on the Sabbath was working on the Sabbath.

Then Jesus asked them, "If one of you were to have a sheep fall into a deep pit on the Sabbath, wouldn't you reach down and pull it out? Can't you see that a person is far more valuable than a sheep? So, it should be obvious that doing what is good on the Sabbath, by taking care of an emergency, does not break the Law."

Then Jesus spoke to the man with the shriveled hand. "Stand up here where everyone can see you."

Jesus asked the people, "Which is the best way to keep the Sabbath: doing good or doing evil, to save a life, or to kill?" But the crowd kept silent.

Jesus had anger in his eyes and was greatly disturbed because their hearts were so stubborn. He told the man, "Reach out your hand." And as he did, his hand became completely normal. This made the Pharisees and Herodians begin to plot together how they might be able to bring a death sentence against Jesus.

58. Jesus Withdraws to the Sea of Galilee, but a Great Multitude Follows Him - Matt 4:25; 12:17-21; Mark 3:7-12

Jesus took his disciples and went away to the lake. The crowd of people from Galilee followed him there. As word of his miracles spread, many came there from as far away as Judea, Jerusalem, Idumea, and places across the Jordan River. They came from Decapolis [those places were also known as the Ten Cities] and from around Tyre and Sidon.

The crowd was so big, he told his disciples to have a small boat ready in order to prevent all those people from crowding him. Whenever unclean spirits saw him—those who were possessed—fell in front of Jesus crying loudly, "You are the Son of God!" So in order to keep the crowds from growing too large to handle, Jesus ordered those who were healed or delivered not to spread the word about his miracles. This fulfilled the prophecy spoken by Isaiah:

This is my chosen servant,
the one I love and who brings me delight;
I will place my Spirit on him.
He will announce justice to the nations.
He will not argue nor shout.
In fact, his voice will scarcely be heard in the streets.
He won't harm those who are already bruised and hurting.
He will not snuff out those who have only a little spark left,
until he has finally enabled justice to triumph.
And the nations of the world will finally place their hope
in the name of Jesus. (Isaiah 42:1-4)

59. Jesus Appoints Twelve Apostles - Matt 10:2-4; Mark 3:14-15; Luke 6:12-16

One day, Jesus went up to the side of a mountain where he spent the night praying. The next morning, he called his followers around him, and he chose twelve from among his disciples. He named them apostles. [This refers to those he called out to represent him.] They would be with him as an inner circle of his followers. He also planned to send them out to teach and preach with authority, and even to have power to drive out demons. Following is the list of these twelve:

First Simon, whom he named Peter, and his brother Andrew; James, son of Zebedee, and his brother, John; Philip, Bartholomew, Thomas, Matthew [or Levi, the tax collector], and James [both Levi and James were sons of Alphaeus], Thaddaeus [also known as Judas, son of James], Simon who was called the Zealot [a political activist], and Judas Iscariot, who betrayed him.

60. Jesus Teaches His Followers on a Mountainside – Matt 5:1; Luke 6:17-19

Jesus noticed that crowds were gathering to hear him, so he climbed up the side of a mountain, then descended a short distance to a small level place where he sat down while he taught the people.

61. Jesus Promises Happiness to the Subjects of His Kingdom, but Woe to Those Who Are Self-Sufficient ~ Matt 5:1-12; Luke 6:22-26

As Jesus began to teach them, he spoke the following blessings:

> God blesses people who are humble in spirit.
>> The kingdom of heaven belongs to them.
> God blesses people who have grieved over their great losses.
>> Their time of comfort and rejoicing will certainly come.
> God blesses people who are gentle and self-controlled.
>> The world will belong to them.
> God blesses people who are hungry and thirsty
>> to grow in godly character. They will be satisfied.
> God blesses people who offer undeserved kindness,
>> for in return, they will receive mercy.
> God blesses people whose hearts are filled with pure love,
>> for they will come to really know God.
> God blesses people who negotiate peace,
>> for they will be known as sons and daughters of God.
> God blesses people who are persecuted because they
>> are godly,
>>> for the kingdom of heaven belongs to them.

"You are truly blessed when people ignore, insult, and persecute you and even call you an evil, self-righteous person just because you honor Jesus as your Lord and Savior. And some even speak all kinds of insults because you trust in me. But in spite of all this, you have a good reason to rejoice and be glad. You can be absolutely sure that a great reward awaits you in heaven. Remember this: Evil people also persecuted God's faithful prophets who came before you.

> Woe to you rich people.
>> You already received what you paid for.
> Woe to you who have had all you want to eat.
>> You will surely learn what it's like to be hungry.
> Woe to you who are partying and laughing now.
>> In time, you will cry and mourn your losses.
> Woe to you if everyone is telling you how great you are.

"Don't forget that is exactly how your ancestors treated the false prophets."

62. Jesus Announces the Responsibility of the Kingdom People: They Are Salt and Light - Matt 5:13-16; Mark 9:50; Luke 8:16-17, 11:33; 14:34-35

Here are some of the things Jesus said as he taught the people:

"My followers are like salt that flavors and preserves the earth. Unspoiled salt is very useful and good. However, if salt loses its freshness, how can you restore its usefulness? In fact, it no longer serves any purpose. You must throw it out to be trampled on the ground. It doesn't even help the soil. A manure pile is the best place for it. However, you need to become like salt, flavoring the earth with your wisdom and love. Like salt, your life should help preserve peace by your commitment to please God among those you are able to influence.

"If you are truly my followers, then you are like a light for the part of the world where you have an influence. At night, a little town up on a hill cannot be hidden. Its lights can be seen for miles around. Also, people don't bring a lamp into the room only to cover it with a big clay pot or jar. Why would anyone place a light under a bed or some hidden place?

"No, people put lights where they can light up the whole surrounding area. Then they can see everything near the light. That's how your influence must be. Your life should spread love and truth to all those around you. Then they will realize that only your heavenly Father could change you into a person who radiates God's blessings. They will honor God for what he is doing in your life. Eventually everything comes into the light. Those things that are concealed now, will eventually be brought out into the open for all to see."

63. Jesus Explains How the Kingdom of God Relates to the Law of Righteousness - Matt 5:17-20

As Jesus continued his teaching, he said, "Don't imagine that I have come to get rid of the Law or the teachings of the prophets. No, I have come to fulfill them, not to abolish them. I'm telling you the truth. Not a dot over an 'i' or the cross of a 't', or even the least stroke of a pen, will in any way disappear from the Law, until everything planned by God has been accomplished. Anyone who rejects even one of the so-called unimportant commands, and encourages others to do the same will be called least in the kingdom of heaven. However, whoever teaches and practices these commands will be considered great in the kingdom of heaven. Also, think about this: Unless you are more righteous than those nit-picking Pharisees and those so-called teachers of the Law, you have no chance of even entering the Kingdom of Heaven."

64. Jesus Teaches about Anger - Matt 5:21-22

"People have often quoted the Law that says, 'You shall not murder, and whoever murders will be brought to justice.' However, I say that anyone who holds anger toward another person will face judgment. Also, anyone who says, 'You fool!' or dishonors a fellow human being deserves to face the court. In fact, anyone who angrily says things such as, 'You fool!' is in danger of the eternal fire of hell."

65. Jesus Teaches about Reconciliation - Matt 5:23-26; Luke 12:57-58

"If you are worshiping in church and contributing your offering to the Lord, and suddenly you remember that a fellow believer has something against you, just forget about your contribution for a moment. Your highest priority should be to make peace with your fellow believer. After that, you can go back and take care of your contributions.

"Can't you judge for yourself the best way to make your contributions, and at the same time preserve the peace? Settle conflicts quickly while you have a better chance to succeed. If someone is bringing a case against you in court, try your best to make things right so it doesn't need to go that far. Whenever possible, avoid being forced to face the judge, because he has authority to place you in the custody of a police officer. He could put you into prison. I'm warning you: it is very unlikely that you will be released until you have served your complete time and paid the last penny you owe."

66. Jesus Teaches about Adultery, Lust, Divorce and Hell - Matt 5:27-32; 18:8; Mark 9:47-48; Luke 16:18

"No doubt you have heard about God's Law that says, 'You must not commit adultery.' (Exodus 20:14) But I say: Whoever looks at someone with lustful intentions has already inwardly agreed to carry out that sinful desire just as soon as there is a good opportunity. So, if what you are choosing to see causes you to stumble, it's better to gouge out your eyes and throw them away. In fact, even if you must lose an arm or a leg to avoid hell, you would still be better off than keeping them only to end up spending eternity in hell. It is better to lose an important body part than for your whole body to be thrown into hell. So, if your best hand or foot causes you to stumble into sin, it would be better to cut them off and throw them away. Entering life crippled or maimed is better than suffering hell's eternal fire. For in the fire that will never be put out, not even the worm of conscience can die. However, everyone will be seasoned with fire." (Isaiah 66:24)

[Some Bible scholars have suggested that the worm may likely refer to a person's conscience. Jesus repeated this same warning another time. He applied it to people who offend children or who offend adults who are childlike.]

"The Law says, 'Anyone who divorces his wife must give her a certificate of divorce.' (Deut. 24:1) But I say that any man who divorces his wife, except for sexual unfaithfulness, causes her to become a victim of adultery. Also, a man is guilty of adultery if he marries a divorced woman who does not have a basis for divorce that is acceptable in the eyes of God."

67. Jesus Teaches on Keeping One's Word - Matt 5:33-37

"You have heard that long ago people were told, 'Do not break a promise, but fulfill to the Lord, every vow you have made.' But I say, don't back up any promise by taking an oath. Don't swear by heaven, because it is God's throne; don't swear by the earth, because it is God's footstool; or by Jerusalem, because it is the city of the Great King.

"Furthermore, don't swear by your head because you have no power to make your hair change its color naturally. If you want people to know that you are telling the truth, just make sure you have a reputation of always saying what you truly mean. If you answer, 'Yes' or 'No' make sure you mean it. Anything else is evil and it comes from the evil one."

68. Jesus Teaches about Merciful Behavior - Matt 5:38-42; Luke 6:30

"No doubt you have heard the saying, 'Eye for an eye, and tooth for a tooth.' But I say, don't try to get revenge against an evil person. If someone slaps you on one cheek, show him the other. If someone tries to force you to give up your shirt, give away your coat also. If a person forces you to help carry his load for a mile, then help him carry it for two miles. In fact, you should do your best to help those who request it. If someone takes something that is yours, don't demand it back, and don't turn your back on a person who asks you for a loan."

69. Jesus Teaches about Love for All Persons - Matt 5:43-48; Luke 6:27-36

"In the past, you have heard about the law that said, 'Love your neighbor and hate your enemy.' But I say this: Love your enemies. Do good even to those who hate you. Try to find ways to bless those who curse you. Also, pray for people who mistreat you. If you do these things you will be demonstrating that you really are behaving like the children of your heavenly Father. After all, he makes his sun shine on evil people as well as on good people. Doesn't God also send rain to water the ground of both godly and ungodly people?

"If you only love those who return your love, how will that credit you with godliness? Even sinners return kindness to those who are kind to them. What credit are you expecting if you limit your kindness to people who always treat you well? Even sinners do that. But you must love even your enemies and treat them well. When you lend to them, don't do it just because you expect to be fully repaid. What credit would that bring to you?

"Be a compassionate person by following the example of your merciful Heavenly Father. That will demonstrate that you are truly children of the Most High God. Remember, he is kind even to those who are wicked and ungrateful. Just as your Heavenly Father expresses perfect love, let your love be perfect, also. If you do this, you will surely be greatly rewarded."

70. Jesus Cautions against Self-Righteous Practices that Don't Belong in the Kingdom of God - Matt 6:1-8

"Avoid practicing your goodness in a conspicuous way just to impress others. Their approval is the only reward you'll ever get. But don't expect your Heavenly Father to reward you for that.

"So, if you plan to give to charity, don't make a show of it. Hypocrites want everybody to know how generous they are. They want all to know all about their charitable giving so everyone will give them praise. But that's absolutely all the honor they will ever get. However, when you help those in need, don't let your left hand know what your right hand is doing. Let your giving be a secret between you and your Heavenly Father. You can be sure that he will see what you have done and he will reward you."

71. Jesus Teaches How to Pray and the Importance of Forgiveness - Matt 6:9-15

"Here is a model of how you should pray:

Heavenly Father,
may your holy character be forever honored.
Make known your kingdom everywhere.
And may your will be fulfilled here on earth,
as it is already fulfilled in heaven.
Mercifully provide for each of our daily needs.
Please forgive our shortcomings,
just as we forgive the offenses of others.
Protect us in our times of testing,
and help us conquer all the deceptions of the evil one.

[The traditional ending is "For yours is the kingdom, and the power, and the glory forever. Amen."]

"If you forgive those who wrong you, then your Heavenly Father will surely forgive you. But if you are unforgiving toward others, how can you expect your Heavenly Father to forgive you?"

72. Jesus Teaches How to Fast - Matt 6:16-18

"Don't let it show outwardly when you go without food, or deny yourself in some way in order to seek God and learn his will. It is likely that the only reward you will ever get is the way people may respect you for your devotion. So, don't seek their sympathy by trying to look weak and pitiful. When you fast, comb your hair and wash your face. Do your best to avoid making it obvious that you are fasting. If your Heavenly Father is the only One who knows what you have done in secret, then he will be the One who rewards you for your devotion."

73. Jesus Warns against Slavery to Materialistic Values - Matt 6:19-23; Luke 11:34-36

"How secure are your earthly treasures? Think about it. Thieves can break in and rob them. Even moths and other pests can destroy them. However, heaven is actually the only safe place for storing up treasures. Nothing can steal or destroy them, if heaven is where your treasures are. You can't escape the fact that your heart will always be focused on the place where your most important treasures are kept.

"Your eyes can light up your whole body. If light penetrates your whole life leaving no part dark, you will be a truly generous and healthy person. However, if your focus in life is stingy and unhealthy, your whole body will be wrapped in darkness. If inwardly there is only darkness and no light at all, how hopeless you will be! So, make absolutely certain that you never allow anything to extinguish your inner light of God's truth and love.

"It is impossible to serve two masters. You are bound to hate one and love the other, or you will be loyal to one and despise the other. It is impossible to be a true servant of God and money at the same time."

74. Jesus Teaches about God's Care and the Foolishness of Worry - Matt 6:25-34; Luke 12:24

"Don't overlook the fact that God knows all about your circumstances. So why should you be anxious about things you might need? Don't worry about your food and drink or what you will wear, or about any other physical need. Isn't your life worth more than food and clothing? Look up at the sky and see the ravens and the many other kinds of birds God has created. They don't have to sow or reap or store up their food. Yet your Heavenly Father constantly takes care of them. Aren't you worth much more than the birds? Can even one single person live a moment longer or grow an inch taller by worrying? Since you can't possibly do such small things, what good does it do for you to worry about everything else?

"So, why do you worry about clothes? Look at the wild flowers out in the fields. Notice how they grow. They don't need to design and sew their clothes in order to have something to wear. Not even the great King Solomon was better dressed than any one of these little flowers. If God pays such careful attention to all the plants in the fields that are here today and burned as trash tomorrow, won't he show even more concern to your need for clothes? You of weak faith!

"Why worry? Why do you keep acting like pagan unbelievers? Like them, you're always asking, 'Where are we going to get the food and drink and clothes that we need?' Have you forgotten that your Heavenly Father knows you need these things? But here's what you ought to do: Make it your top priority to submit to God as your King, and live a godly life. If you do this, everything you really need will be yours as well. So, why worry about what might happen tomorrow? There will always be enough to worry about when tomorrow comes. Just take one day at a time. You can be sure that each day will have enough trouble of its own."

75. Jesus Teaches about Judging, Forgiveness and Generosity - Matt 7:1-5; Luke 6:37-40

"When you judge people, they will certainly turn around and judge you. Whatever measure you use when you judge them, they will surely evaluate you with the same measure. That is why you can often avoid being condemned by simply refusing to condemn others. In contrast, when you choose to forgive, you will surely be forgiven. And God will forgive you as well. Likewise, if you give generously to people, they will often return the favor. In fact, abundant blessings that have been pressed down, shaken together, and running over will be poured into your lap.

"Why do you notice the tiny speck of sawdust in your good friend's eye, while all the time you are overlooking the board in your own eye? How can you dare say to your friend, 'Hold still while I remove that tiny speck from your eye,' when all the time you have a board blocking your own view? What a hypocrite! Start by getting the board out of your eye. Then you'll be able to see clearly when you take the little speck from your fellow believer's eye.

"Can a blind person safely guide another blind person? If they try to do that, won't they both fall hand-in-hand down an unexpected stairway? Students are not often honored above their teacher. Yet all who master what their teacher has taught them will in many ways become like their teacher."

76. Jesus Warns against Sharing Spiritual Truths with Rebels - Matt 7:6

[Jesus compared self-serving people to dogs and pigs. They selfishly do whatever they want to do for their own personal benefit. They sometimes misuse deep spiritual truths as an excuse to do whatever they want to do.]

"Don't be too trusting with people who act like hungry dogs when it comes to their disrespect for spiritual truth and sacred experiences. Furthermore, don't toss your treasured spiritual pearls into a pigpen. If you do, they will fail to see any value at all in what you have given them. They are likely to trample on them, then turn against you and try to tear you to pieces."

77. Jesus Encourages Sincere Seeking, then Offers a "Golden Rule" - Matt 7:7-14; Luke 11:9-13

"You will receive what you ask for; you will find what you are looking for; the door will be opened if you simply knock. All who ask will receive; all who search will find; and the door will be opened to those who knock.

"What father would give his children a snake when they are asking for a fish dinner? Or would he give them a scorpion when they want an egg? Or would he give them a stone when they ask for bread? If you who live sinful lives know how to do what's best for your children, how much more should you be able to trust your Heavenly Father to give you the Holy Spirit along with all his other good gifts? You just need to ask him.

"Now here is the simple meaning of everything the Law requires and all that the prophets have proclaimed: 'In every circumstance, treat others in the same way you wish they would treat you.' [This is the Golden Rule.]

"Pass through the small gate and go up the narrow road that leads into a never-ending good life. In contrast, the highway to destruction is smooth and wide. Many will be attracted to go down that road."

78. Jesus Warns against False Prophets, Then Tells the Way to Recognize Truth and Falsehood - Matt 7:15-23; Luke 6:44-46

"Be careful not to be deceived by hypocritical religious leaders. They are like fierce wolves disguised as sheep. Just look at the results of their unworthy ministries. Do grapes grow on vines covered with thorns? Or do figs grow on thistle bushes? It's obvious that good fruit comes from good trees, and worthless fruit grows on bad trees. When a fruit tree never produces good fruit, it has to be cut down and burned up. Clearly the value of a tree depends on the kind of fruit and the quality of fruit that it produces.

"Why do some of you call me, 'Lord,' and never follow my instructions? Not everyone who calls me, 'Lord,' will get into the kingdom of heaven. Only those who do the will of my Father in heaven will enter heaven. On the Judgment Day there will be many who plead, 'Lord, didn't we speak messages in your name, and even cast out demons and do miracles in your name? But I will tell them plainly, 'I don't even know who you are. Get out of my sight you evildoers!'"

79. The Way You Relate to Christ's Teachings Will Determine Your Survival or Destruction - Matt 7:24-29; Luke 6:49

"All those who hear my teaching and put my words into practice will be like a wise person who built a house upon a rock foundation. Then rainstorms poured down, causing the streams to overflow. Powerful windstorms beat against that house, but it stood firm because its foundation had been built on solid rock. On the other hand, all who hear my words but fail to put them into practice, are like a foolish person who tried to build a house on sand. That foolish person failed to start with a solid foundation. Then rain poured down, streams flooded, and winds battered that house. Suddenly, it fell with a huge crash!"

After Jesus finished his message, the crowds were amazed at the way he taught. He spoke with authority, unlike the teachers of Jewish law.

80. Jesus Honors the Faith of the Roman Centurion - Matt 8:1-13; Luke 7:1-10

After Jesus finished speaking to the crowd that had been listening to him, he descended the mountain and entered the town of Capernaum. Large crowds continued to follow him. A certain Roman centurion had a highly valued servant. His servant was sick and near to death. The centurion heard about Jesus, so he requested some Jewish elders to go to Jesus and ask him to please come and heal his servant. Those elders brought Jesus his request: "Lord, my servant lies paralyzed at my home. He is suffering terribly." They earnestly pleaded, "This man is worthy of your help. Even though he is Roman, he loves our Jewish people. He even sponsored the building of our house of worship." Then Jesus went with them.

When he was not far from the centurion's house, the centurion sent some friends with this message: "Lord, you don't need to trouble yourself, because I don't deserve to have you come under my roof. That's why I didn't come in person to make my request. I know what it's like to have authority and to give orders to my soldiers. I can tell a particular soldier, 'Go,' and he goes; or to another, 'Come,' and he comes. Or I can tell my servant, 'Do this,' and he immediately obeys."

When Jesus heard what the Roman centurion had to say, he was amazed. Turning to the crowd following him, Jesus said, "The truth is, I have never seen such great faith, not even in Israel. I tell you that many people will come from both east and west to celebrate the heavenly feast with Abraham, Isaac, and Jacob in God's kingdom. On the other hand, there will be some subjects who fail to submit to the rule of God's eternal kingdom. They will be thrown into outer darkness where there will be weeping and gnashing of teeth."

Then Jesus told the centurion's messengers, "Go ahead! It will happen exactly as the centurion believed it would happen." And at that very moment the centurion's servant was healed. The men who had been sent returned to the house and found the servant had been completely delivered from his paralysis.

81. Jesus Raises a Widow's Son at Nain - Luke 7:11-17

A short time later, Jesus entered a town called Nain. His disciples and a large crowd followed along with him. When he came near to the town's gate, the corpse of a young man was being carried away. He had been his mother's only son. She was also a widow. Another large crowd from the town accompanied her. When the Lord saw her, his heart was moved with compassion. So, he said to her, "Don't cry."

Then Jesus approached the coffin, and when he touched it, those who were carrying it stood still. Then Jesus commanded, "Young man, get up!" Immediately, the dead man sat up and began talking. Then Jesus gave him back to his mother—alive.

Immediately, everyone was completely amazed and began praising God. "A great prophet has come among us," they said. "God has arrived to help his people." News about Jesus spread through the region of Judea and through all the surrounding area.

82. Jesus Commends John the Baptist at a Time when John Was Facing Persecution and Doubts - Matt 11:2-19; Luke 7:18-35

Although John was in prison, his followers kept telling him all about how the crowds were flocking to Jesus and celebrating his ministry. So, he sent two of his disciples to ask the following question: "Are you the promised Messiah, or should we expect someone else?"

When the representatives came to Jesus, they said, "John the Baptist told us to ask you, 'Are you the one who is to come, or should we expect someone else?'"

At that very same moment Jesus was healing many who were suffering from various diseases, sickness, and evil spirits. He was also giving sight to many who were blind. And this is how he answered the messengers. "Return to John and tell him what you have seen and heard: The blind receive their sight, the lame walk, people with leprosy and skin diseases are cleansed and made well, the deaf are able to hear, the dead are raised to life, and the Good News is proclaimed to the poor. Happy are all those who do not become confused and stumble because of me."

When John's messengers had gone, Jesus began to describe John to the crowd: "What did you go out into the desert to see? Was it perhaps a tall reed swaying in the wind? If not, then what did you go out to see? A man dressed in proper clothes? No, those who dress up in fine clothing are found in palaces of kings. So, what did you go out to see—a great prophet? Yes, I tell you much more than just another prophet. He is the one that was predicted in the prophetic writings:

> *I will send my messenger ahead of you,*
> *to prepare the way for you. (Malachi 3:1)*

"I tell you the truth: Among those born of women, John the Baptist is the greatest. However, even the least in the Kingdom of Heaven is greater than John. The fact is, that from John's ministry until now, the Kingdom of Heaven has been forcefully advancing, and violent people have been attacking it. John is merely the latest of all the prophets and messengers of the Law. Surely you can see that John is actually the long-awaited Elijah who was promised. If your ears are tuned to God's truth, then pay careful attention!"

As they listened to Jesus, all those who had been baptized by John agreed that God's way had certainly been the right one. However, the legalistic Pharisees and experts in Mosaic Law had closed their minds to what Jesus said because they had rejected John's baptism.

"How can I illustrate this generation?" Jesus asked. "They are like children playing outdoors. They call to each other:

> 'When we played wedding songs, you wouldn't dance;
> When we sang funeral songs, you wouldn't cry.'

"In a similar way, John the Baptist came fasting food and wine, and you criticized, 'He's demon possessed!' Then the Son of Man came eating and drinking, and you criticize, 'See how he eats and drinks too much! He spends time associating with sinners and with cheating tax collectors.' But when a person's choices are wise, the proof will be clearly seen in the good results."

83. Jesus Rejoices because the Childlike and Burdened Are Invited into God's Kingdom - Matt 11:25-30

Then Jesus said, "Father, Lord of heaven and earth, I praise you because you have hidden many of the deep secrets of your kingdom from those who are wise and educated, but revealed them to those who listen and are childlike. Yes, Father, this is how you like to do it.

"My Father has entrusted everything to me. No one really knows the Son except the Father, and no one really knows the Father except the Son and those to whom the Son chooses to reveal the Father.

"Draw near to me, all of you who are exhausted and weighed down with life's burdens. If you will just let me be your partner, I promise to give you peace and rest. Team up with me and learn from me, because I am gentle-hearted and humble. When you do this, you will find rest for your souls. As long as you remain my partner, the load will never be too heavy. You will surely be able to keep doing your part."

84. A Sinful, yet Repentant Woman Anoints Christ's Feet - Luke 7:36-50

One of the Pharisees invited Jesus for dinner. Jesus accepted the invitation. [Pharisees were experts in all the traditions of Jewish Law.] Jesus accepted the invitation. [According to custom, they were likely sitting on the floor, reclining next to a low table.] A woman of the town known for her sinful life heard that Jesus was eating at the Pharisees house. So, she entered and brought with her an expensive jar of perfume. Her tears fell on the Lord's feet as she knelt behind him. Then she poured some perfume on his feet and was kissing them and wiping them with her hair.

When the Pharisee saw what she was doing, he thought, "If this man were really a prophet, he would certainly know what kind of woman is touching him. He would know what a terrible sinner she is."

Jesus answered his thoughts saying, "Simon, I want to tell you something."

"What is it, teacher?" he said.

"Two people owed money to a moneylender. One owed him the salary for a year and a half. The other owed the salary for a month and a half. However, neither one had the necessary money to pay him back, so the lender forgave both of their debts. Now, which of them do you think will be most appreciative and love the lender more?"

Simon answered, "I guess it would be the one with the biggest debt."

"You're exactly right," Jesus said.

Then looking toward the woman, Jesus said to Simon, "Have you noticed this woman? When I came into your house, you did not follow the usual custom of providing water to wash the street-dust from my feet. But she wet my feet with her tears and kept wiping them with her hair. You didn't give me the customary kiss of greeting, but this woman has not stopped kissing my feet since I first entered. You provided no oil to anoint my head as is the custom, but she poured expensive perfume on my feet. Now, I want you to know that her many sins have been forgiven. She did all of this out of love and gratitude because God's forgiveness has brought her peace. However, those who have been forgiven very little, also love little."

Then Jesus spoke directly to her and said, "Your many sins are all forgiven."

The other guests murmured among each other. "Who does he think he is to be able to even forgive sins?"

Then Jesus told the woman, "Your faith has saved you; now you may go in peace."

85. Jesus and His Disciples Spread the Good News while Many Women Serve their Needs - Luke 8:1-3

Next, Jesus and his twelve disciples went through many towns and villages, announcing the Good News that the Kingdom of God had arrived. Several women who had been delivered from evil spirits and diseases were also traveling with them. Among them was Mary Magdalene who had been delivered from seven demons. There was also Joanna who was Chuza's wife. Chuza managed King Herod's household. Susanna was also there to help support the team that traveled with Jesus.

86. Jesus Identifies Those Who Belong to His True Spiritual Family - Matt 12:48-50; Mark 3:20-32; Luke 8:19-21

When Jesus entered into a certain house, such a large crowd gathered that he and his disciples didn't even have a chance to eat. His mother and brothers heard about what was going on, and they commented, "What is he thinking? He must be out of his mind." They thought that perhaps they could take charge of the situation, but they couldn't even get close to him because of the huge crowd. So, they sent a messenger to tell him, "Your mother and brothers are outside hoping to see you."

When he heard this, Jesus said to the messenger, "Who really is my mother, and who really are my brothers and sisters? They are the ones who hear the word of God and put it into practice. In fact, each person who does the will of my Father in heaven is my brother and sister and mother."

87. Jesus Tells Stories from a Boat to Illustrate the Kingdom of God - Matt 13:1; Mark 4:1-2

Later that same day, Jesus left the house and sat down by the lake. Once again, he began to teach. Since the crowd that gathered was so huge, he got into a boat anchored near the shore. All the people gathered near the water's edge where they listened while Jesus used stories to illustrate most of his teaching.

88. Jesus Describes Four Kinds of Soil and Four Kinds of Listeners - Matt 13:4-23; Mark 4:2-20; Luke 8:11-15

As Jesus spoke to the people, he gave them the following illustration: "Listen carefully! A certain farmer began to plant his crops. As he was scattering the seeds, some fell on the path where the ground was very hard. Then the birds came and ate it all up. Other seeds fell on rocky ground where the soil was very shallow. There the seeds sprang up quickly because the soil wasn't deep enough. After the sun came up, the plants were scorched and quickly withered up. Their roots just couldn't develop in that shallow soil. Other seeds fell where thorns were already growing. The plants had no chance to grow before the thorns multiplied and choked them. But some seeds did fall on good soil where they produced a healthy crop. Some produced a hundred times, or sixty times, or thirty times more than what had been planted. If you have ears to understand spiritual truth, then you must listen and take it to heart!"

Later when Jesus, the Twelve, and others were gathered around, they asked him, "Why do you always speak to the people with stories?"

Then Jesus responded, "Didn't you understand my illustration? Then how will you ever understand any of my stories? The secret to the knowledge of the Kingdom of Heaven is for you to receive, but not for those who are unable to understand. Whoever has a receptive heart and mind will be given more. They will even receive abundantly. On the other hand, those who do not possess a listening heart will even forget what they think they have. That is why I use stories when I speak to them. Though they seem to see, they do not really see. Though they seem to hear, they do not really understand.

"This prophecy spoken by Isaiah has been fulfilled in these people:

> *You will be constantly hearing words,*
> *yet never really understanding what they mean.*
> *You will be constantly seeing, but never perceiving.*
> *For the hearts of these people have become calloused.*
> *They can barely hear with their ears,*
> *and they have closed their eyes.*
> *If they had not done this,*
> *they could have seen with their eyes.*
> *They might have been able to hear with their ears,*
> *and understand with their hearts.*
> *Then they would have repented,*
> *and I could have healed them. (Isaiah 6:9-10)*

"However, God has blessed your eyes so you can truly see, and your ears so you can hear and understand. It is absolutely true that many prophets and godly people longed to see what you have been allowed to see, but they never had the opportunity. They also desired to hear what you have been allowed to hear, but they were never given the chance.

"Now, let me tell you the meaning of the story about the farmer who planted seeds that fell on different kinds of soil. The Word of God is the seed. The farmer is the one who plants God's Word. When a person hears the message about God's Kingdom and doesn't welcome it, then Satan comes and snatches away the truth that was planted in that person's heart. The devil aims to keep the person from believing and receiving salvation. This happens when seeds fall on the path.

"The seed that falls on rocky ground represents people who joyfully receive the message without hesitation. However, they are people whose spiritual roots are shallow, so their faith does not endure. They believe for a little while, but when their faith is tested by trouble or persecution against the message of salvation, they soon fall away.

"The seed that fell among thorns represents those who hear the message of salvation, but they are distracted by daily worries and they are easily deceived by their efforts to gain things like wealth and pleasure. All such things choke out God's Word so it cannot bear spiritual fruit. Such people fail to become mature in their faith.

"On the other hand, the seed that fell on good soil represents the kind of people who possess a worthy and good heart. When they hear the Word, they understand it and accept it. They also retain it and by persevering in faith, they produce a good crop that yields a hundred, or sixty, or thirty times more than what was planted in the beginning."

89. Jesus Speaks about the Importance of Listening Well - Mark 4:23-24; Luke 8:18

"If anyone has ears that can hear and understand spiritual truth, then listen well and pay careful attention. Be thoughtful and wise about how you put into practice the truth you have received from God. The importance you give to it will pay abundant dividends. When you make genuine truth from God a central part of your life, you are then qualified to receive even more. But, if you fail to welcome God's truth, you will surely lose even what little you think you have."

90. Jesus Explains the Natural Growth of the Kingdom of God - Mark 4:26-29

Jesus also gave this illustration: "Here is what the Kingdom of God is like. When people scatter seed on the ground, whether or not they sleep, day or night the seeds keep sprouting and growing. They have no idea how it happened. The soil has within itself the ability to produce grain—from stem to head—it produces the full kernel. As soon as the grain ripens, it is cut off and gathered because the time for harvest has arrived."

91. Jesus Uses Weeds and Wheat to Illustrate God's Strategy against Satan - Matt 13:24-30

Then Jesus gave another illustration: "The Kingdom of Heaven is like a man who planted high-quality wheat seeds in his field. However, when he was asleep, his enemy secretly planted weeds among the wheat and then left. When the wheat sprouted and ripened, the weeds also appeared among the wheat. Then the owner's workmen came to him and asked, 'Sir, we thought you planted good seeds in your field, so how did these weeds get here?'

'An enemy must have done this,' he answered.

'Do you want us to pull up the weeds?' the servants asked.

'No,' the owner answered. 'If you do that, you might uproot the wheat along with the weeds. Just let both grow together. When the time for harvest comes, I'll instruct the harvesters to collect the weeds into bundles to be burned. Then they can gather the wheat for storage.'"

92. Jesus Uses Mustard Seeds to Illustrate the Growth of God's Kingdom - Matt 13:31-32

Jesus told them yet another story as an illustration: "The Kingdom of Heaven is like a little mustard seed that a man planted in his field. It is one of the smallest seeds, but when it is full-grown it is among the larger garden plants. It is like a small tree. The birds can even sit on its branches."

93. Jesus Explains Kingdom Growth by the Way Yeast Grows in Dough - Matt 13:33

Jesus presented still another illustration: "The Kingdom of Heaven is like yeast that a woman mixed into about sixty pounds of flour. It gradually worked its way completely through the whole dough."

94. Jesus Uses Parables Extensively - Matt 13:34-35

As Jesus addressed the crowds, everything he said was illustrated with stories. In this way, what the prophet said was fulfilled:

I will speak to you in a parable.
I will teach you hidden lessons from our past,
even since the creation of the world.
(Psalm 78:2)

95. Jesus Explains the Parable of the Weeds to His Disciples - Matt 13:36-43; Mark 4:34

Once when Jesus was alone with his disciples, they entered a house. At that time, he explained answers to their questions. They asked him, "Please explain the meaning of your story about weeds in a field."

Here is the explanation that he gave to them: "The Son of Man is the One who planted the good seed. The field represents the whole world. The good seed stands for the people of God's Kingdom. In contrast, the weeds are people who belong to the evil one. The enemy who plants the weeds is the devil. The harvest will take place at the end of the age. Angels are the harvesters.

"Just as weeds are pulled up and burned in a fire, this is how it will be at the end of the age. The Son of Man will send out his angels to weed out from his Kingdom everything that leads to sin and those who do evil. The angels will throw them into hell's blazing furnace where there will be crying and grinding of teeth. But those who are righteous will shine like the sun in the Kingdom of their Father. Let those with spiritual ears listen and understand."

96. Jesus Uses Hidden Treasure to Illustrate the Kingdom of Heaven - Matt 13:44

"The Kingdom of Heaven is like a valuable treasure that was hidden in a field. When a man happened to find it, he hid it again. Then he went joyfully to sell everything he owned in order to buy that field."

97. Jesus Compares Seeking the Kingdom with Searching for a Valuable Pearl - Matt 13:45-46

"The Kingdom of Heaven is also like a tradesman searching for fine pearls. When he found an extremely valuable one, he took time to sell everything he owned so he could return and buy that choice pearl."

98. A Fisherman's Net Shows How Angels Separate Believers from Unbelievers - Matt 13:47-50

"The Kingdom of Heaven is also like a fisherman's net that was lowered into a lake and caught many kinds of fish. When it was full, they dragged it up on the bank where they sorted out the valuable fish from the worthless ones. They kept the good ones, but threw the bad ones away. The end of the age will be like that. The angels will come and separate wicked people from godly people. They will throw the wicked into the blazing furnace where there will be torment, crying, and grinding of teeth." [Those who place their trust in Jesus are the godly ones!]

99. Jesus Illustrates How Wise Teachers Integrate Old and New Truths - Matt 13:51-53

Jesus asked his disciples, "Have you understood all of my teachings?"
    "Yes," they answered.
    Then he told them, "Every wise teacher of God's Law who has become a disciple in the Kingdom of Heaven is like a homeowner who has been cleaning out his storeroom. In the process, he keeps finding some unexpected new treasures and also, many old favorite ones."
    When Jesus finished telling these stories as illustrations, he traveled on.

100. Jesus Departs by Boat, then Calms a Storm - Matt 8:18-27; Mark 4:35-39; Luke 8:22-25

One evening at dusk, Jesus noticed that a large crowd was gathering around him. So he told his disciples, "Let's go over to the other side of the lake." They left the crowd behind and got into a boat. The disciples took Jesus along without any special preparations. There were also many other boats that joined them.
    As they sailed along, Jesus fell asleep. But a sudden, terrible wind came up causing the waves to break over the boat. Meanwhile, Jesus was in the back of the boat, sound asleep on a cushion. His disciples woke him up, yelling with great fear, "Teacher, don't you even care if we all drown? Lord, rescue us!"

Then Jesus stood up and commanded the stormy wind and raging waves. "Quiet down now! Be peaceful and still!" And immediately, the wind and waves became absolutely quiet and calm.

Jesus then turned to them and asked, "Why are you so frightened? Haven't you learned to trust in God yet?"

Trembling with fear and amazement, they asked each other, "What kind of man could possibly do the things we have just seen? Why, even the stormy winds and waves have to obey him!"

101. Jesus Sends Demons from Men to Pigs - Matt 8:28-33; Mark 5:1-20; Luke 8:27-39

Jesus and his disciples continued on across the lake to an area known as the Gerasenes. [They were also known as Gadarenes.] Just as Jesus was getting out of the boat, two demon-possessed men met him. They came from a place where there were some tombs. People were afraid to go into that area because the two men had such a reputation of violence. It was impossible for anyone to bind one of the men—not even with a chain. He was always able to tear off his chains and break away from the irons on his feet. No one was ever able to control him. Day and night, he lived naked up in the hills close to some tombs. He kept hitting himself with stones, and people often heard him screaming.

When he saw Jesus from a distance, the man ran and fell down on his knees before him. Here is what the demon was screaming: "What do you want from me, Jesus, Son of the Most High God? I beg you, don't torture me!"

The evil spirit had often taken control of the man, in spite of the fact that he was kept under guard and both his hands and feet were in chains. The demon often forced him out into lonely places.

Then Jesus spoke directly to the demon. "What is your name?"

"Legion," he answered. In fact, many demons had taken control of him. They kept repeatedly begging Jesus, "Don't send us away from our familiar territory, nor into the Bottomless Pit!"

By then, the demons were actually shouting from both demon-possessed men, "Why have you come here to torture us before the appointed time of judgment?"

On a nearby hillside, a large herd of pigs was feeding. The demons pleaded with Jesus saying, "Let us go into those pigs."

So, he let them go. Then the demons left both of the demon-possessed men and entered the pigs, which numbered about two thousand. The whole herd ran down a steep bank and were drowned in the lake.

When those who had been taking care of the pigs saw everything that happened, both to the pigs and to the men, they spread the news all around the nearby countryside and towns. Then many people went to see for themselves what had happened. When they came to Jesus, they were amazed that the men who had been demon-possessed were sitting at the feet of Jesus, clothed and perfectly normal in every way. Then all the people who lived in that area begged Jesus to leave because these events frightened them so much. They just didn't know what to think of it all. So Jesus got into a boat and left.

However, one of the men who had been delivered from demons begged Jesus, "Please, let me go with you!"

But Jesus told him, "Go back home and tell your family and friends all about the wonderful things God has done for you." Then the man left and began to tell everyone all about what Jesus had done for him, and everyone was absolutely amazed. The area where this happened was known as The Ten Cities.

102. Jesus Heals a Woman Who Touched His Robe, then Restores Life to the Daughter of Jairus - Matt 9:23-25; Mark 5:21-43; Luke 8:42-53

Once again, Jesus crossed by boat over to the other side of the lake. While he was still near the lake, a large crowd began to gather around him. A leader of the Jewish house of worship, named Jairus, came to Jesus and fell at his feet pleading, "My little daughter is about to die. I'm sure that if you will just come and place your hands on her, she will be healed and continue to live." And filled with compassion, Jesus went along with him.

The large crowd that followed him was almost crushing him. A woman who had been hemorrhaging for twelve years was also there. She had spent everything she had on many doctors, but her physical problem was only getting worse. When she learned about Jesus, she followed the crowd and took advantage of a chance to reach out and touch the edge of his outer garment. She thought, *If I can just touch his clothing, I'm sure I will be healed.* When she was actually able to do it, her bleeding immediately stopped. Her body felt so relieved that she knew she had been set free from all her suffering.

However, Jesus immediately became aware that healing power had gone out from him. He turned back within the crowd and asked, "Who just touched my clothes?"

His disciples answered, "You can see how many people are crowding all around you, so how can you ask, 'Who touched me?'"

However, Jesus kept scanning the crowd to see if he could tell who did it. "Someone touched me with faith," he insisted, "because I felt healing power passing out through me."

Then the woman realized that she could no longer go unnoticed. She threw herself down at the Lord's feet trembling with fear, and confessed the whole truth. Then Jesus responded, "My child, your faith has healed you. You may go in peace now because you are completely free from your suffering."

Jesus had not even finished speaking when some folks came from the home of Jairus, the leader of the Jewish house of worship. They informed Jairus, "Your daughter has already died, so why bother the Teacher any longer?"

But Jesus overheard what was said, and he told him, "Don't be anxious; just keep trusting in God."

When they reached the home of Jairus, Jesus saw the great disturbance that was caused by all the people who were grieving the death of the Jewish leader's daughter. Some were playing mournful music on pipes; others were crying and wailing loudly.

Jesus asked, "Why all the commotion? You are free to leave because the girl is not dead at all. In fact, she's only sleeping." But they just laughed at him because they were so sure that she was really dead.

After dismissing the crowd, Jesus didn't let anyone accompany him to where the girl was lying except Peter, John, and James, and the little girl's parents. Then he took hold of the child's hand and commanded, *"Talitha koum!"* That means, "Little girl, I tell you, get up!"

Instantly, that little twelve-year-old girl stood up and began to walk around. Everyone was absolutely astonished. But Jesus ordered the witnesses to this miracle not to tell anyone about what had happened. [He clearly understood that a huge, popular response would only hinder his ministry of teaching about the Kingdom of God.] Then Jesus told the girl's parents, "You need to give her something to eat."

103. Jesus Heals Two Blind Men, but Is Blasphemed for Casting Out Demons - Matt 9:27-34

Going on from there, two blind men kept following Jesus, calling out, "Have mercy on us, Son of David!" ["Son of David" refers to the Messiah.]

After Jesus went indoors, he asked the blind men, "Do you believe I can heal your eyes?"

"Yes, Lord, we do believe," they answered.

Then Jesus touched their eyes and said, "Let it be done according to what you are believing right now." Instantly, their sight was restored. But Jesus strictly warned them, "Don't tell anyone how this happened!" Still, they left and spread the news about Jesus all over that area.

As they were leaving, a demon-possessed man who was unable to speak, was brought to Jesus. After the demon was driven out, the man was able to speak. This so amazed the crowd that the people were saying, "We have never seen anything like this in all of Israel."

Yet, the legalistic Pharisees gave this explanation: "He uses the power of the prince of demons to drive out the other demons."

104. Jesus Again Visits His Unbelieving Hometown of Nazareth - Mark 6:1-6

Then Jesus took his disciples with him to visit his hometown. On the Sabbath Day, he began to teach in the Jewish house of worship. Many of his hometown people were amazed when they heard him speak.

They asked each other, "Where did he learn all of this? Where did he get all this wisdom? What do his amazing miracles mean? Isn't he the boy who was trained to be a carpenter? We know all about his family! He is Mary's son. His brothers are James, Joses, Judas, and Simon. His sisters live here, too." The honor that followed him was offensive to his hometown people.

This is how Jesus himself explained this lack of respect in the area of his hometown: "Each Prophet is honored everywhere except in his hometown among relatives, friends, and family." Even Jesus was amazed at the way their lack of faith prevented him from doing any miracles there. He was merely able to lay his hands on a few sick people and heal them.

105. Jesus Urges His Disciples to Pray for the Needed Workers - Matt 9:35-38

As Jesus traveled through many villages and towns, he taught in the Jewish houses of worship. He announced the Good News that the Kingdom of God had arrived. He also healed every kind of sickness and disease. When he saw how the people were oppressed and helpless, like sheep needing a shepherd, he was filled with compassion for them.

This is how he explained it to his disciples: "Abundant crops are ready for harvesting, but there are very few workers! Pray that the Lord of the harvest will enlist and quickly send out workers to do the harvesting that is so greatly needed."

106. Jesus Gives Special Instructions and Authority to the Twelve Apostles - Matt 10:1-42; Mark 6:6-9, Luke 9:1-5; 10:5-7; 12:5-12

As Jesus was teaching from place to place, he called his twelve disciples to come to him. Then he gave them ability and authority to drive out demons and to heal all kinds of sickness and diseases.

Jesus sent his disciples out in teams of two with these instructions: "Before you go to the Gentiles [non-Jews] or Samaritans, [mixed Jews and Gentiles] you must give the first opportunity to the lost sheep of Israel. As you go from place to place, announce this message: 'The Kingdom of Heaven has come near.' Minister healing to the sick, raise up the dead, bring healing and cleansing to those suffering from leprosy and skin diseases, and also drive out demons. You have freely received from me. Now freely give.

"However, don't carry everything you need along with you; just take a walking staff. Don't take bread, or a backpack, or money belts. Wear sandals, but don't even take an extra shirt. When you come to a town or village, try to find an honorable person who will allow you to stay in their home until you move on. As you enter, if you see that the home is worthy, greet the family like this: 'May God's peace rest on this home.' If peace loving people live there, your blessing will rest upon them. If not, your blessing will come back to you. Do not move around from place to place. Stay in the place that welcomes you, eating and drinking whatever they provide. As a worker in God's

Kingdom, you deserve your wages. If people refuse to welcome you or listen to your message, leave that town. As you go, shake the dust from your feet as a witness against that place. I'm telling you the truth, on the Day of Judgment, even Sodom and Gomorrah will have it better than any town that rejects my messengers.

"I'm sending you out like sheep living around wolves. Because of that, you must be as smart as snakes and as innocent and harmless as doves. Be on your guard; you will be delivered to local authorities and sometimes even beaten and accused of false religion. Because of your faith in me, you will be brought before all kinds of government authorities, but this will give you many opportunities to be my witnesses. However, don't worry ahead of time what you will say or how you will answer. At the time when you need it, the Holy Spirit will teach you what to say and how to defend yourself. You won't be the one speaking; the Spirit of your Heavenly Father will be talking through you.

"Family members will betray one another to death; brother against brother, father against his children, and children against their own parents. Everyone will hate you because of your faith in me. But those who stand firm to the end will be saved. If you are persecuted in one place, escape to another place. I tell you the absolute truth, this message will not be received in every single town and village of Israel before the Son of Man returns.

"Students are not honored above their teachers, nor are workers honored above their employers. It is sufficient for students to be like their teachers and workers to be like their employers. When even the head of God's house is called *Beelzebulb*, it is certainly no wonder that the members of his household are also insulted!" [Beelzebub was the god of Ekron referred to in 1 Kings 1:1-4. This means prince of demons, or lord of flies.]

Jesus continued, "Don't fear those who have power to kill your body but have no power to destroy your soul. However, let me tell you whom to fear: Be afraid of the One who can destroy both your soul and body in hell, even after your body has been killed.

"In the Jewish market place near the Temple, two sparrows sell for a penny, or five for two pennies. Not one of them falls to the ground without your Heavenly Father's concern. He even knows exactly how many hairs are on your head. So why should you ever fear? Aren't you worth far more than many sparrows?

"Do you think I have come to bring peace between people and nations? No, just the opposite is true. My coming brings conflict. Because of me . . .

A man will turn against his own father,
a daughter against her own mother,
a daughter-in-law against her mother-in-law.
A man's enemies will be members
of his own household. (Micah 7:6)

At this point, Jesus began to teach the importance of loving him above all other relationships.

"Those who welcome my followers are also welcoming me. And those who welcome me are also welcoming the One who sent me. Those who welcome a prophet because he is a prophet will receive a prophet's reward, and those who welcome a godly person because he is a godly person will receive a godly person's reward. I tell you the truth, those who give just a cup of cool water to a child, or to one of my teachable and childlike followers, will certainly not lose their reward."

107. Jesus and the Twelve Minister to the Surrounding Towns - Matt 11:1; Mark 6:12-13; Luke 9:6

When Jesus completed instructing the twelve disciples, they went from town to town in the area of Galilee preaching that people need to repent of their sins. They also drove out many demons and anointed many sick people with oil, and they were healed.

108. Herod Kills John the Baptist, then Wonders if John Has Returned from the Dead - Matt 14:12; Mark 6:14-29; Luke 9:7-9

When Herod the Tetrarch heard about all that was happening, [Herod Antipas was the Roman ruler over Galilee] he was confused. Some thought John the Baptist must have been raised from the dead. That seemed to explain the reason behind the miraculous powers at work. Others thought Elijah, or one of the ancient prophets, must have come back to life. However, Herod said, "I beheaded John, so who could this be that is causing such a stir among the people?" He looked for a good opportunity to see Jesus for himself. Actually, Herod had previously given orders to arrest John. He had him bound and thrown into prison in order to please his wife, Herodias. She was both

Herod's wife and his sister-in-law because she had previously been his brother's wife, as well. Herodias hated John because he had publicly condemned King Herod as an adulterer for marrying Herodias.

However, Herod respected John as a righteous and holy man. When Herod listened to John, he didn't know what to think. He truly liked to hear what John had to say.

On Herod's birthday during a great banquet in his honor—with all the leading officials in Galilee present—the daughter of Herodias came in and danced in front of Herod and his guests. [Tradition says her name was Salome.]

King Herod was so excited and pleased by her dance, that he called her over and said to her, "I swear to give you absolutely anything you want—even up to half of my kingdom. Just say what you want and you will have it."

She went to her mother, Herodias, and said, "What shall I ask for?"

Immediately, Herodias answered, "Ask for the head of John the Baptist."

The girl went quickly to the king and said, "I ask you to give me the head of John the Baptist right now on a platter."

King Herod was terribly frustrated by her request, but to break an oath in front of his dinner quests was out of the question. So, he ordered an executioner to bring in John's head. The man went quickly to the prison and beheaded John. Then he brought back his head on a platter. He gave it to the girl who passed it on to her mother.

When John's disciples heard what had happened, they went right away and carried his body to a tomb. Then they came to Jesus and told him what had happened.

109. The Twelve Return to Report Their Ministry Experiences - Mark 6:30

When the twelve apostles returned from their ministry, they gathered around Jesus and gave him a complete report of their teachings and all the things they had done.

110. Jesus Calls His Disciples to a Place of Retreat and Rest - Mark 6:31-34; Luke 9:10-11; John 6:1-4

There were crowds of people constantly coming and going around Jesus to the extent that he and his disciples could hardly find a chance to eat. He said to them, "Let's get away from the crowds to a quiet place and get some rest."

They left by boat to a solitary place, and came to the town of Bethsaida that was on the other side of the Sea of Galilee. However, people from many other towns saw which way he was heading, and they ran along the shore to get there ahead of Jesus. Then as Jesus looked all around at the great throng, he felt compassion for them. They seemed to him like sheep trying to find their shepherd. Because of this, Jesus welcomed them and began to teach them about the Kingdom of God. He also healed all those who needed healing.

Afterward, Jesus climbed to a flat place on the side of a mountain where he sat down with his disciples. It was almost the time of year to celebrate the Jewish Passover.

111. Jesus Feeds Five Thousand Men Plus Women and Children - Matt 14:13-21; Mark 6:40; Luke 9:12-16; John 6:5-15

Late one afternoon, the Twelve came to Jesus and said to him, "Don't you think it is time now to send the crowd away? They need to look for food and lodging in the nearby villages and countryside. This place where we are is very isolated."

Jesus answered, "Then you must feed them."

Then he asked Philip, "Where do you think we could buy enough bread to feed so many people?" He was only testing Philip because Jesus already knew what he was planning to do.

Philip answered, "I think we would need more than half a year's wages just to buy enough bread for each person to have even one bite."

Andrew, Peter's brother spoke up and said, "There's a boy here who brought a small lunch containing five barley loaves and two little fish. How could they possibly feed such a huge crowd?"

Then Jesus instructed, "Organize the people into groups of hundreds and fifties and have them all sit down."

Since there was plenty of grass in that location, they were all able to find an appropriate place to sit. There were about five thousand men present, not counting the women and children.

Jesus held up some loaves and he looked up to heaven as he offered thanks. Then he broke the bread, and his disciples distributed to each person as much as they wanted. He followed the same procedure with the fish.

After everyone had enough to eat, he told his disciples, "Collect the leftover pieces so that nothing will be wasted." When they had done this, the crowd returned twelve baskets filled with fish and barley loaves that were left over.

When the people realized the importance of this great sign that Jesus had performed, they began to say to each other, "He certainly must be the great Prophet everyone has been waiting for." But Jesus realized they were making plans to gather around and force him to become their king. [Of course, the Romans would see this as a threat.]

Jesus quickly had his disciples return to their boat and take it on ahead of him to the town of Capernaum on the other side of the lake while he dismissed the crowd. Then Jesus went up on the side of a mountain where he spent time alone praying. Later that night, he was still alone as the disciples in their boat had traveled quite some distance from land, and were being buffeted by stormy wind and waves.

112. Jesus Walks to His Disciples on Stormy Seas; Peter also Begins to Walk on Water – Matt 14:25-33; Mark 6:48-52; John 6:17-21

It was dark, and Jesus had not yet joined the disciples. But he saw them straining on the oars against the strong wind and rough waters. And as the storm grew even stronger as the morning began to dawn, Jesus went toward them, walking on the water of the lake. He was about to walk on past them when suddenly they saw him there, walking on the water. They were extremely terrified and cried out in fear, "It's a ghost!"

But Jesus responded quickly, "Be brave! It is I. There is no reason to be afraid."

Peter answered, "Lord, if it really is you, order me to come to you on the water."

"Come on," Jesus said.

Amazed, Peter climbed down out of the boat and started walking on the water toward Jesus. But his attention was quickly distracted by the wind-driven waves. He became terribly frightened. Immediately, he began to sink and he called out, "Lord, save me!"

Jesus quickly reached out and caught him. "You have such small faith," Jesus said. "What made you doubt?"

The disciples were completely amazed because they hadn't fully understood the significance of the earlier miracle of the loaves and fish when Jesus fed the multitude. Their hearts kept on resisting truth whenever they couldn't comprehend it.

Finally, they were sure it was Jesus, and they were willing to let him get into their boat. And as Jesus and Peter were climbing into the boat, the wind suddenly died down. All those in the boat worshiped Jesus as they exclaimed, "Truly you are the Son of God!" and the boat instantly reached the shore where they were heading.

113. Jesus Heals Many at Gennesaret - Mark 6:53-56

When Jesus and his disciples reached Gennesaret, they anchored their boat. Then all the people there quickly recognized Jesus. Wherever he went, in all the towns and villages, and throughout the countryside, people started bringing all those who were sick to the marketplaces. They begged Jesus to let them reach out and touch just the edge of his outer garment, and every person who touched him was immediately healed.

114. Jesus Announces the "Work God Requires" - John 6:22-29

The following day, many people stayed on the shore of the lake where Jesus and his disciples had been. They learned that only one boat had passed that way, but Jesus had not boarded it. However, his disciples left without him. Later some boats from Tiberias landed near the place where he had blessed the bread and fish and had fed thousands of people. Once the crowd understood that Jesus and his disciples were no longer there, they got into their boats and went to Capernaum searching for him. When they finally found him over on the other side of the lake, they were puzzled and asked, "Teacher, how did you get here?" [In fact, Jesus had walked on water, then joined his disciples in their boat.]

78

Jesus answered, "I'll tell you the truth: you are anxious to find me, but not because you understood the meaning of my miracles. It was only because your appetite was satisfied with the loaves I gave you. Don't try so hard to get the kind of food that can spoil. Instead, you need to do whatever it takes to obtain the spiritual kind of food given to you by the Son of Man. That will result in eternal life. For God the Father has placed his seal of approval upon his Son."

Then his disciples asked Jesus, "What do we need to do in order to fulfill what God requires of us?"

Jesus answered, "Here is what God requires: Place your faith in the One that God has sent into the world."

115. Jesus Teaches Concerning the True Bread of Life— His Own Flesh and Blood - John 6:30-59

Some in the crowd near Jesus asked him, "What sign can you give us as proof, so we can place our faith in you? What great thing will you do? After all, our ancestors ate the miraculous manna that God gave to them when they were starving in the wilderness. The Scriptures say, 'He gave them bread from heaven to eat.'" (Ex. 16:4; Neh. 9:15; Ps. 78:24-25)

Jesus said this to them, "Here is the absolute truth. It wasn't Moses who gave you the bread from heaven. It is my Father who gives you the true bread from heaven. Actually, God's bread is the bread that has come down from heaven and provides life for the whole world."

"Teacher," they said, "please keep giving us this bread."

Then Jesus proclaimed, "I am the bread of life. All who seek what I can give to them will surely satisfy their hunger. And all who put their trust in me will surely satisfy their thirst. So why is it that even after seeing all the evidence I have provided, you still refuse to believe in me? Everyone the Father gives to me will come to me. And I will never send away anyone who comes to me. I did not come down from heaven to do what I choose to do, but rather to do what my Father has sent me to do. It is my Father's will that all who turn to the Son and place faith in him, shall have everlasting life. I will raise them up at the last day. It is also my Father's will that none of those who come to me should be lost."

When they heard this, the Jews began complaining about his statement, "I am the bread that came down from heaven." They objected saying, "Isn't this Jesus who is the son of Joseph? We know

79

who his father and mother are! How can he tell us, 'I came down from heaven?'"

"Don't complain among yourselves," Jesus responded. "No one is able to place confidence in me unless my Father who sent me draws them to me. And I promise you that I will raise them up at the last day. The prophets have written, 'God will teach them all.' (Isaiah 54:13)

"Everyone who listens to the Father and learns from him will also come to me. Only the One who has come from God has actually seen the Father. I tell you the truth, each person who genuinely places trust in me has eternal life. I am the bread that is the source of life. Your ancestors ate the manna* in the wilderness and they all died. But I am standing before you as the living bread that came down from heaven. All who eat this bread will live forever. This bread is my body that I will sacrifice in order to bring life to the world." [*Manna was little wafers that were miraculously sent from God to provide food.]

Then the Jews started arguing among themselves, "How can he give us his own body to eat?"

116. Many Forsake Jesus for Teaching about His Flesh and Blood, but Peter Affirms His Faith - John 6:60-71

When his disciples heard what Jesus said about eating his body, they said, "This teaching is really hard to understand. How many will be able to accept this?"

Jesus knew that his disciples were complaining about this, so he said to them, "Are you offended by this? Then what will you think if you witness the Son of Man rise up to where he came from? The Holy Spirit is the One who gives life. The human body doesn't count for much. I have spoken words to you that are filled with the Spirit and with life. However, some of you still don't believe."

Actually, Jesus knew from the beginning who did not trust in him and which disciple would eventually betray him. Then he added, "Do you understand now why I said that none can come to me unless the Father has helped them?"

At this point, many turned away and no longer followed him. Jesus asked the Twelve, "Are you going to leave me, too?"

Simon Peter spoke up, "Lord, where else can we go? Only you have the words that offer everlasting life. We have placed our trust in you. In fact, we believe and are absolutely certain that you are the Holy One who has come to us from God."

Then Jesus responded, "Didn't I choose the Twelve who are my closest followers? But among you is a devil." He was referring to Judas, son of Simon Iscariot. Even though he was one of the Twelve, he was also the one who would eventually betray Jesus.

117. Conflict Arises When the Followers of Jesus Disregard the Customs of Jewish Cleansing - Matt 15:12-15; Mark 7:1-23; John 7:1

Jesus traveled from place to place in the area of Galilee. He knew it would be a dangerous time for him to minister from town to town in Judea. The Jewish leaders there were looking for circumstances that might give them a good excuse for putting him to death.

Some legalistic Pharisees and teachers of the Jewish Law traveled from Jerusalem to keep track of what Jesus was doing. Then they discovered that some of his disciples were eating without going through the customary Jewish cleansing ceremonies. [Jesus was failing to keep certain traditions in preparation for eating, but he was not actually breaking any of the Laws of God. According to Jewish custom, when they went shopping in the market, they would never eat until they first carried out their many traditions connected with washing themselves and washing cups, pitchers, kettles, etc.]

The Jewish legalists asked Jesus, "Why don't your followers keep the traditions kept by our elders? Your disciples don't even cleanse their hands before they eat!"

In answer to their question, Jesus said, "When Isaiah prophesied about you hypocrites, here is what he had to say:

> *They are the kind of people who just give me lip service.*
> *However, they have no heart for God.*
> *Their worship is useless.*
> *They just teach human rules that they make up.*
> *(Isaiah 29:13)*

"You abandon God's commands just to follow your own customs!"

Jesus went on rebuking the Jewish legalists. "It doesn't even bother you when you ignore God's commands, just so you can follow your own customs! Moses said it right, 'Honor your father and mother,'

(Ex. 20:12; Deut. 5:16) and 'anyone who curses their father or mother must be put to death.' (Ex. 21:12, 17.) However, you say that if anyone announces that whatever should have been used to help their parents is officially devoted to God, then you no longer have any obligation to help your parents. So, you think it is acceptable to use your traditions, [that have been handed down] in order to cancel out God's holy Word. And this is only one example of many other similar things that you do."

Then Jesus called the crowd to come near. "Listen carefully, everyone," he said. "There isn't anything on the outside that can make a person spiritually unclean by eating it. On the other hand, people can be defiled by the words that come out of their mouths. If your ears are tuned to spiritual truth, then listen carefully and think about what I have said to you."

After Jesus had dismissed the crowd and entered a house, his disciples came to him and asked, "Are you aware that the Pharisees objected to the way you criticized their religious customs?"

Jesus responded this way: "Every plant my Heavenly Father did not plant will be pulled up by the roots. Don't let them disturb you. They are blind guides. If a blind person tries to guide another blind person, both will fall into a deep hole."

Peter spoke up saying, "Please, help us understand this parable."

"Are you really that slow to comprehend?" Jesus said. "The things that people take into their body from outside cannot corrupt them. Those things don't enter their heart; they just enter the stomach and pass on through the body." [When Jesus said this, he was declaring all foods clean, even some foods that were forbidden under the Law of Moses.]

118. Jesus Ministers to a Believing Gentile Woman Near Tyre - Matt 15:22-28; Mark 7:24-30

Jesus left the area near Tyre and Sidon. Since he didn't want anyone to know where he was, he secretly entered a house. There, he found a Greek Canaanite woman who, by birth, was from the region of Syrian Phoenicia. An unclean spirit had taken possession of her little daughter. Just as soon as she heard about Jesus and where he was, she came and fell at his feet calling out, "Lord, Son of David, please have mercy on me! A demon has possessed my little girl, causing her to suffer terribly."

But Jesus remained silent. Then his disciples pleaded with him, "Get rid of her because she just keeps calling out to us."

Then Jesus answered her, "I have been commissioned to serve only the lost sheep of Israel." [He certainly knew that though she was a Gentile, her faith in the Son of God would persevere.]

However, kneeling at Jesus feet, she pleaded, "Lord, help me!"

"Is it right to toss the children's bread to the dogs?" Jesus asked. [Jesus seems to speak with some tongue in cheek humor, as he refers to the people of Israel as children, and the Gentiles as dogs.]

"I believe it is right," she said, "because even dogs get to eat crumbs that fall near their master's table."

Then Jesus told her, "Dear woman, your answer proves that your faith is truly great! Therefore, your request has been granted. You may go to your daughter and see for yourself that the demon has left her."

Sure enough, she went home and found her daughter lying peacefully on her bed—the demon had fled!

119. Jesus Heals Many in the Ten Cities Region - Matt 15:29-31; Mark 7:31-36

Next, Jesus left the area near Tyre, then passed through Sidon on his way to the Sea of Galilee, and into the Ten Cities area known as Decapolis. It was there that some people brought a man to him who was unable to hear and whose speech was also impaired. They begged Jesus to heal him.

Jesus took him away from the crowd and placed his fingers in the man's ears. He then spat on his own fingers and touched the man's tongue. Jesus sighed deeply, looked up to heaven and commanded, "Be opened!" Suddenly, the man's ears were opened so he could hear, and his tongue was freed, allowing him to speak clearly.

However, Jesus told everyone, "Don't tell anyone what happened here." But the more he insisted, the more those who witnessed this kept on talking about it.

After this, Jesus climbed up the side of a mountain and large crowds came to where he was. They brought those who were lame, blind, crippled, unable to speak, and those with all kinds of sicknesses and disabilities. As they laid them at his feet, he healed each one of them.

Everyone was amazed when they witnessed all the miracles: The crippled were given ability to walk and function normally, the blind could see, the deaf could hear, and the mute could speak. Everyone was praising the God of Israel. They said, "Everything he does is just right; he even makes the deaf hear and gives ability to speak to those who could not speak."

120. Jesus Feeds Four Thousand Men Plus Women and Children - Matt 15:34-39; Mark 8:1-10

After healing many diseases, another large crowd gathered to hear Jesus. After they had been with him for three days without having anything to eat, Jesus called his disciples over and said, "I feel sorry for all these people. They have been with me for three days and haven't had a thing to eat. I can't send them away hungry, because they would surely faint on the way home. Some of them have actually traveled a great distance just to be here."

But his disciples questioned, "Where can we possibly find enough bread to feed them all? We are in a very remote area!"

Then Jesus asked them, "Have you counted how many loaves of bread we have available?"

They replied, "We have seven loaves along with a few little fish."

Jesus told all the people in the crowd to find a place to sit on the ground. After that, he offered thanks and told his disciples to distribute the food to the people. Everyone was able to eat and all were satisfied. Then the disciples gathered up seven basketfuls of left over pieces.

There were four thousand men, not counting women and children, who ate and were filled.

Then Jesus dismissed the crowd and got into a boat that took him to the area of Magadan. [It is a place that is also called Dalmanutha.]

121. Jesus Answers the Pharisees and Sadducees Who Seek a Sign - Matt 16:1-4; Mark 8:12-13

The Pharisees who were known for their extreme legalism, and the Sadducees who were known for their materialistic beliefs and lifestyle, approached Jesus intending to test him. They wanted Jesus to prove himself by showing them some miraculous heavenly sign.

This is how Jesus answered them, "In the evening, you often try to forecast the weather. You say, 'Tomorrow there will be good weather because the sky is red.' Then in the morning you say, 'Today there will be stormy weather because the sky is cloudy and red.' You know about how to predict the weather, so why can't you interpret the signs of the times?" Then Jesus sighed deeply and commented, "Why are people today always looking for signs? It's because adulterous and wicked people always want proof. But the only sign they will receive is Jonah's sign." [He was 3 days and nights in the whale's stomach, just as the Son of Man would be 3 days and nights in the tomb.] Then Jesus got back in the boat and went away to the other side.

122. Jesus Warns of the Errors of the Pharisees, Sadducees and Herodians - Matt 16:6-12; Mark 8:14-18

Then Jesus warned, "Stay away from the yeast of those legalistic, hard-hearted Pharisees, and those free-thinking Sadducees. Also, don't be like Herod either. He resists the truth." [Yeast spreads very rapidly in warm, fresh bread dough.]

When the disciples discussed this, they said, "Jesus must have talked about this, because we didn't bring enough bread with us." [On one occasion, when traveling by boat, the disciples had forgotten to bring extra bread with them. They had brought only one small loaf.]

However, Jesus knew what they were discussing, so he asked, "Why are you talking with each other about not having bread? Don't you comprehend? Why do you have such hard hearts? Are your eyes unable to see and your ears unable to hear? Don't you remember how we fed five thousand with five loaves and how many basketfuls of leftovers we gathered? Or what about feeding four thousand with seven loaves and how many basketfuls of leftovers we gathered? Why didn't you realize that I wasn't talking about bread? However, you must watch out for the yeast of the Pharisees and Sadducees." It was then they realized he wasn't telling them to avoid yeast used in bread, but to reject the misguided teachings of the Pharisees and Sadducees.

123. Jesus Heals a Blind Man at Bethsaida - Mark 8:22-26

Jesus and his followers soon arrived in Bethsaida where some people brought a blind man to Jesus. They begged him to touch the man. Jesus led him by the hand outside the village, and after putting spit on his eyes, Jesus asked, "What can you see?"

The blind man looked up and said, "I can see some people, but they look a little like trees walking around."

Jesus then put his hands on him once more and the man's eyes were opened completely. He was able to see everything clearly. Then Jesus sent him home with this warning: "Don't tell anyone in the village what has happened to you." [Jesus didn't want the rapidly growing crowds to hinder his ministry.]

124. Peter Correctly Identifies Jesus as the Messiah, then Jesus Prophesies about the Church - Matt 16:13-19; Luke 9:18-21

One time when Jesus arrived in the area near Caesarea Philippi, he was privately praying. Then he asked his disciples, "Who do the crowds think I am?"

They answered, "Some think you are John the Baptist; others say you are Elijah; still others believe Jeremiah, or one of the ancient prophets has been resurrected."

"But who do you say I am?" he asked.

Simon Peter spoke up, "You are the promised Messiah, the Son of the living God."

Jesus responded, "God has blessed you, Simon son of John, for your understanding does not come from human wisdom. Your Heavenly Father has revealed this to you. This is why I gave you the name Peter. It means stone, you know. And I am going to build my church on this solid rock because it is the will of my Father in heaven. Even the kingdom of Hades can never defeat anyone who truly believes that I am the Messiah. I will give those of you who have this kind of faith the keys that are able to open the way into the Kingdom of Heaven. Whatever you confirm on earth, will also be confirmed in heaven. Furthermore, whatever your faith in me has set free on earth, has also been liberated in heaven."

Jesus went on to firmly warn his disciples, "Don't go around announcing to people that I am the Messiah."

125. Jesus Begins to Clearly Predict His Rejection, Death and Resurrection - Matt 16:22-23; Luke 9:22

Jesus added, "The Son of Man is destined to experience many types of pain and suffering. The Jewish elders, the chief priests and teachers of Jewish Law will all conspire to reject him. The Son of Man must then be killed. But on the third day he will be raised from the dead and live."

Later that evening, Peter spoke to Jesus privately. "Lord, don't even suggest such a terrible thing! This can't happen to you!"

Jesus turned toward Peter and spoke firmly saying, "Back off, Satan! You are like a stumbling block on my path. You are not seeing this from God's perspective. You understand only an earthly way of thinking."

126. Jesus Admonishes His Followers to Identify with Him, then Promises a Revelation of the Kingdom of God - Matt 10:32-33; 16:27; Mark 8:38; Luke 9:26; 12:8-9

Jesus continued, "When people are ashamed to be identified with me in the midst of this evil and adulterous culture, then I, the Son of Man, will also be ashamed of them when I return shining in the glory of my Heavenly Father and all the holy angels. I promise you that those who openly and publicly identify with me before others, the Son of Man will also acknowledge them before my Father in heaven and before the angels of God. However, those who disown me before others will also be disowned when they stand before my Father in heaven and before God's angels. God will individually reward them according to what each one has done on earth."

Then Jesus told them, "I tell you the truth. There are some standing here right now who will not die before they see a powerful display of the Kingdom of God."

127. The Kingdom Glory of Jesus Is Revealed when He Is Transfigured - Matt 17:2-7; Mark 9:2-10; Luke 9:28-36

Jesus announced that in about one week, there was going to be an amazing display of God's Kingdom. Actually, it was exactly six days later when Jesus took Peter, James, and John, and led them on a long hike up a high mountain where they were completely alone. In that beautiful setting, his appearance was completely changed right before their eyes. His face was shining like the sun, and his clothing was like shining white light—much whiter than any bleach on earth could ever produce.

Two men also appeared in glorious splendor, Moses and Elijah, talking with Jesus about his ascension. They knew that this event would complete his earthly ministry in Jerusalem. Then Peter and his two companions began to feel very sleepy, but when they completely awakened, they were able to see the Lord's glory, along with the other two men standing there.

When those heavenly visitors were leaving, Peter spoke up to Jesus. "Master, this is an amazing place for us to be! Can we build three shrines—one for you, one for Moses, and one for Elijah?"

Even as Peter was speaking, a cloud moved in and began to cover them. When the cloud had completely enclosed them, they became very frightened. Then a voice spoke out from the cloud, saying, "This is my Son. I have chosen him. Therefore, you must listen to him."

When the disciples heard this voice, they fell down terrified, their faces to the ground. After the voice stopped speaking, they realized that they were alone with Jesus. Then Jesus came over and touched them. "Get up now," he said, "there is nothing to fear."

Jesus ordered them not to tell anyone what they had witnessed until the Son of Man had risen from the dead. So they kept this experience to themselves, but they did question each other about what rising from the dead might mean. At that time, they did not disclose what they had seen.

128. Jesus Explains the Coming of Elijah and John the Baptist - Matt 17:10-13

Then the disciples asked Jesus, "Why do the teachers of the Law declare that Elijah must come first?"

Jesus replied, "It is certainly true that Elijah was to come and restore all things. But I am informing you that Elijah has come already. They just didn't recognize him. They treated him however they wished. The Son of Man is going to suffer in a similar way, at their hands." It was then that the disciples realized he was referring to John the Baptist.

129. Jesus Heals a Demon-Possessed Boy, then Rebukes Those Who Lack Faith - Matt 17:15-20; Mark 9:14-29; Luke 9:37-43

The following day, Jesus, Peter, James, and John descended the mountain and rejoined the other disciples who were surrounded by a large crowd. The teachers of the Law were arguing with them. But when the people saw Jesus, they were overwhelmed with emotion and ran to welcome him.

"What have you been arguing about with them?" Jesus asked.

One of the men in the crowd spoke up, "Teacher, I have come intending to seek your help for my son. He is possessed by a demon that has taken away his ability to speak. He also suffers greatly from seizures. Whenever the demon seizes him, it throws him to the ground. He becomes stiff, grinds his teeth, and foams at the mouth. I begged your disciples to get rid of the evil spirit, but they were unable."

"Oh, you doubting generation!" Jesus answered, "How long must I keep putting up with your lack of faith? Bring me the boy."

They brought him, but when the spirit saw Jesus, right away it threw the boy into a convulsion. He began rolling around on the ground and foaming at the mouth.

Jesus asked the boy's father, "How long has he had this problem?"

"Since he was a small child," his father responded. "The spirit has often thrown my son into the fire or water in order to kill him. But if you are able, please show us mercy and help us now."

"What do you mean, 'If you are able?'" Jesus said, "Everything is possible for the person who believes!"

Then the boy's father quickly answered, "Lord, I really do want to believe: Please help me overcome my doubts."

When Jesus saw a crowd of people running toward them, he spoke directly to the unclean spirit, "You deaf and mute spirit, I command you to come out and never return to this boy again!"

Then the evil spirit gave a shriek, shook the boy violently, and came out. The boy became so much like a corpse that many people said, "The boy is dead." But Jesus reached out his hand and helped him stand up. Then everyone was amazed at God's great power, and marveled at what Jesus had done.

When Jesus went into a home, his disciples privately questioned, "Why couldn't we drive out that demon?"

He responded saying, "It's because your faith is too small*. I am telling you the truth, even if your faith is small like a tiny seed from a mustard plant, then you can even command a mountain, 'Move away from here to over there' and it will move. For you, nothing will be impossible." [*Some manuscripts add, "This kind can come out only by prayer and fasting." (Mark 9:29)]

130. Jesus Again Predicts His Suffering, Death and Resurrection - Matt 17:23; Mark 9:30-31; Luke 9:45

They traveled on through Galilee. Jesus was trying to avoid the crowds because he did not want to be interrupted while he was teaching his disciples.

Then Jesus told them, "The Son of Man will be handed over to those who will kill him, but after three days he will rise from the dead." However, they just could not comprehend what he was talking about. This truth concerning rising from the dead was hidden. It just did not make any sense to them. They simply were afraid to ask him to explain it, and they were filled with sadness.

131. Jesus Answers a Question about Paying the Temple Taxes - Matt 17:24-27

When Jesus and his disciples reached Capernaum, the Temple tax collectors asked Peter, "Isn't your teacher planning to pay the Temple tax?"

"I'm sure he will pay it," Peter answered.

Yet, when Peter entered the house where Jesus was, Jesus said to him, "Simon, tell me what you think about this: When earthly rulers collect taxes and other kinds of fees, do they collect them from their own children or from others?"

"From others, of course," Peter answered.

"So, the children are excused from the tax?" Jesus questioned. "However, we must avoid any appearance of favoritism. I want you to go to the lake and cast out your fish line. Then open the mouth of the first fish you catch. You will find a coin for the exact amount needed. Take it and use it pay for both my tax and yours." [Since Jesus is God, he had a right to everyone's tithe (10%). But rather than challenging Rome's authority, he chose to submit to Rome's taxation.

His example implies that even children of God must submit to government authorities when it does not conflict with Scripture.]

132. Jesus Teaches about the Unity of Those Who Trust in Him - Mark 9:38-41

Then John approached Jesus concerning something he had observed. "Teacher," he said, "we saw somebody using your name to cast out demons. We told him to stop because he was not part of our group."

"You shouldn't stop him! " Jesus responded saying, "For anyone who uses my name to do a miracle cannot in the next breath speak a bad word about me. Whoever is not against us is actually for us. Let me illustrate it this way: Anyone who merely offers you a cup of water in my name, which is to say, because they know you are serving Christ, will certainly not lose their reward."

133. Jesus Explains the Urgency of Making Peace and How to Go about Doing It - Matt 18:15-20

"Whenever a spiritual brother or sister commits an offence or a sin against you, (1) first go privately just between the two of you, in order to point out their offence. If they listen and make amends, you have restored your relationship. However, if your first attempt at making peace fails, don't give up. (2) Then take one or two mature believers along so every detail of the problem is clearly understood by two or three witnesses. If the second attempt also fails, (3) then explain the problem clearly to the elders of the church. (4) If they even reject the authority of the church, they have shown that they are not really fellow believers at all; they are acting like ungodly people of the world.

"I want you to put this truth into practice: If you who are godly leaders of my church agree concerning what must be forbidden, then it will have already been forbidden in heaven. In the same way, when godly people permit something on earth, then surely heaven has already allowed it.

"I also want you to understand this truth: Whenever even two of you (who are my followers) agree concerning anything you are requesting, then my Father in heaven will have already granted it.

And whenever just two or three of you come together in harmony with who I am, you can be sure that I will be right there with you."

134. Jesus Tells a Story about an Unforgiving Servant - Matt 18:23-35

"Now, the kingdom of heaven is similar to a king who wanted all his servants to clear up their debts. The first servant that he confronted owed him more than a million dollars. He couldn't even begin to pay off the debt. When the king was about to sell him and his family as slaves to a king in a far-off country, the man fell on his knees and begged the king, 'Please just be patient and give me a little more time. I plan to pay you everything I owe you.' Then the king felt sorry for him and decided to forgive the whole debt and to set him free.

"However, the servant then found one of his fellow servants who owed him one hundred coins, each worth about a day's work. He grabbed his debtor and started to choke him. 'Pay me back, right now!' he demanded.

"His fellow servant begged on his knees, 'please be patient with me, and I will be able to give you back what I owe you.'

"Still he refused and had him thrown in jail until he could pay back everything he owed. The other servants were outraged when they saw how he had treated his fellow servant. So, they reported to the king everything that had happened.

"Then the king called in that wicked and unmerciful servant. 'You evil servant,' he said, 'because you pleaded for mercy, I forgave everything you owed me. Shouldn't you have also been merciful to your fellow servant, as I was to you?' Then the king gave him to the jailers with instructions to do whatever it took to punish him until he could pay back everything he owed.

"This illustrates exactly how your Father in heaven will treat each one of you if you fail to show heartfelt forgiveness to your fellow brothers and sisters."

135. The Lord's Half Brothers Accuse Jesus of Lacking Boldness - John 7:2-9

It was almost time for the Jewish Festival of Shelters [also known as the Feast of Tabernacles] when Jesus' brothers told him, "You should leave your home here in Galilee and travel down to Judea where the crowds will all be going to celebrate the festival. You should go where your followers can see all your miracles. No one who wants to be famous does his work in secret. Since you are doing all these amazing things, you should let the whole world see what you are doing." Even his own brothers ridiculed him because they didn't believe in him.

Jesus told them, "The time is not right for me. Any time will be acceptable for you. The world is not going to hate you; it hates me because I expose the evil things the world is doing. So, you can go on ahead to the festival. But I'm not going yet because the time appointed for me has not arrived." After saying this, Jesus stayed a while longer in Galilee.

136. Jesus Travels through Samaria among People Despised by the Jews - Luke 9:51-56; John 7:10

After his brothers had left to attend the Festival of Shelters, Jesus also left. However, he went secretly rather than in the public eye. The time was approaching for Jesus to return to heaven, so he committed himself to follow the road to Jerusalem. He sent some messengers on ahead into a Samaritan village. [Strong prejudice existed between Samaritans and Jews.]

The Samaritans did not welcome him because it was evident that he was traveling to Jerusalem. When James and John saw their prejudice, they asked Jesus, "Lord, should we call fire down from heaven and destroy them?" Instead, Jesus corrected them for their unmerciful attitude. Then he led his disciples to another town.

137. Jesus Requires His Followers to Be Completely Committed - Matt 8:19-20, Luke 9:57-62

As Jesus and his disciples were walking along, a teacher of Jewish Law came and offered to volunteer. "Teacher, I am willing to follow you wherever you go."

Jesus then explained in the following words what his decision would mean: "Foxes all have their dens and birds all have their nests, but the Son of Man has no place of his own where he can lay his head."

He told another man, "Come and follow me."

The man replied, "First, please let me wait until after my father dies. Then when his time comes, I will be free to give him an honorable funeral."

But Jesus replied, "Let those who are already spiritually dead go and bury their own dead. As for you, right now is your time to go and announce that the Kingdom of God has come."

Still another man answered the Lord's invitation this way: "Sooner or later, I think I'll be able to follow you, Lord. First, let my family and friends have time to plan a farewell party. I'm sure they'll want to send me off with their blessing. When they have completed all of their celebration, I'll probably be able to go with you."

However, Jesus said, "The person who gets behind a plow to prepare for a harvest and then decides to wait for a better day, is not qualified to work for a spiritual harvest of souls on behalf of the Kingdom of God."

138. People Have Mixed Reactions to Jesus' Teachings and Miracles at the Festival of Shelters - John 7:11-31

When the Festival of Shelters began, the Jewish leaders kept watching for Jesus to come. They were asking each other, "Where is he, anyway?"

There was also widespread whispering about him among the crowd. Some insisted, "We're sure he's a good man."

Others insisted, "No, he's a deceiver of the people." But out of fear of the Jewish leaders, no one wanted to risk talking publicly about him.

Finally, about halfway through the festival, Jesus showed up at the Temple courts where he began to teach openly. Then the Jewish leaders were completely amazed and discussed with each other, "We didn't teach him all these things," they said, "so where did he receive such great understanding and wisdom?"

Then Jesus explained, "What I teach is not merely my own. I received my understanding from the One who sent me. Anyone who determines to please God will soon discover if my teachings come from God, or if they are merely my own ideas. Those who are just sharing their own opinions often hope they will receive honor. But whoever seeks honor from the one who sent him is a person of integrity and truth; such persons have no hidden agendas. Hasn't

Moses delivered to you the Law of God? Yet not one of you has actually kept the whole Law. So why are you trying to kill me?"

"You must be demon possessed," the crowd responded. "Who do you think is trying to kill you?"

Jesus reminded them, "I did one great miracle when I healed a demon possessed man on the Sabbath, and you were all amazed. However, you say that Moses gave you circumcision although it was not really Moses. It was the early fathers of the Jewish people. You allow a boy to be circumcised on the Sabbath. Now, if you can circumcise a boy on the Sabbath in spite of the Sabbath Law, why are you angry with me for healing a man's whole body on the Sabbath? Don't base your decisions on superficial opinions. Think it through carefully, then judge correctly."

Just then, some citizens of Jerusalem began questioning, "Isn't this the one they are seeking to kill? Now here he is speaking publicly, and they are not even saying one word against him. Is it possible that our authorities have decided he really is our Messiah? But we know all about his background. They say that when the Messiah comes, no one will know his background."

As Jesus continued speaking in the courts of the Temple, he shouted, "You say you know me and where I came from. In fact, I am not here merely on my own authority. You don't know the One who sent me. However, the One who sent me is true. And I know Him because He is the One who sent me here, and I am from Him."

When they heard this, they were about to lay hold of him, but no one did because it was not the right time. In spite of these events, there were many in the crowd who placed their trust in him. They argued, "Do you think that when the Messiah appears, he will perform more signs or greater signs than this man has already done?"

139. The Pharisees Fail to Arrest Jesus and Jesus Offers Living Water to All Who Believe in Him - John 7:32-53

The Pharisees knew that many in the crowds surrounding Jesus were whispering to each other that he must surely be the expected Messiah. And when the chief priests and the Pharisees sent guards from the Temple to arrest him, Jesus told them, "I'll be with you only a short time longer. Soon I'll be going back to the One who sent me into the world. Then you won't be able to find me, because it will be impossible for you to come to where I am."

The Jewish leaders questioned each other, "Where does he plan to go so that we will not be able to find him? Will he go and teach those Jews who are living among the Greeks and other Gentiles? What did he mean when he said we would not be able to find him?"

During the water celebration at the climax of the Jewish Festival, Jesus stood up and shouted, "All of you who are thirsty, come to me and drink. For the Scriptures have promised that rivers of living water will flow through all those who place their trust in me." Jesus was referring to the Holy Spirit who would be given later to all those who believe. But the Holy Spirit would not be given to all believers until after Jesus received his glorified body, at the time of his resurrection.

When the crowd heard these promises, the people exclaimed, "Certainly this man is the Prophet we have all been waiting for." Many others insisted, "He surely must be God's chosen Messiah!" Others questioned, "How could the Messiah be from Galilee? Don't the prophecies predict that the Messiah will be one of King David's descendants, born in Bethlehem, in the very town where David lived?"

The people became deeply divided about the claims made by Jesus. Some were prepared to seize him. Yet no one laid a hand on him.

Then the Temple guards finally reported back to the chief priests and Pharisees who asked them, "Why didn't you arrest him?"

"We have never heard anyone speak the way this man does," the guards answered.

"Do you mean he has you fooled, also?" the Pharisees responded. "Do you know any of the religious rulers or leaders among the Pharisees who have believed in him? You certainly don't, but this mob is completely ignorant of our Law. May a curse be upon them!"

Then Nicodemus, who had interviewed Jesus some time before and who was also a member of their council, asked this question: "Does our Law ever condemn a person before investigating his actions and listening to his viewpoint?"

The council responded, "Are you also taking sides with these Galileans? Just look into it more carefully. You'll discover that not one prophet is ever supposed to come from Galilee."

Then all the people returned to their homes.

[The next section from John 7:53-8:11 is not included in some ancient manuscripts. Other manuscripts include these verses—wholly or partially—after John 7:36, John 21:25, Luke 21:38 or Luke 24:53.]

140. Jesus Forgives a Woman Caught in Adultery - John 8:1-11

Jesus went back to the Mount of Olives. At the dawn of a new day, he went to the Temple courts and everybody crowded around him. He sat down there and began teaching the people. Then the teachers of the Law and the Pharisees brought in a woman they had caught in the act of adultery. They made her stand up right in front of the crowd as they asked Jesus, "Teacher, we caught this woman in the very act of committing adultery. In the Law, Moses commanded us to stone a woman like this. Now, tell us what we should do."

Of course, this was a trap question because they intended to use his answer against him. [At that time, only the Romans had authority to require a death sentence.]

Jesus knelt on the ground and started writing with his finger in the dirt. [We don't know what he wrote. Perhaps he wrote, "Where is the man?"]

The Pharisees kept on insisting for an answer because they hoped he would fall into their trap. [If Jesus agreed with the Law of Moses, he would be taking authority that belonged only to the Roman Empire at that time. If he honored Roman authority, he would seem to be rejecting the Law of Moses.]

When the woman's accusers kept on insisting for an answer, Jesus straightened up and replied, "If there is anyone here who has never sinned, let that person throw the first stone at this woman." Then Jesus knelt on the ground again and continued to write.

In response, the witnesses began to leave one at a time, beginning first with the older ones. Finally, only Jesus and the woman were left standing there. Jesus then straightened up and asked the woman, "Where are your accusers? Hasn't anyone condemned you?"

"Not even one, Sir," she answered.

"I don't condemn you either," Jesus affirmed. "So now you are free to go. Don't ever return to those sins that once held you."

141. Jesus Is Criticized for Claiming to Be the "Light of the World" - John 8:12-20

When Jesus returned to teaching the people, he announced, "I am the light of the world. Those who follow me will never live in darkness. They will possess living light."

The Pharisees were angered and challenged him. "Look what you're doing! You are serving as your own witness. How can such testimony be valid?"

Jesus answered, "My testimony certainly is valid, even when I witness in behalf of myself because I know where I came from and I know where I am going. Your judgments are based on human standards. At this time, I am not judging anyone. However, when I do judge, my conclusions are completely reliable because my decisions agree perfectly with my Father who sent me. Your own Law states that the testimony of two witnesses is considered reliable. I am one witness and I have a right to testify for myself, and my Father who sent me is the second witness."

Then they asked Jesus, "Where is your father?"

Jesus answered, "You don't know me or my Father. If you knew me, you would also know my Father."

He said all these things while he was teaching in the courts of the Temple near the place where they leave their offerings. Yet, even there in the center of Jewish authority, no one took him into custody because his appointed time had not arrived.

142. Jesus Calls People to Believe He Is the Christ (or Messiah) - John 8:21-30

Jesus spoke to them again and said, "Soon I will be leaving you. Even if you search for me, you will still die in your sin. But I will be going to a place where you will not be able to come."

This caused the Jewish leaders to ask, "Is he going to commit suicide? Is that why he says, 'You can't follow me to where I am going'?"

Jesus continued speaking, "You are from the earth; I am from above. You belong to this world; I do not belong to this world. I have warned that you are going to die in your sins. In fact, if you do not believe that I am the promised One, you will surely die in your sins."

When they heard this they asked, "Who are you claiming to be?"

"Exactly what I have been telling you all the time," Jesus answered. "I also have much more to reveal to you. However, you should know that the One, who sent me here, is completely dependable. I am announcing to the world the truth I have received from Him."

However, they failed to comprehend that Jesus was telling them about his Father. So he continued speaking, "When you have lifted up and exalted the Son of Man, you will realize that I AM the One you have been waiting for, and I do nothing independently. I make known to you only those things the Father has taught me. The One who sent me here, is now with me. He has not deserted me because I always do exactly those things that please Him."

Even while Jesus was speaking to the crowd, many who were listening also placed their faith in Him.

143. Jesus Teaches Freedom through Truth, then Calls Himself the Eternal "I Am" - John 8:31-59

Then Jesus spoke directly to those Jews who had placed their faith in him. "If you remain loyal to what I have been teaching, then you have offered strong evidence that you truly are my disciples. As a result, you will understand and personally experience truth, and my truth will set you free to be all that you were created to become."

But the Jews answered, "We are descendants of Abraham. We have never been slaves to anyone! Why do you imply that we need to be set free?"

Jesus responded this way: "The truth is that every person who sins becomes a slave to sin. Of course, a slave never has a lasting and secure place in the family. However, a son is a permanent member of the family. And if it is the Son who sets you free, then you are completely free. Yes, you are Abraham's descendants; however, since you have no place in your hearts for my teachings, you keep seeking a way to kill me. I'm teaching you things I learned while in the presence of my Father." [Here is an alternate interpretation: "The things you keep doing imply that you learned them from the wrong father."]

"We aren't illegitimate children," they protested. "Our only Father is God himself."

But Jesus answered, "If God really is your Father, why don't you love me? Don't you realize that I have come here from God? He is the One who sent me here. Why can't you understand? Am I not speaking clearly enough? Do you want to know the true problem? You actually have the devil as your father, and you enjoy carrying out his wishes. From the very first, he's been a murderer. He never practices truth because there is no truth within him. He is only speaking his native language when he lies. He is the true father of all dishonesty. However, when I speak the truth, you don't believe me! Can any of you point to a sin in my life and also prove it? So, if I am speaking only the truth to you, why don't you trust me and believe what I am saying? Everyone who truly belongs to God will listen to what God says. The only reason you don't receive what I am teaching is that you don't really belong to God."

The Jews protested loudly, "What more evidence do we need to prove that you are demon-possessed and speaking like a Samaritan?"

"Obviously, I am not possessed by a demon," Jesus responded, "and it should be very clear to you that I always honor my Father. However, you are showing no honor to me. I am not seeking praise for myself; there is One who does, and He has the right to judge. Here is the absolute truth: All who trust and obey my teaching will never experience death."

In response, they exclaimed, "Now we are sure that you really are demon possessed! We are all sure that Abraham died and so did all of the prophets. Then how can you claim that anyone who obeys your teaching will never experience death? Are you trying to tell us that you are even greater than our ancestor, Abraham? Who do you think you are, anyway?"

Jesus answered, "If I'm honoring myself, it means nothing. However, my Father is the One who honors me. He is also the very same One you claim as your God. I know him, even if you don't. If I were to say, 'I don't know Him,' I would be lying, like you. But I do know him, and I obey whatever he commands. Abraham, your ancestor, celebrated the very thought of witnessing my day. And he did see it and rejoiced."

They objected, "You are not even fifty years old, so how can you claim to have seen Abraham?"

"Here is the absolute truth," Jesus responded. "Before Abraham was even born, I AM!"

When the Jewish religious leaders heard this, they picked up stones intending to stone him to death. Before they could, Jesus slipped right through the crowd and escaped from the Temple grounds.

["I AM" is a translation of *Yahweh*—the Hebrew response God gave to Moses when he asked God, "What is your name?" (Exodus 3:13-15) The escape of Jesus from the crowd must certainly have been another of his miracles.]

144. Jesus Sends Seventy-Two Followers Ahead of Him to Minister - Matt 10:16; Luke 10:1-12

Shortly after that, Jesus appointed seventy-two additional messengers to go two-by-two into each of the towns where he planned to go next.

[He gave them many instructions that were very similar to those he had given to the twelve when he first sent them out.]

He told them, "I am sending you to go out like sheep and lambs that are followed by wolves. Don't take extra money or extra sandals. Also, don't be distracted by those you pass along the road.

"If a town welcomes you when you enter it, stay there long enough to heal those who are physically suffering. Also proclaim, 'The Kingdom of God has come near to you.' However, if you are not welcomed when you enter a town, then go into their streets and announce, 'We wipe off even the dust from our feet, as a rebuke against your rejection.' I promise you that on the Judgment Day, even the wicked city of Sodom will suffer less than that town."

145. Jesus Pronounces Woe upon Towns Where He Had Ministered - Matt 11:20-24; Luke 10:13-16

Jesus began to rebuke the towns where he had performed many miracles because they had failed to turn away from their sins. He called out, "Woe to the towns of Korazin and Bethsaida! If the towns of Tyre and Sidon had witnessed the miracles you have seen, they would have shown humility and repented long ago. I tell you, Tyre and Sidon will encounter the final judgment to be more bearable than what you are sure to experience. And what about you, Capernaum? Do you expect to be lifted up into the heavens? No! That won't happen. Instead, you will go down to Hades! [This refers to the place of the dead.] If only the miracles you have seen had been performed in Sodom, that city would have repented and survived. I'm telling you that it will be more bearable for Sodom on Judgment Day than for you.

"Whoever humbly listens to you will also be listening to me; whoever rejects you will also be rejecting me; and whoever rejects me is also rejecting the One who sent me into the world."

146. The Seventy-Two Witnesses Report Back and Jesus Rejoices - Luke 10:17-24

The seventy-two witnesses returned with great excitement, and reported to Jesus, "Lord, even the demons had to submit to us when we proclaimed your name with authority."

Jesus replied, "If you want to know the absolute truth, I actually witnessed Satan fall like lightning when he was cast down from heaven. And now I have given you authority also. You can even step on snakes and scorpions. [Perhaps these symbolize demons.] You will even be able to overcome all the enemy's power. Nothing can harm you. However, don't celebrate the fact that evil spirits must submit to you. Here is the greatest reason to celebrate: Your names are on the list of those who are to become inhabitants of heaven."

Then the Holy Spirit filled Jesus with joy, and he began to praise God saying, "Father, Lord of heaven and earth, I praise you because it pleased you to hide these things from those who are known for their wisdom and education, while you have allowed those who are humble and childlike to understand the kind of truth that will survive. Father, I am so glad that this is what you decided to do."

"My Father has trusted me with all things. Only the Father knows who the Son really is, and no one knows what the Father is really like except the Son and those chosen by the Son to truly understand the Father."

Then Jesus spoke the following words in private to his disciples: "How blessed are the eyes of those who are able to see what you are seeing! In fact, many prophets and rulers have wanted to witness the things that you see, but they did not, and they wanted to hear what you are hearing, but they did not."

147. Jesus Tells about a Good Samaritan - Luke 10:25-37

One day, an expert in Jewish Law decided to challenge Jesus. "Teacher," he said, "what do I need to do in order to be certain that I will inherit everlasting life?"

"What do you understand that the Law says about this?" Jesus asked.

The legal expert answered with this quote from Scripture: "You must love the Lord your God with all your heart, and all your soul, and all your strength, and all your mind and love your neighbor as yourself." [This quote is from Leviticus 19:18 and Deuteronomy 6:5.]

"Your answer is correct," Jesus replied. "Do this and you will surely find the life you are seeking."

However, the man was looking for a loophole, so he asked Jesus, "Tell me, what kind of people must I include as my neighbors?"

In order to answer the man, Jesus told him the following story: "A certain man was traveling down the dangerous road from Jerusalem to

Jericho, when he was suddenly attacked by robbers. They beat him up and stripped off his clothes, leaving him naked and half dead. Soon, it happened that a Jewish priest was traveling down the same road, and when he saw the man lying there, he just went to the other side of the road and walked right on by.

"The same thing happened when an expert in Jewish Law came by the same place. He just avoided the man and walked right past him.

"However, a Samaritan also traveled to the place where the man was lying. [Samaritans and Jews generally held strong prejudice against each other.] But when that Samaritan saw the man, he felt sorry for him. He went over to him and poured some oil and wine on him as medicine for his wounds. Then he bandaged him and lifted him up onto his donkey, and brought him to a roadside hotel where he cared for him. He paid the innkeeper the equivalent of a day's wages and requested, 'Please look after this man, and when I come back, I will reimburse you for any extra expenses he may owe you.'"

Then Jesus asked the expert in Jewish Law, "Which of the three men was a genuine neighbor to the victim who was attacked by robbers? Was it the priest, the legal expert, or the despised Samaritan?"

The expert on Jewish Law responded, "Of course, the one who showed him mercy."

Jesus told him, "Go now and practice loving those who need your help, just like that Good Samaritan."

148. Jesus Visits the Home of Mary and Martha - Luke 10:38-42

As Jesus and his disciples were traveling along, they came to a village near Jerusalem where a woman named Martha welcomed Jesus into her home. When Jesus went inside, Martha's sister, Mary, sat down on the floor by the Lord's feet listening carefully to the things he was saying. Martha, however, was very busy with all her duties as a hostess. She went over to Jesus and asked him, "Lord, haven't you noticed that my sister isn't helping me do all the work?"

"My dear Martha," the Lord answered, "many things distract and worry you, but only a few things are absolutely necessary. In fact, in this case only one thing is truly necessary. Mary has chosen what is best and it should not be taken away from her."

149. Jesus Teaches How to Pray and the Importance of Perseverance in Prayer - Matt 6:9-13, Luke 11:1-8

One day, as Jesus finished praying in a certain place with his disciples, one of them requested, "Lord, please teach us how to pray. You know that John did exactly this for his disciples."

He told them, "Here is a model of what kind of things you should include when you pray:

'Heavenly Father, you are holy by your very nature.
May your Kingdom spread throughout the earth.
Provide for our food and other necessities.
Please forgive our sins and shortcomings,
even as we also forgive others when they fail us.
Deliver us from evil and help us become over-comers
when we fall into temptation.'"

Then Jesus gave them this illustration: "What if you went to one of your friends at midnight and called to him, 'Dear friend, will you please loan me three loaves of bread because one of my friends has been traveling. He just arrived at my house, and I don't have any food to offer him.' What if the one inside the house were to answer, 'Don't disturb me! My door is already locked for the night and my children have gone to bed. Why are you expecting me to get out of bed to help you?' Even if he doesn't care enough to help you out because of your friendship, he may very well take all the trouble to help you anyway, in order to preserve his good name."

150. An Accusation against Jesus of Blasphemy Leads to Teaching about Satan's Kingdom - Matt 12:22-37; Mark 3:22-26; Luke 11:17-28

Some people brought Jesus a demon-possessed man who was also both blind and unable to speak. Jesus healed the man and then he was able to both talk and see. The astonished crowd began to ask, "Could this possibly be the promised Messiah, who is called the Son of David?"

The legalistic Pharisees heard what they said and responded, "This healing was actually done by demonic power. It was really the Lord of demons, known as Beelzebub, who did this miracle. [Beelzebub in Latin, means Lord of the flies.] In fact, the teachers of Jewish Law who were there from Jerusalem even accused Jesus of being possessed by Beelzebub.

Of course, Jesus knew what they were thinking, and he asked them to come closer. Then he began to offer some illustrations about truths he wanted to get across to them.

"Why do you think Satan would try to caste out Satan? How could a kingdom survive if it is divided against itself? Such a kingdom would certainly fall. Or what happens when there is division in a home? Such a family will surely fall apart. In the same way, how could Satan possibly survive if he is fighting against himself? That would be the end of the devil. I am saying these things because you are accusing me of using the power of Beelzebub to drive out demons. So, if I am doing that, then what power are your followers using to drive them out? Let them be your judges. However, if I am driving out demons by the Spirit of God, isn't that good evidence that the Kingdom of God has now come among you?

"When a fully armed strong man is guarding a house, the things inside the house remain safe. How could anyone get into the house and steal its contents? An intruder would first need to overpower the strong man and tie him up. And if someone stronger overpowers the strongman, he can carry off whatever he chooses to take. He can even divide up his plunder and share it with his friends. [When Jesus takes on the strong man—Satan—he is able to set people free. Satan no longer has power to keep his victims bound to old ways. Jesus is the all-powerful Liberator. He sets people free indeed if they will only place their trust in him!]

"When a foul spirit leaves a person, it enters a spiritual desert looking for rest and finds none. It says, 'I'll go back to where I was.' But when it gets there, the place has been cleaned and everything is back in order. So, it goes out and welcomes seven other spirits that are even more evil than it. They go in and stay there, and the end result is that the person is far worse off than before. That is what will happen to this present generation. [The generation that has failed to recognize and welcome the Messiah is implied.]

"Anyone who is not my friend is my enemy; anyone who does not help me gather the harvest is actually scattering it to the wind. Therefore, let me present you with this sober truth: Every type of sin and insult can be forgiven except this one—people who continue throughout their life to resist the Holy Spirit's faithful and patient ministry will never be forgiven; not in this life, nor even in the coming ages. [The previous sentence is an interpretation of what it likely means to blaspheme the Holy Spirit.]

"If you want the fruit growing on a tree to be good fruit, you must first make certain that the tree itself is healthy. When the fruit is not good, it is because the tree is unhealthy. It is quite obvious that the condition of a tree can be seen in its fruit.

"You nest of snakes! How can such evil people say anything good? The words coming out of a person's mouth show what is in a person's heart. Good people practice the good that fills their hearts; evil people practice the evil stored up in their hearts. The mouth exposes the attitude of the heart. But let me warn you: On judgment day, everyone must explain all the worthless words they have ever spoken. The evidence of your own words will be the basis for judging you to be either innocent or guilty."

As Jesus was teaching, a woman in the crowd shouted, "May the Lord greatly reward the mother who gave you birth and nursed you."

Jesus responded, "Happy instead are those who listen to the Word of God and then put into practice the things they have understood."

151. The Jewish Leaders Request a Sign, but Jesus Offers Only the Sign of Jonah - Matt 12:38-40; Luke 11:29-32

Some of the experts and teachers of Jewish Law told Jesus, "Teacher, we want you to show us a sign."

As the crowds were increasing, Jesus answered, "This is an age of evil doers. They are always seeking signs, but the only sign they will get is the sign of the prophet Jonah. Jonah was three days and nights in the stomach of a huge fish, as a sign to the people of Nineveh. In the same way, the Son of Man will be in the heart of the earth for three days and three nights as a sign to this generation.

"The Queen of Sheba, who came from the south to visit Solomon, will rise up at the judgment to condemn this generation. Indeed, she came from a very distant place to listen to Solomon's wisdom. Now One greater than Solomon has arrived. Later on, the people of Nineveh repented when Jonah preached to them. However, One far greater than Jonah has now come. Therefore, Jonah's generation will surely be justified to rise up and condemn this present generation."

152. Jesus Pronounces "Woes" upon the Pharisees While Eating with One of Them - Matt 23:25-26; Luke 11:37-54

After concluding his teaching about miraculous signs, Jesus accepted an invitation to eat dinner at the home of an expert in Jewish Law. Upon Jesus' arrival, the host was shocked when he noticed that Jesus did not observe their detailed cleansing rituals before the meal.

Then perceiving what he was thinking, Jesus said to him, "You experts in Jewish Law and its related customs always follow the ritual of cleansing the outside of each cup and dish. However, within your hearts you are full of greed, wickedness, and self-indulgence. You foolish people! Didn't the One who made the outside also make the inside? What hypocrites you are! You pretend to be experts, but you are actually blind. You should first wash the inside of your cup and dish so the outside will also be clean. Here is how you can really be clean. Simply be generous to those who are poor and everything about you will become clean.

"How sad! You legal experts love the most prominent seats in the places of worship and to be greeted by everyone in the markets, because you are very well known."

Then one of the legal experts answered back. "Teacher, you are insulting us when you say such things."

Jesus continued, "Woe to you legal experts for you place heavy loads on people. They are already struggling to carry them, and you would never lift even one finger to help them out."

When Jesus left from there, the legal experts and teachers of the Law started fiercely opposing him. They bombarded him with many questions every chance they got in hopes of catching him in something that might slip out of his mouth.

153. Jesus Declares, "Shameful Secrets Will Be Exposed, and Kingdom Secrets Must Be Proclaimed" - Matt 10:27; Luke 12:1-3

One day, while Jesus was speaking, many thousands were gathering to listen to him. They were even trampling on each other trying to get closer to him. First, Jesus addressed his disciples with these words: "Watch out for the yeast of the Pharisees, which is hypocrisy. [Yeast has the ability to spread throughout a lump of dough.] Nothing has been hidden that will not eventually be disclosed and understood. Those things whispered in darkness will be broadcast in the light of day, and what you have whispered in someone's ear while in a secluded room will be announced across the roof tops. What I am sharing with you in the dark of night, you must speak in the light of day. What has been whispered in your ears, you must shout from the rooftops."

154. Jesus Warns about Greed and Trusting in Wealth - Luke 12:13-21

A person in the crowd gave Jesus a request. "Teacher, please tell my brother that he must give me an equal share of our family inheritance."

Jesus responded, "Sir, how did you conclude that I have been appointed to settle your family quarrels?" Then he added, "Be careful! Be on guard against every kind of greed. After all, the quality of your life doesn't depend on how many material things you have."

Then he told this story as an illustration: "One year a certain wealthy farmer had an unusually abundant harvest. He kept thinking about the best way to proceed. *What shall I do?* he thought. *I just don't have room anywhere to store all of my crops.*

"Then he came up with an idea, and said, 'Here's what I'll do: I'll tear down my storage barns and build much larger ones. That's where I can store my surplus grain. I'll have plenty of grain to last for many years. I'll just enjoy my life—eating, drinking, and having fun.'

"However, God spoke firmly to his conscience saying, 'You're a fool! This very night you are going to die, and then you must face judgment. Now who is going to get everything you planned to enjoy?'"

Then Jesus concluded, "This is exactly what happens to people when they try to selfishly keep everything for themselves, even when they have achieved nothing of eternal value to offer God.

"Don't fear, my little flock, because your Heavenly Father is pleased to offer you a place in his Kingdom. Therefore, sell whatever you are tempted to keep, then give the proceeds to the poor. In this way, you are providing for yourselves savings in purses that can never wear out. Your heavenly treasure will never be a disappointment. No thief or moth can ever touch it. You can surely count on this: That you will wholeheartedly invest your life in whatever you choose to treasure."

155. Jesus Warns His Followers to Be Ready for the Coming of the Son of Man - Luke 12:35-48

"Be like servants who are watching for their master to return from a wedding banquet. They will be properly dressed and ready to serve him, with their lamps lit. When he arrives and knocks, they will quickly jump up and open the door. Because they were well prepared, their master will surely express his approval. He will dress appropriately and let them sit back and relax while he serves them. When he sees how they were ready and looking for him, he will certainly reward them, regardless of whether he arrives at midnight or daybreak.

"Consider this: If the owner of a house were to be told the exact time when a thief is planning to break into his house, wouldn't he surely do everything possible to keep it from happening? In the same way, you must also be prepared because the Son of Man will return when you least expect it."

Then Peter asked Jesus, "Lord, is this illustration just for us, or does it apply to everyone?"

The Lord answered him like this: "Who then does this wise and faithful manager represent, who is in charge of feeding the servants at the right time? I tell you he will surely be rewarded if his manager comes back and finds him faithfully doing his job. He will certainly be promoted and put in charge of all his master's possessions.

"On the other hand, what if that servant should think that his master has been gone too long? He starts beating the other men servants and woman servants. He also indulges in overeating and getting drunk. When his master returns suddenly and unexpectedly, he will certainly punish him severely. He will separate him and send him to dwell in the place assigned only for unbelievers.

"If a servant knows what the master expects and does not prepare or carry out the assigned tasks, that servant will be severely disciplined. But when servants are unaware of what is expected, yet do things they shouldn't have done, their punishment will be light. Remember that much is required of those who have had the greatest opportunities, and much will be expected of those who have been entrusted with much."

156. Jesus Predicts Divisions as a Result of His Ministry - Luke 12:49-53

"I am here upon the earth to bring fire, and oh, how I wish it were already kindled! First, I must endure a very painful and unforgettable event. It will prove to be both sacrificial and sacred. How pressed I am to complete it! Don't imagine that I came to bring peace on earth. No, let me tell you plainly, not peace but division. From now on, even families will be divided. Families of five will be divided, three against two and two against three. Fathers will even be against their own sons, and sons against their father. Mothers will be against their own daughters, daughters against their mother, mother-in-law against daughter-in-law and daughter-in-law against mother-in-law." [People are divided by their faith or lack of faith in Jesus as Savior.]

157. Jesus Admonishes People about the Importance of Discerning the Times - Luke 12:54-56

Jesus lifted his voice and spoke to the crowd: "When you see clouds rising to the west, right away you say, 'It's about to rain,' and sure enough, it does. Also, if a south wind is blowing, you say, 'It's going to warm up,' and it does. Hypocrites! Why are you such experts when it comes to changes on the earth and in the sky, yet you can't interpret the obvious signs of these times?"

158. Jesus Teaches That Tragedy Does Not Prove Greater Guilt, but All Must Repent or Perish - Luke 13:1-9

Several of those who were present in the crowd reported to Jesus about some Galileans whose blood Governor Pilate had mixed with their Jewish sacrifices.

Jesus responded, "Do you think they suffered this way because they were worse sinners than all the other Galileans? I say that was not the case! Unless all of you repent, you will also die. And what about the eighteen people who died when the tower of Siloam fell on them? Were they more guilty than the rest of the people living in Jerusalem at the time? I say, of course not! However, unless you turn away from sinning and serve God, you will all perish."

He then offered another illustration: "A certain man owned a fig tree that was growing among his grape vines. One day, he went to see if it had any fruit and he couldn't find any. So, he told the workman in charge of his orchard, 'I've been checking on this fig tree for three years and it hasn't produced any fruit at all. You might as well cut it down! There surely must be a better use for this soil!'

"However, the workman replied, 'Sir, why don't you give it a chance for one more year? Let me try digging around it and fertilizing it. If it produces fruit during the year, great! If it doesn't, then we can cut it down.'"

159. Jesus Heals on the Sabbath, Then Teaches the Importance of Mercy - Luke 13:10-17

One Sabbath, when Jesus was teaching in a Jewish place of worship, there was a woman there who had been crippled for eighteen years. She was bent over and completely unable to straighten up. Jesus noticed her and called her to come forward.

"Woman," he announced, "you are now set free from your affliction." Jesus then placed his hands on her, and instantly she stood up straight and began praising God.

But the leader of that worship place became angry because Jesus had done this work of healing on the Sabbath day, He instructed the people, "There are six days given for working, so come on one of those days if you need to be healed, but never the Sabbath!"

The Lord rebuked him saying, "You hypocrites! Who among you would not untie your ox or donkey on the Sabbath and lead it out from its stall to get a drink of water? Don't you realize that Satan has kept this woman bound for eighteen long years? She is also a daughter of Abraham. Why shouldn't she be set free from what has bound her, even if it is on a Sabbath day?"

After he said this, all the critics of Jesus were humiliated. But the people kept celebrating all the amazing things he had been doing.

160. Jesus Heals a Man Who Had Been Born Blind - John 9:1-7

As Jesus was walking along, he noticed a man who had been born blind. His disciples asked, "Teacher, what caused this man to be born blind? Was it because he sinned, or because his parents sinned?"

111

"It wasn't because this man or his parents sinned," Jesus said, "God let it happen in order that God's good work could be revealed through him. While it is day, we must accomplish what the One who sent me has given me to do. However, the night will come when it will be too late to work. While I am here in the world, I am the light of the world."

After he had said this, he spat on the ground and mixed the saliva with the dirt to make a little mud. Next, he put it on the man's eyes and said to him, "Go and wash in the Pool of Siloam." [Siloam means sent.] The man went and washed off the mud, and as he was going home, he was able to see.

161. People React to the Healing of the Blind Man - John 9:8-12

The blind man's neighbors and people who had previously noticed him begging asked, "Can this be the same man we used to see sitting and begging?"

Some thought he was that man, but others said, "No, he just looks like him."

He himself insisted, "Yes, I am that man."

The people were puzzled and asked, "If you are the man that was blind, then explain how your eyes were cured and now you can see."

He replied, "The man called Jesus made a little mud and placed it on my eyes. Then he told me to go and wash it off at the pool called Siloam. I did as he said, and suddenly I could see!"

Then they asked him, "Where is this man who healed you?"

The man answered, "I don't know where he is."

162. The Pharisees Cross-Examine the Blind Man, then Shut Him out of the Temple - John 9:13-34

Then the people brought the man who had been born blind to the Pharisees. [The Pharisees were a religious group known for the way they embraced every traditional detail relating to Jewish Law.] They took note of the fact that the man's eyes had been healed on the Sabbath. [The 7th day the Law does not allow people to work.] And the Pharisees asked him how his eyes had been given the ability to see.

"The man who healed me simply put some mud on my eyes and when I washed it off, I could suddenly see!" he said.

Then some of the Pharisees concluded, "This man could not possibly have God's approval because he did this work of healing on the Sabbath day."

Others asked, "How could a sinner do such great miracles that depend on God's approval and power?" And the religious experts were divided among themselves.

Once again, they turned to the man who had received his sight and asked him, "What is your opinion of this man? After all, it was your eyes that he healed."

The man answered, "I believe he is a prophet of God."

The Pharisees couldn't really believe that the man had been blind and had received his sight. They sent for his parents to examine them as well.

"Tell us," they asked, "is this the one you say was born blind? If so, how is it that he can now see?"

"Yes, we know this is our son, and he certainly was born blind," his parents answered. "But how is it that he can now see? Who did this?"

They answered this way because they were afraid of the Jewish leaders who had already warned that anyone who openly proclaimed that Jesus was the promised Messiah, would be banned from entering the House of Worship. Out of fear, his parents responded, "He is old enough to speak for himself; just ask him."

Then a second time they brought in the man who had been blind, saying, "Honor God by telling us the absolute truth. We know this man [Jesus] surely must be a sinner."

The former blind man replied, "I have no way to know if this man is a sinner, but one thing I do know. Once I was blind and now I can see!"

Then they asked him once again, "How did he go about opening your eyes? What did he actually do to you?"

And he answered, "I have already told you What didn't you understand? Would you like me to repeat the story again? Are you thinking about becoming his disciples also?"

At this, they angrily threw insults at him. "You are this fellow's disciple! We are disciples of Moses! We know God talked to Moses, but as for this man, we don't even know where he came from!"

Then the man said, "This is really amazing! You can't figure out where he comes from, yet he had the power to open my blind eyes! We all know that God doesn't take orders from sinners. Yet he does listen to godly people who trust him and who do God's will. Until now, has anyone ever heard of opening the eyes of a man who was born blind? If this man did not come from God, he wouldn't be able to do such amazing wonders."

"Even from birth, you were already completely full of sin. How dare you lecture us!" They threw him out of the place of worship, declaring that he would never be allowed to enter that place again.

163. Jesus Makes Himself Known to the Blind Man - John 9:35-38

Jesus heard that the religious leaders had thrown out the man who was born blind from the place of worship. Jesus found him and asked, "Do you believe in the Son of Man?"

"Who is he, Sir?" the man asked. "Please tell me, because I really do want to believe in him."

Jesus said to him, "You have already seen him; in fact, he is the One talking to you right now."

The man answered, "Lord, I do believe," and he worshiped Jesus.

164. The Pharisees Blind Themselves to the Truth - John 9:39-41

Then Jesus said, "I have come into the world to judge it, so the blind will be able to see, and those who think they can see will have their spiritual blindness exposed."

Some of the Pharisees who heard what he had said, asked, "Did you say this for our benefit? Are you also implying that we are blind?"

Jesus responded, "If you were blind to the truth, you would not be guilty of sin. But since you claim you know the truth, you are guilty of falling short of that very truth, and your guilt remains upon you."

165. Jesus Describes the Good Shepherd and His Sheep - John 10:1-18

Jesus added, "I want to illustrate the truth so you Pharisees can see it. If someone fails to enter the sheep pen through the gate, but climbs in by some other way, that person must surely be a thief and a robber.

However, the person who does enter through the gate is the shepherd of the flock. The One in charge opens the gate for him, and the sheep recognize the shepherd's voice. The shepherd calls each sheep of his own flock by name, and he leads them out.

"When he has brought out all of his own sheep, he goes ahead of them and they follow him because they know the sound of his voice. However, they never follow a stranger. In fact, they are afraid of him, and they run away because they don't recognize his voice." Jesus used this illustration, but the Pharisees were not able to understand the meaning behind this story.

Jesus then said this to them: "Listen, and I will explain the meaning. I am the gate through which the sheep may enter or leave. As for everyone else who came pretending to know how people ought to live, they were really thieves and robbers. But my true sheep have not listened to them. You see, I am the gate; each one who enters through me will be kept safe. They will be able to come and go and find satisfying pasture.

"The thief comes to steal, to kill, and destroy. However, I have come to offer life. Those who seek life through me will be able to enjoy it to the full. I am the Good Shepherd. I lay down my life for the sheep. A hired man does not love the sheep because he does not own them. When he sees a wolf coming to attack the flock, he runs away, leaving the sheep defenseless. Then the wolf is able to attack and scatter the flock. The hired man runs because he has no concern for what happens to the flock.

"I am the Good Shepherd; I know all about each one of my sheep and each one knows me—just as the Father knows me and I know the Father, and I am willing to lay down my life to save the sheep. I even have some other sheep that are not a part of this sheep pen. I must go and bring them, also. They, too, will be able to listen and recognize my voice. Nevertheless, there will be only one flock and one shepherd. This is the reason my Father loves me so much: I will lay down my life, but I will take it up again. No one can take it from me; I will voluntarily lay it down. I have authority to lay my life down, and also to take it up again. My Father has commanded me to do this."

166. The Jews Are Divided over the Teachings of Jesus - John 10:19-21

The Jews heard the words of Jesus, but they were once again divided over his teachings. Many said, "He must be crazy or controlled by a demon. Why should we pay any attention to him?"

However, others said, "His teachings don't seem to be the ravings of a man possessed by a demon. Could a demon have power to give blind people their sight?"

167. The Jews Again Attempt to Stone Jesus or at Least Arrest Him for Claiming to Be God - John 10:22-39

The time had come to celebrate Hanukkah at Jerusalem. [It is the Festival of Dedication celebrated in the winter.] Jesus was walking in Solomon's Colonnade in the courts of the Temple. The Jews gathered around and asked him, "How long are you going to keep us wondering? Tell us plainly, are you, or are you not the Messiah?"

Jesus answered, "I have told you, but you would not believe me. The miracles that I perform should prove to you who I am. You don't believe me because you are not sheep from my flock. Those who are my sheep recognize my voice and what I am saying. I know who they are, and they follow me. I give them eternal life. And they will never lose that life. Furthermore, no one can snatch them away from my care. Those who are given to me by my Father are the greatest gift of all. No one can ever remove anyone who is safely protected by my Father. I and the Father are perfectly One."

Again, the Jewish opponents of Jesus picked up stones, intending to stone him to death. But Jesus asked them, "For which one of the many great miracles that I have shown you from the Heavenly Father, are you planning to stone me?"

"It is not because of any good work that we are stoning you," they answered. "You have blasphemed because you are only a man, yet you claim to be God."

Then Jesus gave them this Scriptural answer quoted from Psalm 82:6.

"Isn't it written in your Law? 'I say, you are gods; you are all children of the Most High.' If the Psalmist called those who had received God's word 'gods,'—and don't forget Scripture can't be simply overlooked—then what about the One whom the Father himself has set apart as his very own Son and sent him into the world? Why have you accused me of blaspheming when I spoke this truth: 'I am the Son of God'? But you don't need to believe me unless, in fact, I really am doing the works of my Father in Heaven. If that is indeed what I really am doing, although you don't believe me, at least believe in the miracles I have performed. Then you will be able to recognize and comprehend that the Father really is in me, and I am in the Father."

Once again, they tried to seize him to take him into custody, but he escaped. [His escape was actually another one of his miracles!]

168. People Follow Jesus Beyond the Jordan River - John 10:40-42

Then Jesus returned over the Jordan River to the place where John had previously baptized people. While Jesus was staying there, many people came to hear him and to see everything he was doing. They made this comment: "John never performed a miracle. but everything he told us about this man was certainly true." And in that area many people put their faith in Jesus.

169. Jesus Responds to Questions About Salvation and Entering the Kingdom of God - Luke 13:22-30

Jesus passed through various towns and villages, teaching the people as he made his way toward Jerusalem. As he was doing this, someone asked him, "Lord, are only a few people going to be saved?"

This was his answer: "Try your very best to get through the narrow door, because I tell you that many will try to enter, but will fail. When the owner of the house stands up and closes the door, you will stand outside knocking and begging, 'Sir, please open the door for us.' The homeowner will answer, 'I don't know who you are or where you came from.' Then you will say, 'We ate and drank with you, and you taught in our streets.' However, he will reply, 'I don't know you or where you come from. Get away from me, all you who continue to do evil!' Then you will weep and grind your teeth together when you see Abraham, Isaac and Jacob, along with all the prophets in the Kingdom of God, but you will be thrown out.

"People will come from all parts of the world and will take their places at the great feast in the Kingdom of God. The fact is, some who are last now will be first then, and some who are first now will be last then."

170. Jesus Affirms Control over His Own Destiny and Grieves over Jerusalem - Luke 13:31-35

At that time, some Pharisees came to Jesus and urged him, "You ought to leave this place and go somewhere else because King Herod is trying to have you killed."

Jesus answered, "Go tell that sly old fox, today and tomorrow I'll keep on doing what I've been doing—driving out demons and healing people—and by the third day, I will accomplish my goal. But whatever happens, I must press on today, tomorrow, and the next day. Surely no prophet is destined to die outside of Jerusalem!

"Oh, Jerusalem, Jerusalem, your people kill prophets and stone those God has sent to you. Many times I have longed to gather your children together just as a hen gathers her chicks under her wings. But you were not willing to trust me! This is what is about to happen: Your house will be abandoned. You will not see me again until you are able to say, 'Blessed is he who now comes in the name of the Lord.'" (Psalm 118:26)

171. Jesus Heals a Man with Dropsy on the Sabbath at the Home of a Pharisee - Luke 14:1-6

On a certain Sabbath Day, Jesus was being carefully observed when he went to eat at the home of a prominent Pharisee with a reputation for keeping every tradition concerning the Law. Just then, standing right in front of him was a man who had been suffering from an abnormal swelling in his body. Jesus asked the Pharisee and other experts of the Law who were present, "Is it legal to heal those who are sick on the Sabbath day or not?" But they would not answer a word. So Jesus placed his hands on the man, healed him, and sent him on his way.

Then Jesus asked those experts in Jewish Law, "If your own child or your beast of burden were to fall into a deep well on the Sabbath, wouldn't you immediately make every effort to get them out?" They had nothing to say and would not answer him.

172. Jesus Offers Examples of Humility and Honor - Luke 14:7-11

As Jesus was sitting by a table, he noticed that the guests were trying to be seated in the most honored places around the table, so he gave them this illustration: "If you are invited to a wedding reception, don't assume that you should go and sit in the most honored place. If you do, you may be embarrassed when a more distinguished person shows up. Then the host will tell you, 'Please give this person your seat.' Then you will be humiliated when you have to move to a less important place.

"Here is what you ought to do. When you are invited, you should voluntarily choose to sit at the least important place. Then the host will come over to you and say, 'Friend, I'd like for you to move over to this better place I have saved for you.' As a result, you will be honored in the presence of the other guests. For here is the way it is: Those who try to honor themselves will be humbled, and those who humble themselves will be honored."

173. Jesus Recommends Making the Needy Your Dinner Guests and Tells about a Great Banquet - Matt 22:1-14; Luke 14:12-24

Then Jesus kindly challenged his host: "Whenever you plan a luncheon or a dinner, don't just invite only your friends and relatives, or even your wealthy neighbors. If you do that, they may try to repay you by inviting you back. When you plan a big banquet, invite those who are poor, crippled, blind, and disabled. Then you will be greatly blessed. Although they can't repay you, you will surely be repaid at the resurrection of those God has made righteous by faith."

When someone at the table heard what Jesus had just explained, he said to Jesus, "Happy is the person who will be allowed to eat in the Kingdom of God."

Jesus continued his answer by giving these illustrations: "The Kingdom of Heaven is similar to a king who planned a great wedding banquet for his son, then invited many guests. When the banquet was about to begin, he sent out his servant to urge people to come. 'Everything is ready,' he said, 'Please come right away.'

"However, they refused to come. Instead they began to make excuses. The first person said, 'I'm sorry. I just bought a new property, and I must go see what it is like. Please excuse me.'

"Another invited guest answered, 'I have just bought five teams of oxen, and I'm going to check them out. Please excuse me.'

"Someone else said, 'I just got married, so I can't come.'

"Then the servant came back and reported to his master how each one had responded. Then the king sent additional servants with these instructions, 'Tell everyone who was invited that my dinner has been prepared, my animals have been butchered, and everything is now ready. Please come right away to the wedding banquet.'

"However, they paid no attention and each one left—one to his farm, another to his job, and the rest attacked the servants, abused some, and even murdered others. Of course, the king was enraged. He sent his army and destroyed those killers and burned their city to the ground.

"Then the king gave orders to his servants, 'The wedding banquet has been prepared, but the ones I invited don't deserve to come. Go out to the street corners, the highways, even the country lanes, and invite anyone you find to my banquet. Urge them to come in so my house will be full. I assure you that not one of those who ignored my invitation will get even a small taste of my banquet.'

"The servants carried out his instructions. They went into the streets and sidewalks and brought everybody they could find, both worthy and unworthy, until the wedding hall was completely filled with guests. However, when the king arrived to see who was there, he saw a man who was not properly dressed for the occasion. He asked him, 'Friend, how did you get in here when you have failed to dress respectfully for the occasion?' And the man was speechless.

"Then the king told his attendants, 'Tie this guy up hand and foot and throw him out into the darkness—to a terrible place where people will be crying and grinding their teeth together in pain.'

"Many are invited. Only a few get ready and are chosen."

174. Jesus Urges People to Consider the Cost of True Discipleship - Matt 10:37-39; Mark 8:34-37; Luke 14:25-33

While large crowds were traveling along with Jesus, he called them together with his disciples. As he turned and spoke to them, he warned them that all who planned to follow him must be completely dedicated to him.

He explained his meaning in this way: "In comparison with their loyalty to me," he said, "all who want to follow me must hate their own father, mother, wife, children, brothers, and sisters—yes, even their own lives. Otherwise, they cannot be my disciples. In other words, those who love their father or mother more than me are not worthy of me. And those parents who love their son or daughter more than me are not worthy of me. Those who want to be my disciples must deny themselves. All who fail to follow me and who refuse to take up their cross daily and carry it, cannot even become my disciples. They are unworthy of me. In order to be in control of their own soul, some who find real life will later turn back to seek their own gain. They will surely lose whatever they selfishly tried to keep. However, in order to spread the Good News of salvation, some are willing to surrender everything for my sake. They will find the true meaning of their life and save it as well.

"If gaining the entire world should require forfeiting your eternal soul, how could anyone believe that it would really be worth such a great sacrifice?

"Let's imagine you want to build a tall tower. Wouldn't you first sit down and estimate how much it would cost, so you can decide if you have the financial resources to complete the project? What if you were to lay the foundation, then couldn't finish the tower? You would end up being everybody's laughingstock. They would taunt, 'This guy began to build, but then he couldn't finish what he started.'

"Or can you imagine a national leader who is thinking about starting a war against the leader of another country? Wouldn't he first sit down and carefully consider if his ten thousand soldiers could defeat a leader coming against him with twenty thousand? If he thinks he can't win, he will no doubt send representatives while his opponent is still far away. They will be instructed to seek terms for achieving peace. In a similar way, those of you who are not ready to sacrifice everything you have, cannot be my disciples.

"All of you who have ears capable of comprehending spiritual truth, listen very carefully."

175. Jesus Tells Stories to Vindicate Association with Sinners - Luke 15:1-3

At that time, many notorious sinners were gathering around to listen to Jesus. Included among them were many tax collectors known for cheating. Seeing this, the legalistic Pharisees and those who were well recognized as teachers of Jewish Law muttered, "This man is always welcoming sinners, and he even eats with them."

176. Jesus Tells about a Lost Sheep That Represents a Repentant Sinner - Luke 15:4-7

Jesus sensed what the Pharisees were grumbling and said, "If a certain shepherd owned one hundred sheep, then lost one, wouldn't he leave the ninety-nine unattended while he goes to look for that lost sheep until he finds it? And once he does find it, he would joyfully lift it up on his shoulders and carry it home. Then he would call all his friends and neighbors together and tell them, 'Help me celebrate, because I have found my sheep that was lost.'

"I want you to realize that in a similar way, there is more celebration in heaven over just one sinner who repents than there is for ninety-nine godly people who no longer need to repent."

177. Jesus Tells about a Lost Coin - Luke 15:8-10

Jesus continued, "Imagine a woman who owns ten silver coins and she loses one of them. [Each was worth one day's wages.] Wouldn't she get out her flashlight and carefully search all around until she finds her coin? And when she does find it, she would call her friends and neighbors and say to them, 'Be happy with me because I have found that valuable coin that I lost.' I want you to comprehend that there is a great celebration in the presence of God's holy angels when even one sinner turns from sin and begins to follow God."

178. Jesus Tells about a Son Who Left Home, then Squandered His Inheritance While His Brother Stayed - Luke 15:11-32

As Jesus continued speaking, he told another story: "A certain man had two sons. The younger son made the following request of his father; 'Father, please give me my share of your inheritance.' So, the father went ahead and divided his property between his sons.

"Soon after that, the younger son packed up everything he owned and set off to a distant country. When he got there, he wasted all his money on living a wild life. By the time he had already spent everything he owned, a terrible famine hit that part of the world. Since he had absolutely no money left, he finally accepted a job feeding some pigs that belonged to a citizen of that country. [The Jewish people considered pigs to be very filthy animals and unfit to eat.] When no one shared anything with him, he became so hungry that he was willing to fill his stomach with the food the pigs were eating.

"When he finally came to his senses, he had to face the truth. 'My father's hired help have always had plenty to eat, but here I am starving to death! I have reached a conclusion: I must go back home and admit the truth to my father—that I have sinned against God and him.'

"Then he set out to journey back home to his father. While he was still quite a distance from home, his father saw him coming and was filled with compassion. He ran out to meet his son, and threw his arms around him and kissed him.

"There the son confessed, 'Father, I have sinned against God and also against you. I'm not even worthy to be known as your son anymore. Please consider me as one of your hired servants.'

"But his father called his servants and gave them orders, 'Hurry! Bring the very best clothing to put on him. Also, put the family ring on his finger and place new sandals on his feet. Bring in the calf we have been fattening and get it prepared for a feast. We are going to celebrate because this son of mine was considered dead, but now he is actually alive; the one we thought was lost forever has been found.' And the whole household began to celebrate.

"Meanwhile, the older son was out in the field. As he drew near to the house, he heard the music and dancing. He asked one of the servants what was happening. He replied, 'Your brother has come home! Now we all know he is back safe and sound. Your father has killed the fattened calf in order to celebrate.'

The older brother became very angry and he refused to go into the house. His father went out and begged him to take part in welcoming his brother back. But instead, the son answered his father, 'Why won't you face the truth? All the time my brother was gone, I have been faithfully working like a slave for you. I have obeyed all your orders, and you never gave me even one young goat to celebrate with my friends. Now that this son of yours has come home after wasting everything you gave him on prostitutes and wild living, you kill the fattened calf and plan a big party for him!'

"My dear son, said the father, you've been home with me all the time, and everything I have is yours. It's only right that we celebrate with joy because your brother was as good as dead and now we know he is alive; he was lost, but now he has been found."

179. Jesus Tells about a Shrewd Manager - Luke 16:1-12

Jesus gave this illustration to his disciples: "A wealthy man's manager was accused of carelessly wasting his master's possessions. He called in the manager and asked, 'What is this I hear about you? I have decided to hire a new manager. I order you, give me a report immediately of all the funds you have managed for me.'

"Then the manager asked himself, 'What am I going to do now? My boss has decided to fire me. I'm not strong enough to do heavy labor, and I surely don't want to start begging. I have a plan. I know how to make people want to help me after I lose my job.'

"He called in each of his boss's debtors. He asked the first one, 'How much do you owe my boss?'

"'Eight hundred gallons of olive oil,' he said.

"The manager told him, 'Take your bill, and quickly change it to four hundred fifty gallons.'

"Then the manager asked the second debtor, 'How much do you owe?'

"'A thousand bushels of wheat,' he answered.

"The manager ordered, 'Take your bill and change it to eight hundred.'

"When the master found out what had taken place, he complimented the witty manager for acting so wisely. He explained, 'People in this world are more clever in the way they deal with their own kind than are the people who live in God's light. I advise you to invest your earthly wealth in ways that are wise and generous. In that way, you will make friends for yourselves. Then, when your wealth is all spent, you will receive a welcome into eternal dwellings.'

"Those who can be trusted with the very little they have, can also be trusted with much more. However, if you have not been trustworthy in how you have handled earthly wealth, then who will ever trust you with lasting riches? And if you haven't been trustworthy with what belongs to someone else, who would ever want to give you property of your own?"

180. Jesus Warns Against Greed, Then Speaks About the Good News and the Law - Luke 16:14-17

The Pharisees were money lovers, and when they had heard what Jesus had said about honesty and dishonesty, they sneered at him. But Jesus answered them saying, "You always try to justify yourselves in the eyes of people. However, God sees your hearts. Often, what people value so highly is actually detestable in God's sight.

"The Jewish Law and the writings of the Prophets were constantly proclaimed until John arrived with his ministry. Since then, the Good News of God's Kingdom is being preached, and everyone is anxious to find a way into it. It would be easier for all the stars and the earth to vanish from sight, than for the dotting of an "i" or the crossing of a "t" to be eliminated from the Law of God."

181. Jesus Tells About the Rich Man Who Ignored the Beggar, Lazarus - Luke: 16:19-31

"Once there was a certain rich man who customarily dressed in very expensive clothes. Near his outer gate, a beggar named Lazarus* was placed there each day. He was covered with sores, and he longed to eat whatever fell from the rich man's table. Dogs often came and licked his wounds. [*This Lazarus is not the same one whom Jesus raised from the dead.]

"Eventually the beggar died, and angels carried him into Abraham's arms. The rich man also died and was buried. In the Place of the Dead, [It was called Hades] the rich man was tormented. He looked up and saw Abraham at a great distance. And Lazarus was by his side. He called out to him, 'Father Abraham, take pity on me. Please send

Lazarus to dip the tip of his finger in water and bring it to cool my tongue, even just a little bit, because I am in terrible agony in this fire.'

"However, Abraham answered, 'Son, remember that during your life, you received many good things while Lazarus was suffering unpleasant things. But now, he receives comfort here while you are in agony over there. Furthermore, there is a huge chasm set in place, so anyone who desires to go from here to you is not able, nor can anyone cross from there over to those who are here.'

"The rich man answered, 'Then I plead with you, Father Abraham, please send Lazarus to my family. You see, I have five brothers. Let Lazarus warn them to do whatever it takes, so they will not come into this terrible place of endless torment.'

"But Father Abraham responded, 'They have the writings of Moses and all the Prophets. They must listen to them.'

"'No, Father Abraham,' he said, 'if only someone from the dead were to go to them, then they will surely repent.'

"Abraham answered, 'If they do not pay any attention to Moses and the prophets, they will not be convinced even if someone should rise from the dead to speak with them.'"

182. Jesus Teaches About Childlikeness - Matt 18:1-6; Mark 9:33-37; Luke 9:48 and 17:1-3

At that time, Jesus and his followers arrived at Capernaum. When they had entered a house, he asked his disciples, "What was your argument as we were going down the road?" They were silent, because they were ashamed that they had been arguing about who was the most important.

Finally, they had enough courage to ask Jesus, "What does it take to be considered the greatest in the Kingdom of Heaven?"

Jesus invited the Twelve to sit, and he said, "Whoever wants to be first must be willing to be the very last, even to become a servant to everyone else."

He then took a small child who was standing in their midst. Holding the child in his own arms, he announced to everyone, "I want every one of you to hear this truth! If you don't change your attitude and become humble, just like this little child, you will never be able to get into the Kingdom of Heaven. Anyone who is willing to take the humble position of a child, like this one, will be considered the greatest in the Kingdom of Heaven."

Then Jesus added this as he taught his disciples, "There will always be stumbling blocks in life. However, it will be terrible for those who are the cause of stumbling. It is absolutely true that if anyone causes one of these childlike ones—who place their faith in me—to stumble, it would be better for him to have a huge grindstone from a mill tied to his neck, then be thrown into the deep sea to drown. Hear me. You must be very careful about your attitude."

183. Jesus Again Speaks of a Lost Sheep to Show the Value of a Child - Matt 18:10-14

"Make sure that you have the right attitude toward small children and toward people who are childlike. I want you to know that they have angels who are in touch with heaven, and are always looking into the face of my Heavenly Father.

"What about this? If someone owns one hundred sheep and just one should wander away, won't he leave the ninety-nine up there in the pasture on the hills while he goes out looking for that one sheep? And when he finds it, of course he will be happier about that one sheep that he rescued than about the ninety-nine that were safe. This is why your Heavenly Father is not willing for even one of these childlike ones to be lost."

184. Jesus Teaches About Persevering in Forgiveness - Luke 17:3-4

Peter approached Jesus and asked, "Lord, tell me how many times I should keep on forgiving my spiritual brothers and sisters when they keep offending me? Is seven times sufficient?"

Jesus answered, "No, seven times is not enough. You should make it at least seventy-seven times, or even seventy times seven. If one of your Christian brothers or sisters offends you, go confidentially to correct them. If they are willing to learn from their mistakes and make whatever changes they ought to make, you must forgive them, even if they sin seven times in one day. But if each time, they come back with an attitude of genuine repentance, you must forgive them."

185. Jesus Talks About Faith and Service - Luke 17:5-9

Then the Lord's chosen followers made this request, "Please help us increase our faith!"

Jesus explained, "If you just have faith no bigger than a tiny mustard seed, you will be able to say to this mulberry tree, 'Arise from the dirt and plant yourselves in the sea,' then it will obey your command.

"Imagine that one of you had an employee plowing your fields or taking care of your sheep. Would you tell your worker, 'Come in now and join my family for dinner around our table?' Wouldn't you be more likely to say, 'It's time now for you to get our dinner and drinks prepared? When you finish, you should serve us first; then you may sit down to eat and drink.' Will you greatly compliment your servant for merely doing what he was supposed to do? In the same way, when you have carried out everything God has required you to do, you should just sincerely say, 'We haven't done anything special; we only did our duty.'"

186. Jesus Raises Lazarus from the Dead - John 11:1-44

There was a man named Lazarus from Bethany and his two sisters, Mary and Martha. Lazarus was lying sick in bed. [This was the same Mary who would later pour perfume on the Lord and wipe his feet with her hair.] His sisters sent a message to Jesus, saying, "Lord, we know how much you love our brother, and we want to let you know that he is very ill."

When Jesus heard this news, he said, "This sickness will not end in death; It will bring glory to God by making his mercy and power visible through his Son."

Now Jesus had a special love for Martha, Mary, and Lazarus. When he heard Lazarus was sick, he waited where he was for two more days before telling his disciples, "Let's go back to the area of Judea."

"But Teacher," they said, "just a short time ago, the Jews there tried to stone you to death, and in spite of that, you still want to go back there?"

Jesus replied, "Aren't there 12 hours of daylight? Those who walk during the light of day don't need to worry about stumbling. It is only when a person walks in the dark of night that there is a risk of stumbling."

However, after saying that, he added, "Our friend Lazarus has fallen asleep, but I plan to go there to wake him up."

His disciples replied, "Lord, if he is sleeping well, most likely he is getting better." But Jesus was actually telling them that Lazarus had died. His disciples thought he was talking about natural sleep during the night.

Then he told them plainly, "Lazarus is dead, and for your benefit, I'm glad I wasn't there. In the end, this will strengthen your faith. Let's go to him."

Thomas [sometimes called the Twin] said to the other disciples, "Let's all go and die along with him." [Thomas was likely referring to the persecution by the Jewish leaders against Jesus and his followers.]

When Jesus finally arrived in Judea, they found out that Lazarus had already been four days in the tomb. Since Bethany was less than four miles from Jerusalem, many Jews had been coming out to comfort Mary and Martha because of the loss of their brother. When Martha heard that Jesus was on his way, she went out to greet him; however, Mary remained in their home.

"Lord," Martha said to him, "If you had only been here, I'm sure my brother wouldn't have died. Yet it is not too late for God to do whatever you ask."

Jesus said to her, "I tell you, your brother will be raised."

Martha responded, "I am sure he will rise at the last day when the time for the resurrection comes."

But Jesus proclaimed to her, "I am the Resurrection and the Life. All who place their faith in me will live, even if they do die; anyone who finds life by trusting in me, will never die. Can you believe this?"

"Yes, Lord," Martha replied, "I do believe that you are the promised Messiah—the very Son of God—who has been promised to come into the world."

After saying this, she went back to call her sister, Mary. She told her, "The Teacher is here and is asking for you." When Mary heard this, she quickly got up and went to where he was. Actually, Jesus hadn't entered the town, but he had been waiting at the place where Martha had met him. Just then, the Jews who had been in the house comforting Mary, noticed how quickly she left to go out, and they followed her, thinking she must be going out to grieve near the tomb.

When Mary arrived at the place where Jesus was waiting, she saw him and fell at his feet and said, "Lord, if you had just been here, I'm sure my brother would not have died."

When Jesus saw her crying, and that the Jews with her were also weeping, he was deeply moved and troubled in his spirit.

And Jesus wept.

He asked, "Where have you laid him?"

"Come and see, Lord," they said.

The people who were watching commented, "Just see how greatly he loved him!"

However, others questioned, "Couldn't the One who opened the blind man's eyes have kept this man from dying?"

Once more Jesus, was greatly moved as he approached the tomb. It was a cave with a large stone covering the entrance. "Take the stone away," Jesus said.

Martha objected. "Lord, by this time there will surely be a bad odor. You know he has been four days in the tomb."

Jesus answered, "Didn't I tell you that if you will only believe, you will see God's power shining through and transforming your sorrow?"

After hearing this, they removed the stone. Jesus looked toward the sky and prayed, "Father, I thank you for hearing me. I am sure that you always hear me, but in order to increase the faith of all who are standing here, and so they will know that you sent me into the world, I have said this."

Then Jesus called out in a loud voice, "Lazarus, come out!" All waited and watched as the dead man came out—his body was still wrapped tightly in strips of linen with a cloth covering his face.

Then Jesus ordered them, "Take off those grave clothes and set him free to move."

187. The Jewish Sanhedrin (Council) Plans to Put Jesus to Death - John 11:45-54

After Jesus had raised Lazarus from the dead, many Jews who had come to visit Mary, and also those who had seen the great miracle, placed their faith in Jesus. Some went to the Pharisees and told them what had taken place. The chief priests and the Pharisees called a meeting of the Sanhedrin, which was the highest Jewish council.

"What are all our efforts accomplishing?" they asked. "This man keeps performing great miracles. Unless we put a stop to it, the whole world will end up believing in him. Then the Romans who rule over us will pay attention, and they will get rid of our whole nation and even destroy our Temple."

Then Caiaphas, who was the high priest at that time, spoke up. He asked the council, "Can't you see the obvious? Don't you understand that in the long run, it is best for all concerned that one man should die for all the people? If we don't act, our whole nation will be wiped out."

Caiaphas didn't say this out of his own thoughts. Since he was high priest that year, he was inspired to prophesy that Jesus must die for the Jewish nation and for all of God's scattered children. Then, all nations could be included to form one worldwide people of God. Starting on that day, they began to plot how to take his life.

For that reason, Jesus stopped moving about publicly among the people of Judea. Instead, he went into a small village called Ephraim that was very close to a wilderness area. His disciples were also there with him.

188. Jesus Heals Ten Lepers, Then Answers a Question about the Kingdom of God - Luke 17:11-21

While on his way to Jerusalem, Jesus traveled along the border between Samaria and Galilee. As he was entering a village, ten men met him. They had all contracted a terrible skin disease known as leprosy. Since people were afraid they would catch their illness if they got too close, the men stood at a distance calling out loudly, "Jesus, Master, please have pity on us!"

When Jesus saw their need, he simply said, "Go show the priests, according to the Law of Moses, so they can proclaim that you have been cured." Even while they were still on their way, they suddenly realized that they had been cleansed from their disease. But only one of these ten men turned back, loudly praising God. He threw himself at the feet of Jesus while thanking him. He was a Samaritan. [They were an ethnic group that was completely alienated from the Jews].

Then Jesus asked him, "Were there not ten of you who were cleansed? What happened to the other nine? Why was this man who has been excluded by our Jewish people, the only one willing to come back and give praise to God?" He turned to the man and said, "Get up and go on your way, because your faith has healed you."

Once, when the Pharisees asked Jesus when the Kingdom of God would arrive, Jesus answered, "As the Kingdom of God arrives, it is not something you can outwardly observe. People are not going to say, 'Here, this is it,' or 'look, it's over there.' Actually, the Kingdom of God is within all who welcome the true King. It's right now in your midst."

189. Jesus Illustrates Prayer by Telling about a Persevering Widow - Luke 18:1-8

Then Jesus offered this illustration to help them understand that people should always pray and never give up. "There was a certain town that had a judge who did not fear God or care what people thought. In that town, there was also a widow who kept returning with the same complaint, 'Please rule against my enemy and grant me justice.'

"Over a long period of time, the judge refused her request. In the end, he said to himself, 'It is true, I really don't fear God, nor do I care what people think. But this widow keeps on pestering me. For that reason, I will arrange for her to get the justice she demands, just so she won't come back and try to have me impeached for not performing my duty.'"

The Lord then said, "Pay attention to what that unjust judge had to say. Don't you think God will also bring justice to his faithful followers because they constantly cry out day and night for help? Will God keep putting them off? I tell you, he will make sure that they do get justice and that they will get it quickly. On the other hand, when the Son of Man returns, will he find that there are still people on earth who have faith?"

190. Jesus Compares the Prayers of a Pharisee and a Tax Collector - Luke 18:9-14

Jesus told this story to open the eyes of people who trust in their own goodness and look down on everybody else. "There were two men who went to the Temple to pray. One was a legalistic Pharisee who paid strict attention to all the rules they had added to the Laws of God. The other was a despised tax collector. [Tax collectors were required to take money from the Jews and give it to their Roman oppressors. Furthermore, they often collected more than they should, in order to keep as much as they wanted for themselves.] That particular Pharisee stood apart from everyone else and prayed like this: 'I thank you, God, that I'm not like this tax collector and these other people. They are thieves and adulterers, and they do all kinds of evil. But I fast twice a week, and I always contribute a tenth of all the money I make.'

"However, the tax collector stood at a distance. He couldn't even bring himself to look up to heaven. Instead, he beat his chest and cried out to God, 'Lord, have mercy on me. I'm ashamed of the terrible sinner that I am.'

"I tell you, this tax collector, rather than the Pharisee, went home forgiven and he was accepted by God as a righteous man. It is absolutely true that all who think too highly of themselves will be humbled, and those who confess their unworthiness will be honored."

191. The Pharisees Ask Jesus a Controversial Question about Divorce - Matt 19:1-12; Mark 10:2-12

After finishing these teachings, Jesus left Galilee and crossed over the Jordan River into the region of Judea. Large crowds were following him, and he was healing many people there.

Then some of those Pharisees who were obsessed with all the rules they had added to God's Law, came to him to see if they could catch him in some contradiction of the Law. They began by asking him this: "Is it alright under the Law for a man to divorce his wife?"

"What does the Law of Moses tell you to do?" Jesus replied.

They responded, "Moses let a man write out a certificate of divorce and send his wife away." (Deuteronomy 24:1)

Jesus replied, "Haven't you read that in the beginning God created them to be male and female?" (Genesis 1:27) Jesus continued, "That is why a man leaves his father and mother and is united to his wife. The two of them are then joined in body to become as one. They are no longer merely two separate persons; they have become one in body. So, what God has united, no one should try to separate." (Genesis 2:24, also 1st Cor. 7:7-8; 25-35) Then they asked, "If that is true, why did Moses allow a man to write out a divorce certificate, then tell his wife to leave?"

Here is how Jesus replied, "This regulation is not for everyone. It applies to those who fit these circumstances. There are some people who are born with physical limitations to their sexual abilities. Others have been limited by medical procedures. Some have vowed to God that they will live a chaste, single life, to be free to focus fully on service to God's Kingdom. Those who are able to accept this call should be obedient to what God has planned for them."

133

192. Jesus Teaches That the Kingdom of God Belongs to Children and to Those Who Are Childlike - Matt 19:13-15; Mark 10:14-16; Luke 18:15

Many people were bringing their little children, including babies, to ask Jesus to place his hands on them and pray for them. However, his disciples tried to keep them from letting those little ones become a distraction to Jesus.

Jesus was angry when he discovered what they were doing. He ordered them, "You must let these little children come to me, and don't try to stop them. Don't you know that the Kingdom of God belongs to little children and to people who have a childlike spirit? Here is the truth: Anyone who refuses to receive the Kingdom of God like a little child will never be able to enter it." He then lifted the children into his arms, placed his hands on their heads, and gave them his blessing. After that, Jesus and his disciples traveled on from there.

193. A Rich Ruler Chooses Earthly Wealth Over Eternal Life - Matt 19:19-21; Mark 10:17-27; Luke 18:18-27

When Jesus started on his way, a very wealthy ruler ran to him and fell to his knees in front of Jesus. "Good teacher," he asked, "what must I do to be certain that I will inherit eternal life?"

"Why did you choose to call me good?" Jesus asked. "Surely you must know that only one person is truly good, and that is God alone. But if you want to enter into the kind of life that is eternal, you must keep God's commandments."

"Which commandments?" he inquired.

Jesus replied, "You must not murder, you must not commit adultery, you must not steal, you must not testify falsely, you must not cheat, you must honor your father and mother, and love your neighbor as yourself." (Exodus 20:12-16; Deut. 5:16-20; Lev. 19:18)

"Teacher," he said, "I have kept all of those commandments since I was just a small boy. What else do I still need to do?"

Then Jesus looked at him lovingly. "You lack only one thing," he said. "If you want God to consider you to be perfect, go and sell all your riches, then give the profit to the poor. All your treasures will be truly safe in heaven. After doing that, come and be one of my followers."

When the man heard this, his face fell and he sadly walked away because he owned great wealth and he was not willing to obey Jesus.

Then Jesus looked around toward his disciples and said, "How difficult it is for those who are wealthy to enter the Kingdom of God! To put God's will above everything else takes genuine faith."

That thought amazed the Lord's disciples, but Jesus repeated, "My children, how difficult it is for people who trust in their riches to leave it all and enter the Kingdom of God! In fact, it is easier for a camel to go through a needle's eye than for a rich person to enter the Kingdom of God." [It is said there is a low narrow gate in Jerusalem called the Needle's Eye. A camel can get through it only if you unload it and push or pull it through on its knees.]

The disciples were greatly amazed by what Jesus said. They asked each other, "If this is true, then who can be saved?"

Then Jesus looked at them and said, "People think it can't be done, but not so with God; he can do what people can never do. In fact, all things are possible with God."

194. Jesus Promises Great Rewards to Those Who Leave Everything to Follow Him - Matt 19:27-28; Mark 10:28-31; Luke 18:29

In response to what Jesus said about putting God's will above riches, Peter spoke up. "Lord, we have left everything behind us to follow you! What will our reward be?"

Jesus answered him this way: "Here's the truth. When the Son of Man sits on his beautiful throne and everything is being made new, those of you who have followed me will also be sitting on twelve thrones. You will be given responsibility to judge all twelve tribes of Israel. No one who sacrifices their house, or brothers, or sisters, or mother, or father, or their children, or wife, or their property for my sake and for the sake of the Good News will ever fail to get back a hundred times more during their lifetime. Although there will be persecutions in this life, those who place their trust in me will be rewarded in the coming ages with everlasting life. However, many who are first now will be last then, and many who are last now will be first then."

195. Jesus Tells About a Landowner Who Paid Generous Wages - Matt 20:1-16

"The Kingdom of Heaven is similar to the owner of a vineyard who started early in the morning to hire his workers. He agreed to pay them the usual amount for a full day's work. Then he sent them out to work in his vineyard.

"Around nine in the morning, he noticed others standing around the marketplace with nothing to do. He said to them, 'If you will go to work in my vineyard, I will pay you whatever is fair.' So, they went to work.

"He went out again around noon, and again about three in the afternoon to repeat the same offer. About five o'clock, he still found others standing around with no work to do, and he invited them, as well. 'In addition to all my other workers, you may work in my vineyard, also.'

"Then at evening, the owner told his foreman, 'Call in the laborers and pay their wages. Start with the last ones I hired and end up with the first ones.'

"Those who had been hired around five in the evening received a full day's wages. Of course, those who were hired first expected to get more than those who were hired last. However, each one also received the same full day's wages. But when they received their pay, they started complaining against the landowner. 'Why did those hired last and who worked for only one hour get equal pay along with us who had to work all day, even when it was the hottest?'

"The landowner responded to one of them, 'Friend, I am not being unfair when I pay you the exact amount we agreed on. Take your pay and go on your way. I desire to give the man I hired last the same amount that I gave to you. Isn't it my right to do what I want to do with my own money? Or are you jealous because I am a generous man?'

"So the last will be first and the first will be last."

196. Jesus Again Predicts His Own Resurrection From the Dead - Mark 10:32-34 Luke 18:31-34

Jesus was leading the way while they traveled toward Jerusalem, and the disciples were afraid and amazed. [They doubtless knew that the Jewish leaders were jealous and were plotting to get rid of Jesus.]

Then, Jesus took the Twelve to one side and explained to them what was about to happen to him.

"We're going to Jerusalem," he said, "and all that the prophets have written about the Son of Man will be fulfilled. The Son of Man will fall into the hands of the chief priests and teachers of the Law. They will succeed in getting him handed over to the Gentile rulers. They will ridicule him, spit on him, beat him, and finally kill him. But three days later he will rise from the dead."

However, the disciples couldn't comprehend what he was saying. It just didn't make any sense to them. The meaning was hidden.

197. Jesus Reveals the Pathway to True Greatness - Matt 20:20; Mark 10:35-45

At that time, the sons of Zebedee, James and John, came with their mother to Jesus. They knelt before him and asked a favor. "Teacher, when you come into your place of glory, will you let one of us sit at your right hand and the other at your left hand?"

Jesus replied, "You don't understand what you're asking. Do you think you will be able to drink the cup I must drink, or be baptized the way I will soon be baptized?"

"Yes, we can," they responded.

Then Jesus told them this: "You certainly will drink the cup I must drink and be baptized with the baptism I must face, but I am not the one who will determine who can sit at my right and at my left hand. That honor will belong to those for whom it has been prepared."

When the other ten heard what had been said, they became angry with James and John. Knowing this, Jesus called them together to explain. "Whoever desires to be considered great among you must become like your servant, and whoever seeks the top place must be like your slave. You must understand that even the Son of Man didn't come into this world to be served, but he came to give up his life to deliver many who have been enslaved by the evil one."

198. Jesus Brings Salvation to the Household of Zacchaeus - Mark 10:46; Luke 19:1-10

Jesus and his disciples passed through a town called Jericho. A man lived there whose name was Zacchaeus. He was a chief tax collector [for the Romans] and very wealthy. [Perhaps he became wealthy by collecting extra money for himself.] He had heard about Jesus and wanted to see him. Since he was quite short he wasn't able to see Jesus in the crowd that followed along, So he decided to run on ahead and climb up into a sycamore fig tree where he would have a better chance to see him. As Jesus drew near that spot, he looked up and called, "Zachaeus, come down right away. I would like to visit you in your own home today."

Astounded, Zachaeus leapt down and gladly welcomed Jesus.

When all the people saw what had happened, they complained, "He has entered as a guest into the home of an evil man."

But Zacchaeus stood and declared, "Listen, Lord. Right here and now I promise to give half of all my possessions to help the poor, and if I have in any way cheated anyone, I promise to pay back four times the amount that I owe."

Hearing this, Jesus proclaimed, "This very day salvation has come to this house, because this man is also a son of Abraham. For I, the Son of Man, have come to find those who are lost and to save them."

199. Jesus Teaches the Need for Faithfulness while Waiting for the Kingdom to Arrive - Luke 19:11-28

As the people continued to listen to Jesus, he told them another story. At that time, he was nearing Jerusalem, and the people were expecting that the Kingdom of God was about to appear.

Jesus told them this: "There was a man who was born into nobility and he traveled to a distant country where he expected to be appointed as their king. After that, he planned to return. He called ten servants and gave each one wages that equaled what was generally paid over a period of two and one-half years. He said to them, 'Invest this money until I return.'

"However, his subjects hated him and they sent representatives saying, 'We don't want this man as our king.'

"In spite of that, he became king, and went back home. Later, he sent for a report from his servants who had received the money. He wanted to find out what they had gained from their investments.

"The first one came and reported, 'Sir, your money has earned ten times as much as you put in.'

"'Well done, my faithful servant!' his master replied. 'Since you have proved to be trustworthy with a small investment, I will put you in charge of ten cities.'

"Then the second servant returned and reported, 'Sir, your money has earned five times as much as you put in.'

"His master told him, 'Take charge of five of my cities.'

"However, another servant came back and reported, 'Here is the money you loaned me. I hid it in a safe place because I was afraid of what you might do if I were to risk investing your money and it turned out to be a bad investment. I know you're a hard man who takes back more than you put in and who reaps what you did not plant.'

"Then his master replied, 'You wicked servant! Your very own words condemn you. If you think I am such a hard man taking what I didn't put in and reaping what I did not sow, why didn't you invest my money so it could have gained interest by the time I came back?'

"With that, he ordered those standing by, 'Take back my money and give it to the one who was able to earn ten times more.'

"'But Sir,' they complained, 'he already has ten!'

"He replied, 'Here's the truth. More will be given to all who are faithful with what they have received, but as for those who have gained nothing, even what they think they have will be taken away. As for those enemies who rejected me as king over them, bring them here and let me witness their execution.'"

After finishing this story, Jesus went on ahead, leading his followers toward Jerusalem.

200. Jesus Heals Blind Bartimaeus and His Companion - Matt 20:30-34; Mark 10:46-50; Luke 18:36-43

As Jesus was leaving the city of Jericho with his disciples, a large crowd was following him. Two blind men were sitting by the roadside begging. One was named Bartimaeus (which means Son of Timaeus). When he heard the crowd passing by, he asked what was going on. They told him, "Jesus of Nazareth is passing by."

He called out loudly, "Jesus, Son of David, please have mercy on me!"

Those who were leading the way told him to be quiet and stop making such a commotion. But he shouted even more loudly, "Son of David, please have mercy on me!"

Hearing him cry out, Jesus stopped and said, "Bring him over to me."

They quickly called to the blind man, "Be encouraged. He's calling for you. Get on your feet and come." He threw his coat aside, jumped up, and started toward Jesus.

When he got there, Jesus asked, "What do you want me to do for you?"

"Lord, I want to be able to see," he pleaded.

Jesus said to him, "Your faith is active and it has healed you. Receive your sight."

Jesus also had compassion on both blind men. When he touched their eyes, immediately both of them received their sight and began praising God and following Jesus. When all the people saw what had happened, they, too, began praising God.

201. Jesus Arrives in Bethany - John 11:55-12:1

The time for the Jewish Passover was near. Many people from all over the country were going toward Jerusalem to take part in the cleansing ceremony in preparation. Many were also looking for Jesus to arrive. As they stood in the courts of the Temple, they were asking each other, "Isn't he even planning to come to the Passover, at all? What do you think?" In fact, the chief priests and the Pharisees had already announced that anyone who discovered where Jesus was should report it so they could arrest him.

Just six days before the Passover began, Jesus arrived in Bethany. That is where Lazarus lived, not far from Jerusalem. He was the brother of Mary and Martha, whom Jesus had raised from the dead.

202. Mary Anoints Jesus for Burial at a Celebration in His Honor - Matt 26:7-8; Mark 14:3-9; John 12:3-1

While Jesus was in Bethany in the home of a man people called Simon the Leper, Mary, Martha and Lazarus gave a dinner to honor Jesus. Martha was serving, while Lazarus was one of those reclining with Jesus at the table. Mary brought in an alabaster jar containing nearly a pint of expensive pure nard perfume. Then she poured the perfume on the Lord's head and wiped his feet with her hair. The whole house became filled with the fragrance of her perfume.

The disciples were upset when they saw what she had done. Judas Iscariot, who would later betray Jesus, and a few others that were present angrily complained, "Why wasn't this expensive perfume sold for a year's wages, so the payment could be used to help the poor? Why such a waste?" Now Judas had no compassion for the poor. The fact is that he was in charge of the moneybag, and he used to dip into it and take some for himself.

Hearing this, Jesus demanded, "Let her alone. Why are you bothering her? She has done a precious, loving thing to me. You will always have people who are poor among you. You can help them anytime you want to. But you won't always have me near. She did what she was able to do. She poured perfume on my body in preparation for my burial. The fact is, wherever the Good News is proclaimed throughout the whole world, the story of what she has just done will be told to honor her memory."

Meanwhile, a large crowd of Jews heard where Jesus was. They came not only to see Jesus, but also to see Lazarus—the man who had been raised from the dead. This got the attention of the chief priests. They saw how many Jews had begun to believe in Jesus because he had raised Lazarus from the dead. And they plotted to kill Lazarus.

203. Jesus Enters Jerusalem As the Triumphant Servant King - Matt 21:1-9; Mark 11:2-10; Luke 19:29-40; John 12:12-19

The following day, the multitude that was coming to the festival learned that Jesus was approaching Jerusalem. As he came near to Bethphage and Bethany, not far from the Mount of Olives, he told two of his disciples, "Go to the next village, and when you are entering it, there will be a donkey tied there next to her colt. Untie them and bring them to me. If someone asks, 'Why are you doing this?' simply say, 'The Lord needs the colt and will soon return them.'"

They did exactly as they were told, and went and found the colt tied to a doorway. While they were untying it, some people nearby asked, "Why are you untying that colt?"

They replied, "The Lord needs it." Then the people decided not to interfere. They brought the colt to Jesus and threw their coats over it, and he sat upon it.

This fulfilled what the prophets had spoken:

Tell the Daughter of Zion,
'Celebrate, Oh people of Jerusalem!

141

Look, your king is now approaching.
He brings victory through the power of God.
Yet, he rides in humbly on a donkey's colt.' (Zechariah 9:9)

Then the crowd picked up palm branches and began to spread them on the road, along with their robes. They hurried out to meet him, shouting:

Save us, Son of David!
Happy and honored is the One who comes
in the name of the Lord! (Matt 21:9)
God, in the highest heaven, has come
to save us! (Psalm 118:25-26)
The promised Kingdom descends now from
our father David and is greatly honored!
(John 12:13, Mark 11:10)
Peace shines down upon the earth from
the highest heaven. (Luke 19:38)

The Lord's disciples did not understand all these things at first. However, after Jesus had received his glorified body, then they recognized that he had fulfilled all these ancient prophecies.

The crowd of witnesses that surrounded him had seen Lazarus resurrected from the tomb. They kept spreading the news. Many of those who heard that Jesus had performed this miracle went out to meet him. His popularity frightened the Pharisees. They complained, "Look! We are getting absolutely nowhere. See how the whole world has gone after him!"

Some of the Pharisees in the crowd even dared to tell Jesus, "Teacher, you should rebuke your followers!"

But Jesus answered them, "If they were to keep quiet, even the stones would loudly announce the Messiah's arrival."

204. Jesus Weeps over a City That Is Divided Concerning Him - Matt 21:10-17; Mark 11:11; Luke 19:41-44

When Jesus was approaching Jerusalem, he looked down on the city and wept over it. He spoke to the city in these words: "If today you could only know the remedy that would bring you real peace—but that is hidden now from your eyes. The time will come when your enemies will build ramparts against your walls. They will surround you on all sides. They will level you to the ground with your children trapped within your walls. Not a single stone will be left resting upon another. All this will happen because you shut your eyes to the time when God came to visit you."

Then, when Jesus came into Jerusalem, the whole city was disturbed. They were asking each other, "Who is this man?"

Some in the crowd answered, "This is Jesus from Nazareth in Galilee. He is a great prophet!"

Blind and crippled people came to him at the Temple, and he healed them. The chief priests and teachers of the Law saw all of the amazing things he did and how the children were celebrating, shouting, "Son of David, save us!" The Jewish leaders became offended and angry.

They asked Jesus, "Are you going to let these children talk like this?"

"I certainly will," Jesus replied. "Haven't you read what the Psalmist said? 'You have taught children and even infants to speak of your power, in this way silencing all who oppose you.'" (Psalm 8:2)

When Jesus entered Jerusalem, he went into the courts of the Temple. He looked all around. Because it was already getting late, he went back to Bethany with the twelve disciples, and they spent the night there.

205. Jesus Curses a Fig Tree with Leaves but No Fruit - Matt 21:18; Mark 11:12-14

The following day, when they were leaving Bethany early in the morning, Jesus was hungry. In the distance, he noticed a fig tree with lots of leaves on it. When he went closer to see if it was producing any fruit, he discovered it had only leaves growing on it. But it was not yet the season for figs.

Jesus commanded the tree, "Let no one ever eat fruit from you again." And his disciples heard what he had said. [Some Bible teachers have warned that there is never any valid excuse for becoming unfruitful believers.]

206. Jesus Cleanses the Temple During the Passover Season - Mark 11:15-18; Luke 19:47-48; John 2:13-22

It was very close to the time for the Jewish Passover Festival to begin. As Jesus arrived in Jerusalem and was approaching the Temple area, he found people selling sacrificial cattle, sheep, and doves. Others were at tables exchanging ordinary money into sacred money to be used for worship and the purchase of sacrifices. Then Jesus made a whip out of ropes, and started driving the sheep and cattle out of the Temple courts. He also drove out the merchants who were doing the buying and selling.

He spoke firmly to those who had been selling doves as sacrifices saying, "Get away from here! Stop turning my Father's house into a common market!"

Then he threw over the tables and benches that belonged to the moneychangers and those who were selling doves. He scattered the coins around, and refused to let anyone carry merchandise through the Temple area. He also explained why he had done all of this, reminding them of what the prophets Isaiah and Jeremiah had written:

My Temple will be called a house of prayer
for all nations. (Isaiah 56:7)
But this Temple, which bears my name,
has become a den of thieves. (Jeremiah 7:11)

When the chief priests, the teachers of the Law, and other leaders among the people had seen what he did and heard what he said, they began to seek some means by which to have him killed. He frightened them because his teachings got the attention of masses of people all over the nation. However, they couldn't find any way to do it because all the people clung to every one of his words.

His disciples then remembered this prophecy:

Passion for your house has consumed me. (Psalm 69:9)

Then the Jews answered him with a question, "Can you show us a miracle that will prove your authority to do all of this in our Temple?"

Jesus spoke this prophecy: "Destroy this temple, and in three days I will raise it again." [He was referring to his own body as a temple.]

To this, they replied, "Don't you realize that it took forty-six years to build this Temple, so how could you possibly rebuild it in three days?" However, the temple Jesus spoke of was actually his own body.

Later, after Jesus was raised from the dead, his disciples remembered his prediction, "Destroy this temple, and in three days I will raise it again." They also remembered other prophecies and words Jesus had spoken.

207. Jesus Answers Some Greeks, by Reminding Them of the Law of Life Springing from Death - John 12:20-36

Now it happened that there were some Greeks among the people who traveled to the Passover Festival. They approached Philip who was from the town of Bethsaida in Galilee. [*Philip* is a Greek name.] This was their request: "Sir, we would like to ask you to please arrange for us to talk to Jesus." Then Philip consulted with Andrew, and both in turn went to inform Jesus. [However, Jesus responded with a philosophical illustration. Of course, Greeks were famous for their interest in philosophy.]

Jesus replied, "The time has come for the Son of Man to shine out in the glory of a new kind of life. Here is a simple illustration: When a wheat seed falls to the ground, it is just one little seed. However, if it sinks into the soil and dies, then it produces many seeds. [Seeds are crushed into flour to make bread that feeds many.]

"All who (selfishly) love their life are bound to lose it. But those who are willing to give their life away in humble service to God and to bless other people, will certainly keep their life for all eternity. All those who are willing to serve should follow me. My true servants will stand with me wherever I take them. You can be certain of this: My Father will honor each person who serves me.

"Now, at this time as I look ahead, I am very deeply troubled. What can I say? 'Father, save me from all that is about to come in the hour that is quickly approaching? No. It was for this very purpose that I have come to this appointed time. So, Father, let the full meaning of your character shine out for all to see! Now glorify your name!'"

A voice then spoke from heaven saying, "I have glorified it, and will do it again." Then the crowd that was present heard something they couldn't quite comprehend. Some thought it had thundered; others thought an angel must have spoken to him.

Jesus explained, "The voice you have just heard was for your benefit, not mine. The time has arrived for judgment to descend. The evil prince of this world is about to lose his ultimate authority. But

when I am lifted up, then exalted, I will draw all humanity to myself."
By saying this, he revealed the kind of death he would soon die.

Some in the crowd questioned, "We have understood that the Law
indicates the Messiah will live forever. Where is there any evidence
that the Son of Man must be lifted up on a cross and die? What 'Son
of Man' are you talking about?"

Jesus replied, "For just a little while longer the light will be shining
for you. You must walk while you still have the light, before darkness
descends upon you. Those who walk in the dark can't see where they
are going. You must place your trust in the light while it is within
reach. If you do this, you will become children of the light."

208. Jesus Withdraws from the Crowds, Then Speaks about Faith and Unbelief - John 12:36-50

When Jesus finished teaching, he withdrew from the crowds to a
solitary place where they would not likely follow him.

Although he had done many miracles to demonstrate the truth of
his claims, they would not place their faith in him. In fact, their
rejection actually fulfilled the predictions of Isaiah the prophet:

> *Who has trusted our message*
> *and to whom has the Lord actually*
> *revealed his powerful arm? (Isaiah 53:1)*

However, the real reason they could not believe was because of
what Isaiah had explained in another one of his prophecies:

> *The Lord has blinded their eyes,*
> *so they will not see,*
> *nor understand with their hearts,*
> *nor turn to me for healing. (Isaiah 6:10)*

Isaiah could speak about this because God had revealed the glory
of Jesus to him.

Even though this prophecy was true, there were very few among
the Jewish leaders who actually believed in him. In order to avoid the
disapproval of the Pharisees, those believers kept silent so they
wouldn't be refused admittance to the Jewish place of worship. The

truth is, they loved the approval of people more than they cared about God's approval.

Then Jesus called out loudly, "Whoever trusts in me, not only believes in me, but is also trusting the One who sent me into the world. Whoever looks at me, also sees the One who sent me. I have come to this earth like a powerful light that delivers all who believe in me from the darkness, where they have been trapped.

"I do not judge anyone who learns about my teachings, then fails to put them into practice. That is because I did not enter the world to judge it, but to save it. However, there is one thing that will judge those who reject me and also refuse to accept my teachings. The very words I have spoken will condemn them on the last day. For what I taught was not by my own authority, but by my Father who sent me here. He commanded me to say everything I have proclaimed. I am absolutely certain that his commands lead toward eternal life. Therefore, everything I am saying is exactly what the Father has told me to say."

209. Jesus Uses a Withered Fig Tree to Teach About Faith - Matt 21:19-21; Mark 11:19-25

That evening, Jesus and his disciples left the city. The following morning as they walked along, they saw a fig tree that was dried up from the roots. Then Peter remembered what Jesus had said, so he exclaimed, "Teacher, look! That fig tree you cursed has withered up immediately!"

"You must have faith in God," Jesus answered. "I want you to really hear this truth. If you refuse to doubt in your heart and have faith that what you declare will happen, you can be sure it will be done. You will not only be able to do what was done to this fig tree, but also you could even say to this mountain, 'Go, throw yourself into the sea,' and it will surely happen. I assure you, whatever you pray for, you must believe that you have received it and it will be yours. Also, when you are praying, if you are holding a grudge against anyone, forgive that person. Then you can also be sure that your Heavenly Father will forgive your own sins."

210. The Religious Leaders Challenge the Authority of Jesus - Mark 11:27-33; Luke 20:1-6

Again, Jesus and his disciples entered Jerusalem. When Jesus was walking in the courts of the Temple proclaiming the Good News as he taught the people, the chief priests and teachers of the Law along with the elders, came up and said to him, "We want you to tell us who gave you the authority to force the merchants to leave the Temple? Who gave you authority to do this?"

Jesus replied, "I will answer your question with another question. If you are willing to answer me, then I will also tell you why I have authority to do all these things. Here is my question: 'Was John's baptism decreed from heaven, or merely by human origin?' Now tell me!"

They talked it over among themselves and concluded, "If we say that John's authority came from heaven, then he will ask, 'why didn't you believe in him?' However, if we say, 'It came merely from human origin,' all the people will stone us to death because they were all convinced that John was a great prophet."

Finally, they said, "We just don't know."

With that, Jesus said, "Since you are unwilling to answer my question, neither will I tell you why I have authority to do all these things."

211. Jesus Illustrates Responsibility and Faithfulness - Matt 21:28-46; Mark 12:4-12; Luke 20:10-18

As Jesus was teaching, he asked, "What do you think about this? Once there was a man who had two sons. He told the first one, 'Son, go now and work today in our vineyard.'

"'No, I don't want to,' he answered, yet later he changed his mind and actually went anyway. Then the father gave the same order to his other son. That son answered, 'Yes, sir. I'll do it,' but he didn't really go.

"Now tell me, which of the two sons actually did what his father wanted?"

"The first, of course," they answered.

Jesus finished his story. "The truth is that tax collectors and prostitutes will get into the Kingdom of Heaven ahead of you 'religious' people. You know that John came and explained to you the path of righteousness, but you refused to believe him. Yet, the tax collectors and prostitutes did respond to him. Then even after you witnessed this, you still refused to repent and believe his teachings.

"Here's another illustration: Once there was a landowner who planted a vineyard. He also built a wall around it. Then he dug a winepress there and built a watchtower. Next, he rented the vineyard to some farmers. After that, he moved farther away to another location.

"When harvest time came, he sent one of his workers to the renters, rightfully expecting them to give him some of the fruit from his vineyard. But the renters beat him and sent him away empty-handed. When he sent another servant, they treated him badly, too, and even struck him on the head and sent him away empty-handed. Likewise, he sent a third worker, but they even murdered him. He continued to send still others. Some they beat and some they killed.

"The landowner had one other person left to send—his only son, whom he deeply loved. He sent him last of all thinking to himself, *they will surely respect my own son.*

"But when the renters saw his son, they plotted with each other, saying, 'This one is his heir. If we kill him we can steal his inheritance.' They grabbed him, threw him out of the vineyard, and murdered him.

"When the owner of the vineyard comes back, how will he deal with those wicked renters?

"He will certainly bring those awful renters to a terrible end. Then he'll rent his vineyard out to others who will give him a fair share of his crops when they are harvested."

Everyone who had listened to this story responded, "May God forbid that this should ever happen to us!"

Jesus looked directly at them and asked, "Then how would you interpret the meaning of what the Psalmist wrote:

> *The stone the builders rejected*
> *has now become the cornerstone?*
> *(Psalm 118:22)*

"All those who fall on that stone will be broken into pieces, but anyone on whom it falls will be absolutely crushed.

"For that reason, I must warn you that the Kingdom of God will surely be taken away from you and given to others who will produce fruit for the Kingdom."

After the chief priests and Pharisees heard the illustrations Jesus had given, they realized he had actually been referring to them. So, they kept looking for some way to have him arrested, but they feared the crowd because the masses of people believed him to be a great prophet. For the time being, they left him and went on their way.

212. The Pharisees and Herodians Ask a Trap Question about Taxes - Matt 22:17-22; Mark 12:13; Luke 20:20-26

At that time, while pretending to be sincere, King Herod sent some of his supporters and some Pharisees to spy on Jesus. They hoped to catch Jesus saying something that might give them an excuse for turning him over to the governor appointed by the authorities of the Roman Empire.

They sent spies who began to ask him questions. "Teacher," they said, "we recognize that the way you speak is excellent and what you are teaching is very good. We also realize that you never show any partiality. You teach God's ways and they are always backed by truth. Give us your opinion about this: Is it proper for us to pay the taxes that are imposed by the Romans under Caesar, or should we not pay them?"

Jesus knew their intentions were evil, so he answered, "Are you not really hypocrites who are trying to trap me? Bring me a denarius coin and tell me whose image and inscription are on it."

The spies replied, "Caesar's image, of course."

But Jesus answered, "Then just give back to Caesar what is his and give to God what is God's."

The enemies of Jesus could find absolutely no way to catch him in all the things he said in the hearing of the public. They were amazed at his answer, and kept quiet. Because of this, they left Jesus and went on their way.

213. The Sadducees Try to Trap Jesus Concerning Eternal Life - Matt 22:23-33; Mark 12:19-27; Luke 20:34-39

On the same day that the Pharisees and Herodians tried to corner Jesus, the Sadducees, who did not even believe in a resurrection from the dead, also attempted to trap him with a question of their own.

They said, "Teacher, as you know, Moses wrote down the following instructions: 'If a man's brother should die and leave behind a wife, and no children as his heirs, then the man must marry his brother's widow and raise his offspring in behalf of his brother.' Now, consider this example: There were seven brothers. The first one married, and then died without leaving any children. The second brother married the widow, but he also died without leaving her any children. The same thing happened with the third and so on. Not one of the seven left her any children. In the end, the woman also finally died. Our question is, whose wife will that woman be at the resurrection, since all seven were married to her?"

Jesus replied, "Haven't you made a fundamental mistake because you don't fully comprehend the Scriptures nor what God is able to do? People, during their time on earth, may marry and their parents may offer them in marriage. On the other hand, those who are worthy of participating in the coming age following the resurrection from the dead, will not marry nor be offered in marriage.

"There will no longer be any death; they will be eternal beings, like the angels. They are all God's children because they are children of the resurrection. Now regarding the question of life after death, haven't you read in the writings of Moses in his account of the burning bush? God told him, 'I am the God of Abraham, the God of Isaac, and the God of Jacob.' That means God is not the God of the dead. He is the God of the living. From God's perspective, everyone is alive. You have made a big mistake."

After listening to this, the crowds who heard him were amazed at the way Jesus taught. Even some of the teachers of the Law responded, "Well said, Teacher!"

214. An Expert in Jewish Law Asks Jesus about the Greatest Commandment - Matt 22:34-40; Mark 12:29-34

When the Pharisees saw how Jesus had silenced the Sadducees, they united to challenge him further. One of them, an expert in the Law, tested Jesus with this question: "Teacher, which commandment is the greatest in the Law given by Moses?"

Jesus answered, "This is the most important commandment: 'Listen, O Israel. The Lord alone is our God. And you must love the Lord your God with all your heart, all your soul, all your mind, and all the strength of your body.' (Deuteronomy 6:4-5) The second in importance is this commandment: 'Love your neighbor as yourself.'

(Leviticus 19:18) There are no commandments greater than these two. The whole Law and all the Prophets depend upon these two commandments."

The man replied, "You have answered well. You are certainly right when you say that our God is the only true God. You must love him with your whole heart, all of your mind, with all of your soul, and with all the strength of your body. To love God with your whole being and to love your neighbor as yourself, are more important commands than all our ceremonial burnt offerings and sacrifices."

When Jesus saw how wisely the man had answered, he said to him, "You are not far from the Kingdom of God."

215. Jesus Challenges His Critics with a Question of His Own: "Why Does David Address the Messiah as Lord?" - Matt 22:41-46; Mark 12:34-37

Since the Pharisees were all gathered together, Jesus took the opportunity to ask them a question: "What are your thoughts about the Messiah? Whose son is he?"

"He is the son of David," they responded.

Then Jesus went on to ask them, "Why then did David, under the guidance of the Holy Spirit, refer to the Messiah as 'My Lord'?"

"For David quoted this Psalm:

God the Father said to his Son (Jesus), who is David's Lord:
Sit at my right hand until I conquer your enemies
and put them all under your feet, as a footstool. (Psalm 110:1)

"If David called the Messiah his 'Lord,' then how can the Messiah also be his son?" But no one could think of even a single word to answer Jesus. From then on, no one dared to ask him any more questions. However, the large crowds loved to hear everything he had to say.

216. Jesus Pronounces Woes upon the Religious Leaders - Matt 23:1-36; Mark 12:38-40; Luke 11:42-52

As Jesus taught the crowds along with his disciples, he warned, "Watch out for the teachers of the Law and the Pharisees because they claim to take upon themselves the authority of Moses. Think carefully about everything they tell you. Especially, don't follow their example because they don't practice what they preach.

"They take over the houses that belong to poor widows and show off how holy they are by making up long prayers. You can be sure that in the end they will receive the most severe punishment of all. Absolutely everything they do is for show. They even wear tiny boxes on their arms and foreheads containing scriptures, and long tassels on their robes. They love to be honored and to be called 'Teacher.'

"As for you, don't allow people to call you, 'Honorable Teacher,' for you have only one true Master and Teacher, and you are all brothers and sisters. Also, be very careful about using the title 'Father' in ways that might easily cause confusion. Remember, you have only one true Father who is also the Creator of heaven and earth. Neither should you be called 'instructors,' for your ultimate instructor is the Messiah. Here's the absolute truth: The very greatest among you are the persons who serve you. But those who exalt themselves will be humbled, and those who humble themselves will be exalted.

"Oh, what sorrow will surely come upon you teachers—you so called experts in the Law—you Pharisees and you hypocrites! You have hidden the key to knowledge and shut the door in the faces of those who seek to enter the Kingdom of Heaven. You yourselves refuse to enter, and you block the way against those who are desperately trying to get in. You travel over land and sea just to win one convert, and when you win their trust, you turn them into a child of hell just like yourselves.

"Oh, what sorrow awaits you blind guides! You teach, 'If someone swears by the Temple, it is permissible; however, if someone dares to swear by the gold in the Temple, he must keep his promise.' You are blind fools! After all, which is more important: the gold, or the Temple that causes the gold to be sacred?

"And you also say, 'If someone swears by the altar, it is permissible, but if anyone dares to swear by the offering on the altar, he must keep his promise.' How blind you people are! After all, which is more important, the gift on the altar or the altar that makes the gift sacred? So, everyone who swears by the altar is actually swearing both by the altar and everything on it. And anyone who swears by the Temple swears by the Temple and the One who dwells in it. Also, anyone who swears by Heaven swears by the throne of God and the One who sits on it.

"How terrible for you teachers of the Law, you Pharisees and you hypocrites! You are careful in the way you give a tenth of all your spices, your mint, dill, cumin, and every herb in your garden. But you have completely overlooked the most important aspects of God's Law. You fail to practice justice, mercy, faithfulness, and the love of God. In fact, you should have done both. You should have loved both God and people without overlooking careful tithing. You are blind guides! You strain out tiny gnats but swallow a whole camel.

"What sorrow awaits you teachers of the Law, you Pharisees and you hypocrites! You are like unmarked graves that people walk on without knowing they are even there. You are like tombs that have been painted with whitewash. Outside they are temporarily pretty, but on the inside, they are full of the bones of dead people and all kinds of filth. In just the same way, you seem like such wonderful, religious people, but in your hearts, you are full of wickedness and hypocrisy.

"How terrible for you teachers of the Law, you Pharisees and you hypocrites! You have built tombs to honor the prophets and you decorate the graves of godly people. However, it was your own ancestors who killed those prophets. But you say, 'If we had only lived in the time of our forefathers, we wouldn't have had any part in shedding the blood of those great prophets.' In this way, you are testifying against yourselves by admitting that you are the descendants of those who murdered the prophets. You actually approve of what they did when they killed the prophets because you build their tombs to honor them. So, go ahead now and finish what your ancestors started!

"You are like snakes! You are a brood of poisonous vipers! How can you ever escape from being condemned to hell? So, I will send you prophets, godly leaders, teachers, and apostles. You will kill and crucify some of them. You will whip others in your places of worship, and chase some from town to town. Upon you will fall the righteous blood that has been shed on earth from the beginning of the world, starting from the blood of righteous Abel. Upon you also falls the blood of Zechariah, son of Berekiah, whom your ancestors murdered between the Temple and the altar. I proclaim to you the absolute truth. This generation will be held responsible for all such things."

217. Jesus Expresses Compassion and Pity for Jerusalem - Matt 23:37-39

[Looking down from a hill upon the city of Jerusalem, Jesus lamented:]

"Oh, Jerusalem, Jerusalem! You are the city that killed many prophets and stoned many others that God has sent to you! How many times I have wanted to bring you together like children, in the same way that a mother hen gathers her little chicks under her wings, but you were not willing to yield to me. Now, just look at what is about to happen to you. Your house will soon be left empty. I must tell you that the time is quickly nearing when you will not see me again until you exclaim, 'Blessed is he who comes in the name of the Lord.'"

218. Jesus Commends a Poor Widow for Putting All She Has in the Offering - Mark 12:41-44

Then Jesus sat down where he could observe the place where people were depositing their offerings to God into the treasury of the Temple. There were many wealthy people who came by and donated large amounts. However, a poor widow came along and deposited just two little copper coins, worth only a few pennies.

Jesus called his disciples and announced to them, "I want you to all understand this fact. That poor widow has given a bigger offering than all the others put together. Truly, they gave only a small portion of their great wealth. But she donated everything she had to live on."

219. Jesus Teaches His Disciples on the Mount of Olives about Future Events - Matt 24:3; Mark 13:1-4; Luke 21:5

When Jesus was leaving the Temple, one of his disciples exclaimed, "Teacher, just look at the huge, beautiful stones in those walls! They have been dedicated to the Lord to form this Temple, and also some of those other nearby buildings."

But Jesus answered, "Do you see all these great buildings? I tell you, not one stone that you see here will be left standing upon another. Every single one will be thrown down. It has been destined to happen."

Later, as Jesus was sitting on the Mount of Olives across from the Temple, Peter, James, John, and Andrew privately asked him, "Will you tell us when this will happen? What sign will signal the end of the age? How will people know when these predictions are about to be fulfilled?"

220. Jesus Describes the Beginning of Birth Pangs before His Return - Matt 24:5-14; Mark 13:9-13; Luke 21:8-18

Jesus went on to answer several questions that some of his disciples asked him privately. He said, "Be careful. Don't let anyone deceive you. There will be many who will come claiming, 'I am the Messiah.' They will also declare, 'The time has arrived,' and they will be able to deceive many. Don't follow after them. And don't be afraid when you hear rumors about wars and uprisings. These things are sure to happen first, but they are not proof that the end times are already here."

Jesus continued explaining some of the things that would come in the future: "Nations will rise up against other nations, and kingdoms against kingdoms. There will be many fearful events. There will be signs in nature—terrible earthquakes, famines, and natural disasters in many different parts of the world—fearful events and significant signs in the heavens. However, all these things are only the beginning of birth pains.

"As for all of you who are my followers, you must remain alert and on guard. Before the very worst happens, you will be apprehended and brought into local courts and even flogged in the Jewish places of worship. They will carry you away and persecute you. They will arrest you and put you in jail. You will be taken before rulers and governors, all because you are known as Christ-followers.

"But because of these things, you will be given a chance to testify on my behalf. Be determined not to waste your time worrying about how you will defend yourself. If you become one of those who is arrested, just say whatever comes to your mind at the time. After all, it will not actually be you speaking. The Holy Spirit will be inspiring your words. Just remember this: I promise to give you words of wisdom that none of your persecutors will be able to resist or contradict.

"However, you will be betrayed. Even relatives and friends will have some of you executed. Brothers and sisters will betray each other to be killed. Parents will even betray their own children. Children will also rebel and testify against their own parents and have them put to death.

"During that time, you will be hated by all nations because you are Christ-followers. At that time, many will forsake their Christian faith. They will hate and betray one another. Many false preachers will appear and deceive multitudes. Wicked living will become so widespread that the love many Christians have had for the Lord will grow cold.

"Yet the Good News about the Kingdom of God must be preached throughout the whole world as a witness to all nations, before the final age actually comes to an end. Through it, all of you will be protected. Not a hair of your head will be lost. Be strong and stand your ground all the way to the very end, and you will surely be saved. But there will be times of great suffering and punishment."

221. Jesus Describes What Follows the Abomination That Causes Desolation - Matt 24:15-27; Mark 13:19-23; Luke 21:20-25

"When you find out that armies have surrounded Jerusalem, you can be sure the time for its destruction is at hand. When you see a sacrilegious object desecrating the place assigned to the Temple of God—as predicted by the prophet Daniel—readers must pay attention and understand the importance of this sign. At that time, let the people of Judea flee to the mountains, and let those in the city get out, and let those living out in the country stay out of the city."

[In the year 70 A.D., a first fulfillment of this prophecy took place. Many Christians in Jerusalem fled to the town of Pella in Decapolis. In that way, they escaped a time of destruction. It is likely some aspects of this prophecy will also be fulfilled during the end times before the Second Coming of Jesus. The Muslim Dome of the Rock now desecrates the Temple Mount.]

"There will be times of punishment that will fulfill all that has been prophetically written. There will be great trouble in the Holy Land and much hatred against Jews and Christians. Many will become victims of weapons; many others will be imprisoned by nations in various parts of the world. Gentile people will trample upon Jerusalem until the period of Gentile rule is completed. [In 1948, The United Nations decreed that Israel could become a recognized nation once again.]

"How terrible it will be for pregnant women and nursing mothers during those times! [This likely refers to 70 A.D. and the end times.] Pray that your escape will not come during winter weather or on a Sabbath day. At that time, the persecution will be terrible. The hatred against the people of God will be unequaled in the whole history of the world, from the time when God created the world until that time.

It will never be equaled again. If the Lord were not to cut that time short, no one would survive. However, for the sake of God's chosen people, that time will be cut short.

"The time will come when you will long to see the Son of Man with your own eyes, but it will not happen yet. If someone tells you, 'Look, the Messiah has come and he will speak at such and such an event!' or 'You can see him tomorrow at such and such a time!', don't believe it. Don't go chasing after him. For there will be many false prophets who will appear. Some will perform amazing signs and demonic miracles that will come close to fooling even God's chosen people. So be on your guard. I have warned you before this happens in case someone says to you, 'The Messiah is living out in the desert,' don't go out there looking for him. Or if they say, 'He is staying at a certain place,' don't believe it.

"When the Son of Man actually appears on the day of his Second Coming, it will happen like the lightning that flashes in the east but is visible far to the west. However, before all this happens, the Son of Man will suffer many attacks and be rejected by this present generation."

222. Jesus Describes the Return of Christ in the Clouds - Matt 24:29-31; Mark 13:27; Luke 21:25-26

"Immediately after the suffering that takes place during those days, there will be signs in the sun and moon and throughout the universe.

The sun will grow dark, (Isaiah 13:10)
and the moon will turn blood red. (Isaiah 13:10 and Joel 2:31)
The stars will fall from the sky, (Isaiah 34:4)
like withered leaves from a grapevine,
and the powers of the heavens will be shaken. (Matt 24:29)

"People everywhere will become anxious and perplexed because of unusual tides—a great increase in storms at sea—accompanied by many other natural disasters happening all over the earth. These disturbances in nature will accompany a growing number of conflicts between nations, races, and ethnic groups.

"Then the sign of the Son of Man will appear in the sky. People all over the world will weep in remorse when they see Jesus coming in the clouds with great glory and power. Suddenly, with the sound of a great trumpet call, his assigned angels will gather up all those who through faith, have been chosen. [This may imply that they are to receive an eternal inheritance]. They will come from the north, south, east, and west—even from the ends of the earth to the ends of the heavens."

223. Jesus Declares That the Time of the End is Unknown, but Signs Will Be Given - Matt 24:32-41; Luke 21:28-37

"When you realize that all these things are beginning to take place, stand tall and look up because the One who paid for your salvation on the cross is about to appear.

"Now, pay attention to this lesson and learn it from the fig tree and all the other trees, as well. You can tell when the summer is near when you see the small twigs on the trees getting tender and the leaves starting to sprout. In the same way, when you see all these events taking place, you can be certain that the completion of your salvation is near, even right at the door. You can be absolutely sure of this truth: The generation that witnesses all these signs will not pass away before they see them all actually fulfilled. The present heavens and earth will pass away, but my words will endure forever.

"Concerning the day and time when everything will be fulfilled, not even the angels nor the Son know this. [His knowledge was limited while he remained with his disciples on earth.] However, the Father knows. The coming of the Son of Man will be similar to Noah's time. Before the great flood, everyone was living life as usual. They were eating, drinking, offering their girls in marriage and getting married, right up to the day when Noah entered the ark; no one knew what was about to happen until the flood came and carried them all away.

"It happened in a similar way during Lot's time. The very day that Lot escaped from Sodom, fire and sulfur rained down from the sky and destroyed everyone. It will be like that when the Son of Man comes back. Two men will be working on a farm; one will be taken and the other left behind. Two women will be working in a mill, grinding grain into flour; one will be taken and the other left behind.

"On that day, those who happen to be working on a roof should not go back down into the house to save their possessions. All those who are away from home should not even consider going back to save something valuable. Remember what happened to Lot's wife! All

159

those who try to hold on to their life will surely lose it, and all those who are willing to surrender their life will actually keep it. Let me tell you this: on that night, there will be two people in one bed; one will be taken; the other will be left behind."

"Where will this happen, Lord?" they asked.

Jesus answered, "Wherever there is a dead body, there the vultures will gather." [A dead body (Matthew 24:28) may refer here to the faithless and dead end-time churches, like Laodicea (Revelation 3:14-17). The true Church is called the Body of Christ (Ephesians 4:4). Vultures likely refer to evil spiritual powers.]

[Jesus gives five illustrations about being on guard and faithful:]

224. (1) The Guardians of the House - Mark 13:33-37; Luke 21:34-36

"Be on guard; be alert and pray! You do not know when the time of my return will happen. [Jesus is referring to his Second Coming, or when you—his follower—meet Him in eternity at your death.]

"It will be similar to when a wealthy man leaves (on a long trip). When he leaves, he puts his hired workers in charge of everything. Each one is assigned a certain task. He also tells the doorman to be especially watchful.

"In a similar way, you must continually be watchful since you do not know when the owner of the household will return. It could be in the evening, at midnight, when the rooster crows, or just before sunrise. If he comes suddenly, don't let him find you sleeping. I am saying this to warn everyone. Be on your guard! Watch! [Jesus means, "keep trusting the Lord and faithfully following him!"]

"Be careful not to let your hearts become loaded down with partying, getting drunk and the worries of life. If you do, the Day when I return for you will snap down upon you suddenly like a trap. This is what will surely happen to absolutely everyone who lives on the face of the whole earth. Be diligent and continue to keep expecting my return, and pray that you will be delivered from everything that is about to happen. Also pray that you will be able to stand in the presence of the Son of Man."

225. (2) A Homeowner Who Is Unprepared for a Burglary - Matt 24:43-44

"You must understand this: If a homeowner only knew what time during the night a thief was planning to come, he would keep a watchful eye and would not allow his house to be broken into. You must also be alert and prepared, because the Son of Man will come when you least expect him."

226. (3) The Wise and Unwise Overseers of the Master's Servants - Matt 24:45-51

"Who then is qualified to be that wise and faithful servant that the master trusts to feed and direct all his other hired hands? It will certainly go well for that servant, if when the homeowner returns, he is found to be faithfully carrying out his duties. I assure you that the homeowner will put that trustworthy worker in charge of everything he owns. But what if his worker turns out to be wicked and says to himself, 'My overseer is staying away a long time. I doubt he will come back soon.' Then he begins to mistreat the other workers. He even gets into fights with them, and goes out to eat, drink, and party with other drunkards. When the owner returns unexpectedly, he discovers his worker's lack of responsibility. He will throw the book at him, and have him locked up with other hypocrites where they will all keep on weeping and grinding their teeth in pain forever."

227. (4) The Five Wise and the Five Foolish Virgins at a Wedding - Matt 25:1-13

"The Kingdom of Heaven will also be like ten virgins who took their oil lanterns and went to take part in a wedding banquet, scheduled to begin just as soon as the bridegroom arrives.

"However, five of those virgins were foolish and unprepared while the other five were wise and well prepared. The foolish ones took their oil lanterns, but carried no extra oil. On the other hand, the wise virgins took jars full of extra oil along with their lanterns. It turned out that the bridegroom was very slow to arrive. He took so long, that the virgins became tired and fell asleep.

161

"At midnight, there was a loud shout, 'Here comes the bridegroom! Come quickly to meet him!'

"Then all the virgins woke up and turned up the flames in their lanterns. The foolish virgins told the wise ones, 'Give us some of your oil because our lamps are about to go out.'

"They replied, 'No, we fear there will not be enough oil for both you and us. You must go and search for oil venders where you can buy some oil for yourselves.'

"As they were on their way to buy more oil, the bridegroom arrived. The virgins who were prepared went with him to the wedding banquet. Then the door was tightly locked.

"Finally, the others arrived. They called out, 'Lord! Lord! Open the door for us!'

"But the Master of the banquet replied, 'The truth is, I don't even know who you are.'

"Therefore, keep on watching and expecting because you have no way of knowing the exact day or time of day when the Lord will come for his bride."

228. (5) A Traveler Who Entrusts His Investments to His Servants - Matt 25:14-30

"Here is another way to illustrate the Kingdom of Heaven: It will be like a man who is preparing to leave on a long trip. Before he leaves, he calls his household servants and explains that he plans to entrust them with the wealth he has saved up in bags full of gold. He delegated different amounts to each one according to their investment abilities.

"To one, he gave five bags of gold; to another two bags; and to another one bag. Then he left on his long journey. The servant who received five bags immediately invested the gold and was able to gain five additional bags. The servant with two bags was able to gain two more. But the servant with just one bag dug a hole in the ground and hid his master's gold.

"After a long time, the man returned and called his servants to give an account of the investments they made while he was gone. The one who had received five bags of gold brought him the extra five he had gained. 'Lord,' he said, 'you trusted me to invest five bags of gold. You can see that I have gained an additional five for you.'

"The master replied, 'Well done! You are a good and faithful servant! Since you have been faithful with small things, I will put you in charge of many things that are even more important. You are now invited to share in your master's joy!'

"Then the one who had received two bags of gold brought him the two he had gained. 'Lord,' the servant said, 'you trusted me to invest two bags of gold. You can see I gained an additional two for you.'

"The master replied, 'Well done! You are a good and faithful servant! Since you have been faithful with small things, I will put you in charge of many things that are even more important. You are now invited to share in your master's joy!'

"Then the one who had received just one bag of gold came back. 'Lord,' the servant said, 'I knew you were a hard master, harvesting in fields where you did not sow and picking crops where you did not plant. So, I was afraid of what might happen if my investment should fail to gain money for you. See what I have here: I am returning to you what is yours.'

"But his master answered, 'You are a wicked and lazy servant! You knew, didn't you, that I harvest where I don't sow and I even pick crops I didn't plant? Why then didn't you invest my money in the bank, so I could receive it back with interest when I returned from my trip? Take away the bag of gold from that lazy servant and give it to the one who has ten bags.'

"For the one who has gained wisely can be trusted with more.

"In the end, that servant will have abundantly more than enough! Those who have gained nothing, what little they have will be taken from them. Throw those worthless servants into outer darkness, where there will be great weeping and grinding of teeth."

229. Jesus Reveals Judgment Will Be Based on How We Serve - Matt 25:31-46

"When the Son of Man returns—shining with perfect truth, mercy, peace, justice, and love—he will be accompanied by all the angels of heaven. Then he will sit on his glorious throne, and all the nations of the world will be called to stand before him. At that time, he will separate people from each other just as a shepherd separates his sheep from the goats. He will place the sheep on his right and send the goats to his left.

"Then the King will invite those on his right, 'Come, each of you who the Father has blessed; receive your inheritance—the Kingdom of God that has been undergoing preparation ever since the world was first created. For when I was hungry, you gave me some food to eat;

when I was thirsty, you satisfied my thirst with something to drink; when I came to you as a stranger, you took me in; when I was in need of some clothes, you gave them to me; when I was sick, you took care of me; and when I was in prison, you visited me.'

"Then those who are godly will answer him like this: 'Lord, when did we see you hungry and give you some food, or thirsty and give you something to drink? When did we see you as a stranger and take you in, or needing clothing and give you clothing? When did we see you sick or in prison and come to visit you?'

"And the King will answer, 'Here's the truth: Whatever you have done for the very least of my brothers and sisters, that is what you have also done for me.'

"Then the King will say to those at his left, 'Away from me, all of you who are cursed! You must now be banished forever to the eternal fire that has been prepared for the devil and his doomed angels. For when I was hungry, you gave me nothing to eat; when I was thirsty, you gave me nothing to drink; when I was a stranger, you did not welcome me; when I needed clothes, you gave me nothing to wear; when I was sick and in prison, you never came to see me or find out what I might need.'

"They will also answer, 'Lord, when did we see you hungry, or thirsty, or a stranger, or needing clothing, or sick, or in prison and fail to meet your needs?'

"He will reply, 'Here is the absolute truth: Whatever you have failed to do for even one of the least of these brothers and sisters of mine, that is exactly what you have also failed to do for me.'

"Then all those who have failed to serve in love will depart into eternal punishment, but those who are righteous because of their faith, love, and obedience, will enter into life eternal."

230. As Passover Nears, Jesus Again Predicts His Crucifixion - Matt 26:1-2; Luke 21:37-38

After Jesus had finished saying all these things, he then said this to his disciples, "As you know, the Passover begins in only two days, and during the Festival, the Son of Man will be apprehended and crucified."

Each day during that week, Jesus taught at the Temple. Each evening, he went to spend the night in an area near the hill called the Mount of Olives. Early each morning, crowds of people came to hear him speak at the Jerusalem Temple.

231. Judas Iscariot Plots to Betray Jesus - Matt 26:3-15; Mark 14:10-11; Luke 21:37-22:6

The Passover, also called the Festival of Unleavened Bread, was approaching. At that time, the chief priests, teachers of the Law, and elders of the people gathered in the palace of Caiaphas, the High Priest. They were seeking the best plan for arresting Jesus secretly. In this way, they hoped to avoid a riot among the people.

That was when Satan entered into the mind of Judas Iscariot. He was one of the Twelve who followed Jesus as his disciple. Judas went to the temple guards and suggested a plan for betraying Jesus. They were surprised and happy to learn that Judas was prepared to help them, so they offered to give him money.

He asked, "What will you give me if I can place him in your hands?"

They settled on thirty pieces of silver, and that is when Judas began to look for the best time and place to hand over Jesus to them—when no large crowd would be present.

232. Jesus Instructs His Disciples to Prepare for the Passover Meal - Matt 26:18-19; Mark 14:12-17; Luke 22:8-16; John 13:1

It was the first day of the Festival of Unleavened Bread. That was the usual time for sacrificing the Passover lamb. The disciples asked Jesus, "Where would you like for us to prepare the Passover meal?"

Then Jesus told Peter and John, "Go now and prepare for us to eat the Passover together." He gave them these instructions: "As you enter the city, you will meet a man carrying a jar of water. Follow him to the house where he enters. Say to the owner of that house, 'The Teacher says that his appointed time is near. Show us the guest room where he may eat the Passover with his disciples.' Then he will lead you to a large upstairs room that is completely furnished. That is where you should make preparations."

They quickly left and found everything to be exactly as Jesus had described it. They went ahead and prepared for the Passover.

As evening was settling, Jesus arrived with the Twelve. Since it was just before the Passover Festival, Jesus knew the time had arrived for him to leave this world and go back to the Father. He loved his own followers in this world, and he loved them right to the very end.

As Jesus and his twelve apostles were reclining by the table, he said to them, "I have eagerly wanted to eat this Passover with you, before I face what I must suffer. I want you to know that I will not eat another Passover meal until its full meaning is fulfilled in the Kingdom of God."

233. Jesus Models Serving by Washing the Disciples' Feet - John 13:2-20

The evening Passover meal was already in progress, and the devil had already planted in the mind of Judas, son of Simon Iscariot, a plan for betraying Jesus. The Lord knew that the Father had placed all things in his power. He also knew that he had come from God and was about to return to God, so he stood up from the meal and removed his outer clothing. Placing a towel around his waist, he then poured some water in a basin and began to wash the feet of each of his disciples. He also dried them with the towel. [According to the custom of that time, as each guest entered the house from the dusty street, it was the host's duty to arrange for a servant to wash the feet of each one. Obviously, none of the disciples volunteered to accept the role of servant.]

Then Jesus came to Simon Peter, who asked, "Lord, are you going to wash my feet, also?"

Jesus answered, "You do not understand right now what I am doing, but you will understand later."

"No," Peter objected, "you will never wash my feet."

Jesus gently corrected by saying, "If I don't wash you, you have no part with me."

"Lord, if that's how it is, don't wash just my feet; also wash my hands and head as well."

But Jesus told him, "Those who have already bathed only need to wash their feet; the rest of their body is clean. And truthfully, you are clean, except for one of you."

Since Jesus knew who would betray him, he said that not everyone was clean.

After Jesus had finished washing their feet, he put his clothes back on and returned to his place. "Do you comprehend why I have done this?" he asked. "You all call me 'Teacher' and 'Lord,' and that is the right thing to do because that is who I am. And since the One who is your Lord and Teacher has washed your feet, you should follow my example and wash each other's feet. This is my example for you: You ought to treat each other the same way I have treated you. I tell you very truthfully that servants are never greater than their master, nor are messengers greater than the one who sent them. Since you now understand these things, God will greatly bless you if you practice them.

"I am not applying this to every one of you; I know very well each one that I have chosen. But this passage of Scripture is about to be fulfilled: 'The one who shared my food has turned against me.' (Psalm 41:9)

"I'm telling you ahead of time what will happen, so that when it does happen, you will believe that I am who I claim to be. I tell you truthfully, all those who receive anyone I send to them are actually accepting me; whoever accepts me, also accepts the One who sent me into the world."

234. Jesus Identifies His Betrayer - Matt 26:22-25; Mark 14:18; Luke 22:21; John 13:21-30

After saying these things, Jesus was troubled in his spirit. As they were reclining around the table and eating, he said, "I want you to know the truth: The hand of the disciple who will betray me is with my hand on the table. He is trying to act like a friend."

This caused them great upset and worry. One after another, they began to ask, "Lord, you surely don't mean me, do you?"

Jesus replied, "The one who has just eaten with me from this bowl is the person who will betray me. The Son of Man must die, as was prophesied, but it will be terrible for the one who betrays the Son of Man! It would have been better if he had never been born."

The disciple, John, who was deeply loved by Jesus, was reclining right next to him. Simon Peter motioned to John and said, "Ask him who he's talking about."

John leaned over against Jesus and asked, "Lord, who is it?"

And Jesus answered, "It is the one that will receive this piece of unleavened bread after I have dipped it in the bowl." Then he dipped it and gave it directly to Judas, son of Simon Iscariot.

After receiving it, Judas, who would later betray him, asked, "Teacher, am I the one?"

Jesus answered, "It will be exactly as you have said."

Just as Judas took the bread, Satan entered into him.

Then Jesus said this to Judas, "Do right away what you are planning to do." However, no one else who was there understood why Jesus said this. But since Judas was in charge of the money, some thought Jesus was telling him to buy what they needed in order to prepare for the festival, or perhaps that he should make a donation to the poor. Then just as soon as Judas had taken the bread, he left and went out into the night, and it was very dark.

235. Jesus Institutes the Sacrament of the Lord's Supper - Matt 26:26-29; Luke 22:17-20; 1 Cor. 11:25-26

After Jesus picked up the cup of grape wine, he said, "Take this and share it among each other." Then during the meal, Jesus took some of the Jewish *mitzvah* bread, and after giving thanks, broke it and gave some to each of his disciples saying, "This is my body given for you; eat this in remembrance of me."

In a similar way, after the supper, he picked up the cup. "Drink this, each one of you. This is my blood of the new covenant, [Hebrew: "testament"] which is poured out for the forgiveness of sins. Whenever you drink this, do it to remember what I have done for you. I tell you that I will not drink from this fruit of the vine from now until that day when I drink it again with you in my Father's kingdom."

[Apostle Paul:] That is why whenever you eat this bread and drink this cup, you are proclaiming the Lord's death until he comes again.

236. The Disciples Argue about Who is the Greatest - Mark 10:42; Luke 22:24-30

After receiving the bread and wine, an argument arose among the disciples about which one of them should be considered as the most important. Then Jesus explained: "You are aware that among the kings and leaders of the Gentiles, they regard as their rulers those who lord it over them. Those with authority call themselves benefactors. But you should not act like that. Instead, you must treat the greatest among you as you do the youngest. And you must treat the one who rules as you treat the one who serves all the others.

"For who is considered the most important at a banquet, those who sit at the table and eat, or the person who serves them? Isn't it those at the table? Yet, I am the one who is serving you. You are the ones who have stood by me in all my trials. Now, I hereby grant you a kingdom, just as my Father has given me a Kingdom. You will sit by me, and eat and drink at my table in my Kingdom. You will also sit on thrones, judging the twelve tribes of Israel."

237. Jesus Prepares His Disciples for His Departure - John 13:31-33

After Judas had left, Jesus also said this to his disciples: "The Son of Man is now shining out with God's character so that God can be honored in his Son. And when God is honored in this way, he himself will also shine out with his Son, and he will do it right away.

"My children, I will remain with you just a little longer. You will try to find me, and even as I told the Jewish leaders, I am also telling you now: At this time, you can't come to where I am about to go."

238. Jesus Gives a New Command, Then Warns Peter of His Denial - Matt 26:31-35; Luke 22:31-34; John 13:34-38

Then Jesus said, "I am giving you this new commandment: You must love each other in the same way that I have loved you. This is how everyone will know that you are my true followers, by the way you love each other." [The Greek word *agape* translated here as love means to love the way God loves—without conditions.]

Then Simon Peter asked him, "Where are you going, Lord?"

Jesus replied, "You will not be able to follow where I am going at this time; you will follow me later."

Peter insisted, "Lord, why can't I come now? I'm even ready to lose my life for you!"

Jesus replied, "Would you really lay down your life for me? Oh, Simon, Satan has asked for the right to sift all of you as if you were wheat. But I have prayed especially for you that you will not completely lose your faith. When you are restored, strengthen your brothers."

Simon insisted, "Lord, I am prepared to go to prison or even die for you."

Then Jesus warned his disciples, "This very night your faith will be severely tested by what happens to me. You will turn away and even abandon me, just as the prophet warned: 'Strike down the shepherd, and the sheep will be scattered.' (Zechariah 13:7)

"However, after I have risen, I will go on ahead of you to Galilee."

But Peter argued, "Even if everybody else gives up because of you, I will never fail you."

Jesus answered softly, "Here's the truth, Peter. This very night, before the early morning rooster crows, you will deny three times that you even know me."

Peter insisted, "Even if I must die with you, I will never disown you." And the rest of the disciples also joined in affirming their loyalty.

239. Jesus Tells His Disciples to Get Money, Clothing and Weapons - Luke 22:35-38

Then Jesus asked his disciples, "When I sent you out as witnesses, you left with no money in your purse, no handbag, or even extra sandals. But did you lack anything while you were fulfilling your mission?"

"Nothing at all," they answered.

This time, Jesus gave them these instructions: "Now," he said, "if you own a purse, take it, and also carry a handbag. If you don't have a sword for protection, sell your coat and buy one. For it is written, "He was treated like those who were sinners." (Isaiah 53:12)

"And I tell you that this must be fulfilled through me. Yes, and you can be certain the things written about me are now about to reach complete fulfillment."

"See, Lord, we have two swords," the disciples answered.

"That will do," Jesus replied.

240. Jesus Explains the Way to the Father and to His Home - John 14:1-14

"Don't let your hearts be disturbed. Trust in God and also believe in me. There are many excellent dwelling places in my Father's house. My promises are absolutely true. I will definitely get a place ready for you. You can rest assured that since I am going to prepare a place for you, I will surely come back and bring you to be with me. You know where I am going, and you know how to get there."

Then Thomas questioned, "Lord, we don't really know where you are going. How can we possibly know how to get there?"

That's when Jesus explained: "I am the way, and I am the source of truth, as well as the source of everlasting life. No one can approach the Father except through faith in me. Once you really know who I am, knowing my Father just comes naturally to you. So, from now on, you do know the Father. If you have seen me, you've seen the Father."

But Philip said, "Lord, just show us the Father and we'll be satisfied."

Jesus answered, "Philip, we've been together a long time now, and anyone who has seen me has also seen the Father. Why do you keep saying, 'Show us the Father'? Simply believe that I am in the Father and the Father is in me.

"Just look at the evidence of the miracles you have seen me perform. Here is the absolute truth: Anyone who really believes in me, will be able to do the miracles I've been doing, and all who come to believe in me will accomplish even greater things* because I am going to be with my Father. I will do anything you ask if it is in harmony with who I am, as revealed by my name. Then, the Father's authority will shine through the Son. You will be able to ask for anything in my name, and I will surely do it." [*The earthly life of Jesus was limited to one person living in Israel. In our time, the Spirit of Jesus works through his followers throughout the whole world.]

241. Jesus Promises to Be Present through the Holy Spirit
- John 14:15-31

"You must keep my commandments. When you do, you are showing that you truly love me. Then I will ask the Father to give you another companion to faithfully stand by you as your Helper. He is the Spirit of Truth. He will be with you forever. The godless world cannot receive him because they are blind to him and do not know who he really is. However, you do know him because he is your Counselor and Companion. He will actually dwell within you.

"I will not abandon you like orphans in a storm; I will come to be with you. Soon, the people of this world will no longer see me, but by means of your faith you will see me. And since I will be alive, you will live, also. When that time of fulfillment arrives, you will understand that I am living in my Father. You are living in me, also, and I am living in you.

"Anyone who hears my commands and puts them into practice really loves me. My Father will surely love all those who truly love me. I will also love them and reveal myself to them."

Then Judas (not Judas Iscariot) said, "Lord, why are you planning to reveal yourself to us only, and not to the rest of the world?"

"All those who love me," Jesus answered, "will live in harmony with what I teach. My Father will also love them, and we will come and dwell with them. But all those who fail to love me will also reject the things I have been teaching. The things I have been telling you do not originate with me. They come from the Father who sent me.

"I am telling you these things while I am still with you. However, the Holy Spirit will serve as your Counselor. He will stand by you to help you whenever you need him. The Father will send him in my name. He will teach you everything you need to know. He will also remind you of everything I have told you. I am leaving you with my peace—it is my gift to you. My gift of peace is very different from what the world offers you. Don't let your hearts be disturbed and don't be afraid.

"You have heard me say this before, 'I am going away, and I will also come back to you.' If you truly love me, you should be glad that I am going to be with the Father, since he is greater than I am. I am speaking this truth now, before it happens, so you will believe when it does happen. I have little more to say right now, and the evil prince of this world is coming against me. However, he has no power over me. But all these things will happen so the people of this world can see how much I love the Father. Then everyone will understand how I obediently carry out absolutely everything my Father has ordered me to do.

"Come now, my followers. Let us be on our way."

242. Jesus Offers an Illustration of the Vine and the Branches - John 15:1-17

As they walked toward the Garden of Gethsemane, Jesus was teaching them in these words. "I am the true vine. My Father is the gardener. He trims away each of my branches that fail to bear fruit. He trims them so the vine will bear even more fruit. In the same way, my teaching keeps purifying each of you who are true followers of mine. Stay connected to me, just as I remain in you. No branch that is disconnected can bear fruit by itself; it must remain connected to the vine. In the same way, you cannot bear fruit unless you stay connected to me.

"I am the Spiritual Vine and you are my branches. If you remain connected to me, my life will flow through you and you will bear abundant fruit. Apart from me, you can do nothing. If you become disconnected from me, you will be like branches that are tossed aside. After they dry up, they are thrown into the fire and burned. But if you stay connected to me and if my teaching remains in your hearts, you may ask whatever you wish. If you ask in harmony with my will, it will surely be done for you. When you bear much fruit, you show that you are truly my disciples. Then my Father's character will shine out through you for all to see.

"I have loved you in the same way my Father has loved me. Therefore, remain within my love. If you do the things I have commanded, you will remain in my love. Since I have obeyed my Father's commands, I also remain in his love.

"I have shared these things with you, so you will have my joy within you. You will even overflow with my joy. Now, here is my new command: Love each other in the same way I have loved you. There is no greater love than laying down your life for your friends. All of you who do the things I have commanded, are my friends. I no longer consider you to be merely servants because servants are not aware of their master's plans. But I have called you 'my friends.' I have taught you everything my Father has taught me. You haven't chosen me; I have chosen you and commissioned you to go and bear lasting fruit.

"Now the Father will give you whatever you ask if it is in harmony with my name and in harmony with my character. Here is my new command: 'Love one another.'"

243. Jesus Warns of the World's Opposition - John 15:18-16:4

"Whenever it seems like the ungodly people of the world hate you, remember they hated me first. If you were one of them, they would claim you as their own. But you don't belong to them—I have chosen you out from the world. That's why they don't like you. Remember what I have told you: 'Servants are not more important than their master.' Since they have persecuted me, they will also do the same to you.

"If they have obeyed my teaching, they will also obey yours. They will treat you the way they do because of your identity with my name. They do this because they do not realize who sent me. They don't even know him. If I had not come and spoken to the people of the world, they would be innocent of sin. Now that I have come, they have no excuse for their disobedience. Whoever rejects me has also rejected my Father, as well. If I had not done mighty miracles that no one else could ever do, they would be innocent of sin. Yet, they have seen the power of God the Father working through me. Now, they have hated both me and my Father. This only fulfills what the Law says:

Don't let those who hate me without cause gloat over my sorrow.
(Psalm 35:19)
These enemies who seek to destroy me are doing so without cause.
(Psalm 69:4)

"However, when the Helper who will plead your case arrives, He is the One I promise to send you from the Father. He is the Spirit of Truth who represents the Father, and he also testifies about me. You must also be my witnesses since you have been with me from the first.

"I have explained all of this to you in order to protect you from giving up. You will be persecuted in many different ways. They will expel you from their Jewish houses of worship; in fact, there will be a time when those who kill you will believe they are doing God's will. They will do such things because they do not really know the Father or me.

"I have told you this ahead of time so that when it happens, you will remember that I warned you that this would take place. I did not need to tell you this before because I have been with you until now."

244. Jesus Speaks of His Departure and the Holy Spirit's Coming - John 16:5-15

"Now, I'll be leaving soon and going back to the One who sent me. You haven't asked me, 'Where are you going?' However, you are full of sadness because I have said these things to you. The truth is, it will actually be good for you that I'm going away. If I don't go, the Standby-Helper will not come to you. However, if I do leave, I will send him to you. And when he comes, he will prove that the people of this world have been mistaken about sin and righteousness and judgment. Sin is about refusing to believe in me. Righteousness will be available now that I am going to be with the Father, even though you will no longer be able to see me. Judgment will surely take place because the evil prince of this world already stands condemned.

"There is much more I would like to say to you, but you are not ready to comprehend it. When the Spirit of Truth arrives, he will be able to lead you into all truth. What he says will not be his own ideas; he will tell you only what he hears from the Father. He will reveal things that are to happen in the future. He will honor me by making known to you the truth he receives from me. Whatever belongs to the Father is mine, also. That's why I told you that the Holy Spirit will first receive from me the truth that he will reveal to you."

245. Jesus Predicts the Joy of His Disciples When Death Is Finally Conquered - John 16:16-22

As Jesus continued speaking to his disciples, he said, "Soon, you will not see me, but after a little while, you will see me again."

This caused some of his disciples to ask, "What does he mean by telling us, 'Soon we won't see him; then after a little while we will see him?' What does he mean when he talks about 'going to the Father'? And what does 'a little while' mean? What is he trying to tell us? We just don't understand all these things."

Jesus realized they wanted to ask him more about these things, so he said, "Would you like to know more about what I meant when I said, 'in a little while you will not see me, then after a little while you will see me'? Here's the truth about what will soon take place: You will weep and be sad because of what will happen to me. However, the evil world will celebrate. You will grieve, but your grief will suddenly be transformed into great joy when you see me again. It will be like a woman experiencing labor pains. After her baby is born, she quickly forgets her suffering because she is so happy with her new baby. It will be just like that with you; your time of grief is at hand, but I will see you again very soon. Then you will celebrate with great joy that no one can take away."

175

246. Jesus Assures His Followers of Security in the Father's Love - John 16:23-33

"The day will come when instead of asking me for things, you will be able to go directly to my Father and ask him. If you ask using my name, he will surely grant your requests. You haven't done this before, but from now on, ask using my name and it shall be done. This will bring you great joy that no one can take away.

"Until now, I have been using stories to illustrate truth. Soon that will no longer be necessary. I will simply speak clearly about my Father. Then you can ask in my name. I don't mean that I must represent you before the Father, because the Father himself already loves you. He realizes that you really love me, and that you also believe that I have come representing God to you. I have come from the Father into this world. Soon, I will leave and return to the Father."

His disciples responded, "You are finally speaking clearly rather than using stories as illustrations. Now, we can see that there is nothing you don't know. We can only conclude that you really have come to us from God."

"Do you now finally believe?" Jesus asked. "The time is at hand. In truth, it has already arrived. You will be scattered, and each one will go his own way. You will abandon me! Even then, I won't really be alone because my Father always remains with me. Remember this truth because it will bring you peace: On earth, you will surely have many tests and troubles. But take courage! I have won victory over the world."

247. Jesus Prays for His Disciples and for All Future Believers - John 17:1-26

After Jesus completed these teachings, he lifted his eyes toward heaven and began to pray: "Father, the time has now arrived. Let your Son shine out with your presence so that he may reflect it back to you. You have given him authority to rule over all humanity. Now, all who place their trust in your Son will receive eternal life. And the purpose of eternal life is so people may really know you—the only true God— and also know the One who represents you, Jesus, the Messiah. I have honored you on earth by completing everything you assigned for me to do. Now, Father, I ask you to let your presence shine through me, just like you did before the earth was created.

"I have revealed your presence to all those you have given to me out of this world. They belonged to you; now you have also given them to me, and they have obeyed your word. They now realize that you have given to me everything I have. I have passed on to them the truths you have given to me, and they have accepted my message. They are absolutely certain that I did come from you and that you are the One who sent me.

"I am not only praying for those who are tied to this present age. No, I am praying also for all those you have given to me out of this world because they are all yours. And because they are mine, all of them are also yours. You have given them back to me so that because of them, I am now able to receive honor.

"Since I am about to leave this world, I am leaving them here. Then I will come to you. Holy Father, guard them. Take care of them—each one who belongs to me—so they will enjoy the same kind of unity we have, as Father and Son.

"While I was here on earth, I protected them and guarded them by the power of my own name. Therefore, in order to fulfill prophecy, not one was lost except the one who is doomed for destruction.

"Now, I will soon be coming to you. However, while I am still here, I have told them these things so they can be filled with my joy. I have taught them your word. The unbelieving world hates them because they do not belong to its evil system, just as I don't belong to it either. I don't ask you, Father, to take them out of the world, but to protect them from the evil one. They do not belong to the ungodly spirit of this age any more than I do. Purify them and dedicate them to live by the power of the Holy Spirit as they welcome the truth found in your word.

"In the same way that you have sent me into the world, I am also sending them into the world. I sanctify myself entirely for them so that they might be entirely sanctified. [Sanctify means to be dedicated, or set apart for God's Holy use.]

"I am not just praying for my present disciples, but also for everyone in the future who will place their trust in me because of the testimony of these followers of mine. I pray that they will all be united into one body, just as you and I are one, Father. In the same way that you are in me and I am in you, I pray that they will be in us, so people all over the world will come to believe that you have sent me.

"The light of your presence in me is the very light I have given to them. That light was given to me in order to unite them, just as you and I are united—I in them, and you in me—and all of us made into perfect unity. This is how the world will come to understand that you really did send me here. They will also know that you have loved them, just as you have loved me.

"Oh, righteous Father, even though the world doesn't know you, I know you, and my disciples know that you sent me. I have now revealed you to them, and I will continue making you known. My purpose is that your love for me will also be in my followers, and that I may be in them, also."

248. Jesus Struggles in Prayer at Gethsemane - Matt 26:30-44; Mark 14:33-40; Luke 22:43-45; John 18:1

After Jesus finished praying, they sang a hymn. Then he led his disciples from Jerusalem across the Kidron Valley to the Mount of Olives, and into a grove of olive trees. A garden there was called Gethsemane.

He said to them, "Sit down here while I go a little farther to pray."

Then he took Peter, James, and John aside, and he began to be deeply distressed. He told those three, "My soul is crushed to the point of death. I need you to stay here and watch with me." Then he went a little farther and fell face down to the ground, and began to pray, "Father, if there is any possible way, please don't make me drink this cup of suffering. But I'm not pleading for you to fulfill my own desires. Father, just let your will be carried out completely."

Then, an angel from heaven came and gave him strength to go on. In the suffering of his soul, he prayed even more earnestly. His sweat was even falling to the ground in drops of blood.

When he went back to check on his disciples, he found them sleeping because they were so exhausted by their sorrow. He asked them, "Couldn't you keep watch with me for even one hour? You must learn to watch and pray in order to keep from falling in times of temptation. The spirit may be willing, but the body is weak."

He went back a second time and prayed with the same words. When he returned to his disciples, he again found them sleeping. They just couldn't keep their eyes open, and they couldn't think of what to say to him. He left them again to pray in the same way, a final time.

249. Jesus Is Betrayed and Arrested, Then Forsaken by His Disciples - Matt 26:45-56; Mark 14:41-52; Luke 22:48-54; John 18:2-12

When Jesus went back to his disciples a third time, he asked them, "Are you still sleeping? Listen carefully! The time has come now for the Son of Man to be delivered into the hands of evil people. Get up! We must go. See, there comes my betrayer!"

At those words, Judas—who was planning to betray him, and knew where they would be since Jesus had often taken them there—entered the garden with a group of soldiers and officials from the chief priests, Pharisees, teachers of the Law, and the elders. Accompanying Judas was a group of soldiers armed with swords and clubs. They were also carrying torches and lanterns.

Jesus knew what was about to happen to him, so he went forward and asked, "Who are you looking for?"

"Jesus of Nazareth," they said.

"I am the one," Jesus responded. And just as he said this, the soldiers drew back and fell to the ground.

So he asked them again, "Who is it that you want?"

Again they said, "Jesus of Nazareth."

Once again Jesus said, "I have told you that I am the one you are looking for, so let these other men go."

As he said this, his own prediction was fulfilled: I have come down from heaven and it is God's will that I should not lose even one of those you gave me. (John 6:39)

Now Judas had prearranged a signal: "I will kiss the man you are wanting to arrest." He walked right up and greeted Jesus and said, "Teacher!" Then, he kissed him.

Sorrowfully, Jesus asked, "Judas, would you deliberately betray the Son of Man with a kiss?"

Just then, the Jesus' followers could see what was about to happen. They asked, "Lord, should we use our swords to fight?" But Simon Peter had already drawn his sword, and he cut off the right ear of the high priest's servant, whose name was Malchus.

Jesus shouted, "Peter, put your sword away! I must drink the cup the Father has given to me." Then, Jesus touched the man's ear and healed him.

Jesus turned to Peter and said, "Those who use the sword will die by the sword. Don't you realize that I could call on my Father, and immediately he would send me an army of seventy-two thousand angels? But then how would the Scriptures be fulfilled that have predicted what is about to happen?"

Then Jesus asked the crowd, "Why are you coming with weapons to capture me? Do you think I am leading an armed revolution? Every day I sat teaching at the Temple, so why didn't you arrest me then? But this is the time when darkness rules. It must happen like this in order to fulfill what the prophets have predicted in their writings."

The group of soldiers and their commanders, along with the Temple guards, arrested Jesus. They tied him up and led him away. As soon as this happened, all the disciples deserted him and ran into the darkness. However, Peter was following along behind.

Later, he went into the courtyard of the High Priest. Peter waited there to keep track of what was going to happen to Jesus.

A young man was following far behind, wearing only a linen nightshirt. When the mob seized him, they tore off his clothes, and he ran away naked. [Some have speculated that this man was John.]

250. The Jews Take Jesus First to Be Tried by Annas, the Deposed High Priest - John 18:13-14 and 19-23

The soldiers brought Jesus to Annas, the father-in-law of Caiaphas. He was the High Priest that year. Earlier, he had advised the other Jewish leaders, "It is better for one to die for the people, than for all to die." Then the High Priest began asking Jesus about his followers and what type of things he had been teaching them.

Jesus responded, "My teaching is well-known everywhere, because I have been teaching openly and regularly in many Jewish places of worship and in the Jerusalem Temple, as well. Whatever I have said in private, I have also said in public. Instead of asking me, why don't you question those who have heard me? They will tell you what I said."

With that, one of the Temple guards hit him in the face and demanded, "Is that the way you should answer the High Priest?"

Jesus replied, "If I said something that is not allowed, you should explain it to me. So what right do you have to hit a man for speaking the truth?"

Then Annas had Jesus bound and sent to Caiaphas, the High Priest.

251. Peter Denies His Lord - Matt 26:58-74; Mark 14:54; Luke 22:55-62; John 18:15-26

Since it was cold, the servants and guards were standing around a fire they had kindled in the center of the courtyard. Peter slipped in, and sat with the guards by the fire to find out what was going to happen to Jesus.

A servant girl noticed him seated there in the firelight, and she kept staring at him. Finally, she spoke up, "I'm sure this man was one of the followers of Jesus," she said.

And in front of them all, Peter denied it. "I have no idea what you're talking about," he insisted. [This was his first denial.]

By the gate, another servant girl also saw him and asked Peter, "Aren't you also one of the disciples of Jesus?"

"No, I am not," he insisted.

Speaking out to all the people there, she persisted. "This man was certainly with Jesus of Nazareth!"

Peter denied it again with an oath: "I don't even know this man!" [This was Peter's second denial affirmed twice to the second girl.]

About an hour later, one of the High Priest's servants who was related to the man whose ear Peter had cut off, challenged him. "Weren't you with Jesus in the garden?"

And even more people who were standing around approached Peter saying, "Surely you must be one of them; your Galilean accent gives you away."

Another bystander also insisted, "Yes, he is a Galilean!"

Peter answered sharply, "Man, I don't have any idea what you're talking about!" Then, he cursed at them and insisted, "I don't know that man!"

And just as he said this, a rooster crowed. The Lord turned and looked straight at Peter, and Peter remembered what the Lord had said to him: *Before the rooster crows in the morning, you will deny three times that you know me.* Then Peter went outside and wept bitterly.

252. The High Priest, Caiaphas, and the Sanhedrin Try Jesus - Matt 26:62-68; Mark 14:53-65; Luke 22:65-70; John 18:24

Annas sent Jesus, bound, to Caiaphas, the High Priest. All of the chief priests, elders, and teachers of the Law gathered at daybreak as Jesus was brought before them.

The whole High Court [known as the Sanhedrin] was looking for sufficient evidence against Jesus in order to have him put to death, but they couldn't find any. There were many false witnesses making contradictory statements. They just could not agree.

Some stood up and offered this false testimony: "We heard him say, 'I will destroy this Temple made with human hands, and in three days I will build another not made with hands.'" Even then, their statements did not agree.

Finally, the High Priest stood up and said to Jesus, "Why don't you answer? Can't you explain the testimony these men are bringing against you?"

However, Jesus remained completely silent.

Then the High Priest said to him, "I charge you under oath, in the name of the living God, tell us if you are the Messiah, the Son of God."

So Jesus answered him. "If I do tell you, you still won't believe me, and you would not answer the question that I could ask you. However, soon the Son of Man will be seated at the right hand of the Mighty One, and he will be seen coming on the clouds of heaven."

"Are you then the 'Son of God?'"

"As you say, so 'I Am'." [*Yahweh* is Hebrew for "I Am." When Moses asked God, "What is your name?" God answered that his name is Yahweh. (Exodus 4:14-15)]

Enraged, the High Priest tore his clothes and shouted, "He has spoken blasphemy! We have heard it right from his own lips. Why do we need any more witnesses? You have all heard his blasphemy. What is your judgment?"

They shouted, "He is worthy of death." And they all condemned him.

Those who were guarding Jesus also began to mock him and beat him. They spat in his face; they blindfolded him and hit him with their fists while others slapped him, demanding, "Prophecy, Messiah! Tell us who hit you." And they said many other insulting things.

253. Judas Regrets His Treachery and Commits Suicide - Matt 27:3-10

When Judas, who had betrayed him, saw that Jesus had been condemned, he was filled with regret. He took the thirty pieces of silver and gave them back to the chief priests and elders.

"I have sinned," Judas confessed, "because I have betrayed the blood of an innocent man."

"What is that to us?" they replied, "That's your responsibility."

Judas then threw the money on the Temple floor. From there he went out and hanged himself.

The chief priests picked up the coins and discussed what to do with them. They said, "It is against the Law to put blood money into our treasury."

They finally decided to use the money to buy the potter's field. [This field was outside the walls of Jerusalem.] They assigned it as a burial place for foreigners. It was at that very place where Judas fell head first and his body burst open, leaving his intestines spilling out. That place has been permanently called, "The Field of Blood."

This happened to fulfill what Zechariah the prophet said, "Give me my wages, whatever I am worth, but only if you want to. So they counted out for my wages, thirty pieces of silver. And the Lord said, 'Throw it to the potters—this magnificent sum at which they valued me!' I took the thirty coins and threw them to the potters in the Temple of the Lord." (Zechariah 11:12-13)

254. The Roman Trial of Jesus Begins before Pilate - Matt 27:1-14; Luke 23:2-5; John 18:28-38

It was very early in the morning when all the chief priests and elders of the people began planning how they could have Jesus executed. After bringing him before Caiaphas, they tied him up and led him to the palace of Pilate who was the Roman governor.

The Jews, however, did not enter the palace because they did not want to become ceremonially unclean during the Passover celebration. Knowing this, Pilate came out to where they were and asked, "What are your charges against this man?"

"We wouldn't have brought him to you if he were not a criminal," they replied. "He has been leading our people into trouble by telling us not to pay taxes to the Roman government, and by claiming that he is the Messiah—a King."

"Then take him away and judge him by your laws," Pilate told them.

"But he deserves to be crucified," the Jews objected, "and we have no right to do that!" This fulfilled what Jesus had previously said about how he was going to die. (John 12:32 - Section 207)

Pilate went back into his palace and ordered Jesus to be brought to him. Then he asked Jesus, "Are you the King of the Jews?"

"Is this your own idea, or have others accused me of making such a claim?" Jesus asked.

"Don't expect me to know all about what the Jews are thinking," Pilate said. "It was your people and your chief priests who have turned you over to me. So, what is it that you have done?"

Jesus answered, "My Kingdom is from another place. It does not belong to this world. If that were so, my servants would fight to prevent me from being arrested by the Jewish leaders."

"So, you are a King!" Pilate said.

"You have called me a king. And it is the truth: I was born into this world and came here for this one reason to announce the truth. Everyone who loves truth knows that what I teach is completely true."

"What is truth?" Pilate responded. But he gained no reply.

He then went back to the Jews who had gathered and announced to them, "I have found absolutely no basis for charging him of any crime!"

When the chief priests and elders of the people kept accusing Jesus, he kept silent and gave them no answer at all.

Pilate asked Jesus, "Haven't you heard their testimonies against you?" Again, Jesus made no reply to any of their charges. This greatly surprised the governor.

However, Jesus' accusers kept on insisting, "He has stirred up the people by his teaching all over the region of Judea. He began in the area of Galilee, and now he has come all the way here."

255. Pilate Sends Jesus to Herod Antipas for Further Trial - Luke 23:6-12

After hearing this, Pilate asked if Jesus was a Galilean. Since Galileans were under Herod's jurisdiction, Pilate sent Jesus to Herod who happened to be in Jerusalem at the time.

When Jesus was sent, Herod was delighted because he had heard so much about Jesus, and wanted to see him perform a miracle. He asked him one question after another, but Jesus didn't give him even a single answer. During that time, the priests and teachers of the Law kept shouting their accusations against him.

Losing patience, Herod and the soldiers began to make fun of Jesus. Dressing him in a royal robe, he sent him back to Pilate. Herod and Pilate had previously been enemies. On that day, they became friends.

256. Jesus Returns to Pilate Who Offers to Release a Prisoner - Matt 27:15-22; Mark 15:7-8; Luke 23:19-21; John 18:39-40

A man named Barabbas had been put into prison for murder and for taking part in an uprising in the city. It was the governor's custom during the Jewish Festival to release a prisoner who was chosen by the people. The crowd came to Pilate and requested for him to do what he usually did.

Pilate called together the chief priests, the people, and their rulers. He told them, "You have accused this man, Jesus, of leading a revolt. Now, I have carefully examined him in your presence and found him to be completely innocent of your charges against him. Herod has come to the same conclusion, and has sent him back here to me. It is obvious that he has done nothing deserving death. I will have him flogged and release him.

"According to your custom, I will release one prisoner during the Passover. Now, which one do you want me to release: Barabbas or Jesus, who is called the Messiah?" [Pilate knew very well that the Jewish leaders had arrested Jesus out of envy.]

And as Pilate sat on the judgment seat, his wife sent him a message. "Don't condemn that innocent man. Last night, I was warned by a terrible dream concerning him."

However, the chief priests and elders convinced the crowds to ask for Barabbas to be released, and for Jesus to be executed.

Again, the governor asked, "Which of these two do you want me to release? If you want me to, I'll release the 'King of the Jews'."

"No!" they shouted back, "Not that man! Let us have Barabbas!"

"If I let Barabbas go, then what shall I do with Jesus who is called the Messiah?" Pilate asked.

They all began to shout in unison, "Crucify him! Crucify him!"

Still desiring to release Jesus, Pilate appealed to them once again. But they kept on shouting, "Crucify him! Crucify him!"

257. The Roman Soldiers Mock Jesus - Matt 27:24-30; Mark 15:15-19; Luke 23:22-24; John 19:1-15

Pushed into a corner, Pilate had Jesus flogged with a whip laced with pieces of lead. Next, the governor's soldiers took him into their headquarters, and called in the whole battalion. They stripped him and dressed him in a scarlet robe. Then they twisted together a crown made of long, sharp thorns and put it on his head. They also put a stick in his right hand to be used as a scepter. Then they knelt in front of him, mocking and yelling, "Hail! King of the Jews!"

They also spat on him, slapped his face, then grabbed his stick and used it to strike him again and again on the head.

Once again, Pilate came out and announced to all the Jews that were gathered there, "I am bringing him out to you now, but I must tell you that I clearly find him not guilty!"

When Jesus came out wearing the crown of thorns and the purple robe, Pilate said, "Here is the man!"

As soon as the crowd saw him, they shouted, "Crucify him! Crucify him!"

For a third time, Pilate asked the people, "Why? What crime has this man committed? I have found no grounds at all for approving the death penalty. You take him and crucify him. As for me, I find him not guilty!"

However, the Jewish leaders answered, "According to our laws, he must die because he called himself the Son of God."

When Pilate heard this, he was more frightened than ever. He went back into the palace and asked Jesus, "Where did you come from?" But Jesus remained silent. "Are you refusing to speak to me?" Pilate asked. Jesus remained quiet. Then Pilate said, "Don't you realize that I have power either to set you free or to crucify you?"

Then Jesus responded, "You would have no power over me at all unless it were given to you from above. The one who delivered me into your hands is guilty of a greater offence."

From that time on, Pilate looked for a way to release Jesus. However, the Jewish leaders kept reminding him, "If you let this man go, you are no friend of Caesar. Anyone who claims to be a king is a rebel against Caesar's throne."

When they told him this, he decided to bring Jesus out. Pilate then sat down on the judgment seat at a place called "The Stone Pavement."
[It was called *Gabbatha* in Aramaic/Hebrew. It was about noon on the Preparation Day for the Passover.]

"Here is your king," Pilate said to the Jews.

But they kept shouting, "Away with him! Kill him! Crucify him!"

"Do you want me to crucify your king?" Pilate asked.

The chief priests said, "Caesar is our only king. We have no other."

Pilate finally realized that he was getting nowhere, and a riot was developing. He took a bowl of water and washed his hands in front of the crowd. Then Pilate declared, "I am innocent of this man's blood! You are responsible!"

All the people yelled back, "We take responsibility for his death! Let his blood be upon us and upon our children!"

The crowd kept shouting louder and louder, and kept calling for his death. Since Pilate wanted to please the crowd, he sentenced Jesus to die according to their demands. He then set Barabbas free, and handed over Jesus to be crucified.

258. A Procession Follows Jesus to Calvary - Matt 27:31; Mark 15:21; Luke 23:26-31; John 19:16-17

Pilate turned Jesus over to the Roman soldiers, and gave them orders to crucify him. When the soldiers grew tired of mocking him, they removed the royal robe and put back on his own clothes.

Jesus carried his own cross alone as they led him toward the place of crucifixion. [According to tradition, he was weakened by the terrible abuse he had suffered. Jesus fell under the load of the heavy crossbeam.] (John 19:16-17)

Simon was a man from Cyrene in North Africa who happened to be passing by on his way in from the country. The soldiers forced him to carry the heavy crossbeam in the procession behind Jesus. Simon had two sons named Alexander and Rufus.

Large crowds followed along behind Jesus. Among them were many sorrowing women. When Jesus saw their grief, he turned and spoke to them saying, "Daughters of Jerusalem, you don't have to weep for me; rather, cry for yourselves and for your children. The time will come when people will declare, 'How fortunate are the women who are childless, the wombs that have never given birth to a child and the breasts that have never fed a baby!'"

[As the prophet Hosea said:]

> *They will beg the mountains, 'Bury us!'*
> *and plead with the hills, 'Fall on us!' (Hosea 10:8)*

"For if people can do such things when the tree is fresh and green, what will they be capable of doing when it has dried up?" [Perhaps Jesus was implying: "If people can do this while Jesus was still on earth announcing his Kingdom, what will they be capable of doing when his Kingdom is under attack from many places?"]

259. Jesus Is Crucified - Matt 27:33-49; Mark 15:23-35; Luke 23:32-46; John 19:18-30; John 20:25; Col. 2:14

The procession reached a place called Golgotha, meaning Skull Hill. [The Romans called it *Calvaria* (Calvary).]

Then, the soldiers gave Jesus wine mixed with myrrh [bitter gall]. After tasting it, he wouldn't drink it.

There they nailed Jesus to the cross and crucified him.

Two other men, who were both criminals, were brought with him to be executed. One was on each side, and Jesus was in the middle.

The soldiers divided Jesus' clothes into four piles—one for each soldier. His undergarment was seamless. It was woven from top to bottom into one single piece. Rather than tearing it into four equal parts, the soldiers decided to cast lots to see who would get to keep it.

[As the Scriptures predicted:]

> *They are dividing my clothes among themselves*
> *and throwing dice for my garments." (Psalm 22:18)*

[This was written by David, author of Psalm 22. He lived about 1000 years before Jesus came.]

In doing this, the soldiers did not realize they had fulfilled prophecy!

Then Jesus prayed, "Father, forgive these people for they don't actually understand what they are really doing."

It was nine o'clock in the morning when they crucified Jesus. Pilate prepared a sign in Hebrew, Latin, and Greek. It read, "Jesus of

Nazareth, the King of the Jews." The place where Jesus was crucified was close to Jerusalem. For that reason, many Jews read the sign.

However, the Jewish chief priests objected to Pilate, saying, "You shouldn't write, 'The King of the Jews', but that he claimed to be King of the Jews."

Pilate answered, "What I have written, I have written."

The crowds that passed by the cross shouted insults. They wagged their heads and yelled, "So, you were going to destroy our Temple and rebuild it in three days? See if you can save yourself now! Yes, come on down from that cross if you really are the Son of God!"

In a similar way, the chief priests, the teachers of the Law, and the elders of the people also mocked him. They called out, "He saved other people. Now, he can't even save himself! He's the King of Israel, so he says! Well, let's see if he can come down from the cross. Then we'll believe in him. Does he really trust in God? Let's see if God wants to rescue him since he said, 'I am the Son of God'."

The soldiers also came closer and joined in ridiculing him.

One of the criminals hanging near him also threw insults. "Aren't you supposed to be the Messiah? Then why don't you save yourself? And while you're at it, save us too!"

But the other criminal rebuked him. "Don't you fear God, even while you are dying? We deserve to die for our crimes. This man hasn't done one thing wrong!"

Then he spoke to Jesus. "Remember me when you come into your Kingdom."

Jesus answered, "I promise you that today, you will be with me in paradise."

While all these things were happening, several women stood close to the cross. Among them were Mary, the mother of Jesus, her sister, Mary the wife of Clopas, and also Mary Magdalene. When Jesus looked down and saw his mother there along with John, the disciple he especially loved, he spoke to his mother, "Dear woman, here is your son." Then looking toward John, he said, "Here is your mother." And from that time on, John took Mary into his home.

At noon, a great darkness descended over the whole land until three in the afternoon. At that moment, Jesus called out loudly, *"Eloi, Eloi, lema sabachthani?"* This means, "My God, my God, why have you forsaken me?" (Psalm 22)

Some who were close enough to hear, commented, "Listen, I think he's calling for Elijah."

After a while, with Jesus aware that prophecies were being fulfilled, he said, "I am thirsty." (Psalm 69:21)

There was a jar of sour wine sitting nearby. They soaked a sponge in it, attached it to a branch from a hyssop plant, and raised it up to Jesus' lips. But some who were near said, "Just leave him alone. We want to see if Elijah will actually come and deliver him."

After Jesus had received the drink, he said, "It is finished." Then he called out loudly, "Father, I now trust my spirit into your hands."

After saying this, he bowed his head and took his last breath.

260. Unusual Events Follow the Death of Jesus - Matt 27:51-56; Mark 15:39-41; Luke 23:47-49

Just as Jesus' body shuddered and gave up the ghost, the sacred curtain in the Temple was torn in two from top to bottom*. There was a great earthquake; rocks were splitting apart as some tombs broke open. Many godly people who had previously died, came out of their tombs after the resurrection of Jesus. They entered the holy city of Jerusalem and appeared to many people. [*The Temple curtain protected the Holy of Holies. It was so sacred that only the High Priest could enter there once a year. The splitting of the curtain from top to bottom represents that through the blood of Jesus, the entrance to the dwelling place of God is now open. Forgiveness and salvation are now available to all who place their trust in the sacrifice of Jesus.]

One of the Roman captains—over one hundred soldiers—was standing in front of the cross, and saw how Jesus died. He exclaimed, "This was certainly a righteous man and truly the Son of God!" When those who had been guarding Jesus experienced the earthquake and everything that was happening, they were terrified. They were beating their chests in fear as they left.

Among the people who had been watching from a distance were many women who had followed Jesus from Galilee, caring for his needs. Among them were Mary Magdalene, Mary, the mother of James and Joseph, the mother of Zebedee's sons, James and John, and also Salome.

While in Galilee, all these women had followed him. There were also many other women there who had come up with him from Jerusalem. Everyone who knew him, including these women who had followed him from Galilee, stood at a distance watching everything that happened.

261. Jesus' Death Is Certified and His Body Delivered for Burial - Mark 15:42-45; Luke 23:50-51; John 19:31-38

It was Preparation Day, just before the annual special Passover Sabbath. [This does not refer to the regular weekly Sabbath.] Since the Jewish leaders did not want any bodies left on crosses during the Sabbath, they asked Pilate to verify the deaths of each one who had been crucified.

The soldiers came, as ordered, and broke the legs of one of the men who was crucified with Jesus. Then they did the same with the other man. However, when they came to Jesus, they discovered that he was already dead—they didn't need to break his legs. Instead, one of the soldiers took a spear and pierced his side. Then blood and water came flowing out.

The disciple, John, saw this and declared that he was absolutely certain that his report was true. He verified this so all might believe that these things really did happen in fulfillment of the Scriptures that say: "Not one of his bones will be broken. You may not break any of the bones of your sacrifice." (Exodus 12:46, Numbers 9:12, and Psalm 34:20)

"They will look on the one they have pierced." (Zechariah 12:10)

Joseph of Arimathea was one of the people who were expecting God's Kingdom to be revealed soon. He was a prominent member of the Jewish High Council. He had not agreed with their decision to take action against Jesus, but was secretly one of the Lord's followers. Joseph was also an honest, godly man. That evening, he went boldly to Pilate and asked to be given custody of the body of Jesus.

Pilate was surprised to learn that Jesus was already dead. He called in the Roman commander who had been assigned to the crucifixion, and asked him if it was true—if Jesus had already died. After learning from the officer that it was true, he then gave the body to Joseph.

262. The Body of Jesus Is Placed in the Tomb - Matt 27:60; Luke 23:53; John 19:39-42

Nicodemus accompanied Joseph. He was the same man who had previously visited Jesus one evening. (John 3:1-21) Nicodemus brought a mixture of about seventy-five pounds of myrrh and aloes to be used for anointing the body. After lowering the body from the cross, Joseph and Nicodemus wrapped it with strips of linen according to Jewish burial customs.

There was a garden near the location where the crucifixion had taken place, and in it was Joseph's new tomb that had never been used. (Isaiah 53:9) Because Preparation Day for the Jewish Passover was so near, and the tomb was so close, they laid Jesus in Joseph's own new tomb that had been cut out of a rock wall. Then they rolled a large stone in front of the tomb and left.

263. The Tomb Is Watched by Women and Guarded by Soldiers - Matt 27:61-66; Mark 15:47; Luke 23:55-56

Some women who had traveled with Jesus from Galilee, followed Joseph, and saw everything he and Nicodemus had done with the Lord's body. Mary Magdalene and the other Mary were sitting across from the tomb. [The other Mary mentioned here was probably the mother of James and John.]

The chief priests and Pharisees went to see Pilate. "Sir," they said, "while that deceiver was still alive, he predicted: 'After three days I will rise again.' You must give orders to secure the tomb through the third day. If not, his disciples might come and steal the body. If they do this and tell the people that he rose from the dead, their lie will make things even worse than ever."

[Jesus predicted that he would be in the tomb three days and three nights. A Friday crucifixion would result in only two days and two nights before his resurrection. It seems likely that Jesus must have been crucified and entombed on Thursday some time before sunset. The three days and three nights must have referred to Thursday, Friday, and Saturday. Sunday does not count as a day because Jesus was resurrected at the break of dawn on Sunday.]

Then Pilate gave the order, "Take a guard and make the tomb as secure as you can." They made it very secure, placing the Roman seal on the stone and also posted a guard.

The women left and prepared spices and perfumes; however, they obeyed the command to rest on the Sabbath day. [The Jewish Sabbath is from sundown Friday to sundown Saturday.]

264. Women Visit the Tomb, Followed Later by Peter and John ~ Matt 28:2-6; Mark 16:1-7; Luke 24:3-8

After the Sabbath—at sunrise on Sunday—Mary Magdalene, Mary, the mother of James and Salome, brought spices for anointing Jesus' body. Very early that morning as they were on their way to the tomb, they asked each other, "Who will help us roll the stone away from the tomb's entrance?"

Suddenly, there was a violent earthquake, just as an angel of the Lord came down from heaven. He went right to the tomb and rolled back the stone, then he sat on it. He appeared to be very bright, like lightning. Even his clothes were as white like snow. The guards at the tomb trembled with fear, then fell to the ground like dead men.

When the women recovered, they looked up and realized that the huge stone had already been rolled away. When they went into the tomb, the body of the Lord Jesus was missing. Just as they began to wonder what had happened, suddenly, two men dressed in clothing that shined like lightening, stood there next to them.

They told them, "Don't be alarmed. We know you are looking for Jesus of Nazareth, who was crucified. He isn't here because he has risen! Come and see where he was lying. Don't you remember what he told you while he was in Galilee: 'The Son of Man must fall into the hands of sinners to be crucified. But he will rise again on the third day.' Now, go tell his disciples, including Peter, that Jesus is going on ahead of you into Galilee. He will meet you there just as he instructed you." Upon hearing this, they remembered what he had told them.

265. The Chief Priests Devise a Plan to Cover Up the Resurrection ~ Matt 28:11-15

As the women were leaving, some of the guards returned to the chief priests to report everything that had been happening. They, in turn, met with the elders and devised a plan. They bribed the soldiers with a large sum of money to spread a lie.

"You must say, 'His disciples stole his body during the night while we were sleeping.' If the governor hears about it, we'll find a way to satisfy him so that you won't be blamed."

Then they accepted the money and carried out the plot. As a result, this story has been passed on among many of the Jews. Some even repeat it yet today.

266. The Truth about the Resurrection Begins to Dawn upon the Followers of Jesus - Mark 16:9-20; Luke 24:12; John 20:2-17

Meanwhile, Mary Magdalene ran to Simon Peter and to the other disciple that Jesus loved. [This refers to John.] She announced, "They took the Lord from the tomb, and we don't have any idea where they have put him!"

Peter and John immediately ran toward the tomb. John outran Peter and was the first to arrive. When John stooped to look in, he saw the strips of linen lying there that were used for wrapping the body. However, he didn't go inside.

When Peter arrived right after him, he went directly into the tomb. He also saw the strips of linen and the burial cloth that had covered the head of Jesus. It was lying in its place, separate from the linen strips.

As Peter left, he kept wondering what could have happened. [It is likely that Mary Magdalene followed Peter and John back toward the tomb. Many believe that the shroud that has been kept in the European city of Turin is that same burial cloth. On that cloth there is a permanent image of both the front and back of a crucified man.]

Finally, the other disciple, John, who had arrived first, also went inside. As he looked all around at the scene, he believed. Then these disciples returned to the place where they had been staying. [Mark 16:9-20 is not included in some early manuscripts. It is included here with the quotes from Matthew, Luke, and John.]

On that same Sunday morning, Jesus appeared first to Mary Magdalene, from whom he had previously cast out seven demons. She was standing outside the tomb weeping. Finally, she bent down to peer into the tomb, and saw two angels dressed in brilliant white clothing. They were sitting—one at the head and the other at the foot of the place where the body of Jesus had been lying.

The angels asked Mary, "Dear woman, why are you crying?"

"My Lord's body has been carried off," she said, "and I don't have any idea where to look for him." Just then, she turned around, and

Jesus was standing right there. But through her tears, she failed to recognize that it actually was Jesus.

Jesus asked her, "Dear woman, why are you weeping? Who are you looking for?"

Assuming he was the gardener, she answered, "Sir, if you have taken him somewhere, please tell me where you left him. I can make sure that his body is cared for properly."

Then Jesus answered, "Mary!"

Immediately, she turned and recognized him. She exclaimed in their familiar Aramaic language, *"Rabboni!"* [This means "Teacher."]

Jesus responded, "Mary, don't cling to me now, because I haven't yet ascended to my Father. Rather, go and find my brothers. Tell them, 'Our Lord told me to give you this message: I am ascending to my Father, who is also your Father, and to my God, who is also your God.'"

267. The Disciples Cannot Believe the Good News of the Resurrection - Matt 28:8-10; Mark 16:8-11; Luke 24:9-11

Meanwhile when the other women fled from the tomb, they didn't say anything to anyone at first. [The sequence of events here is based upon a careful examination of the evidence provided by the accounts given in the four Gospels.] They hurried away in shock, yet simultaneously, filled with great joy. While they were running to tell the disciples, suddenly Jesus met them and greeted them. They dropped to the ground in worship and grasped his feet.

Then Jesus spoke, "Don't be afraid. Go and tell our brothers to leave for Galilee. I will meet them there."

Mary Magdalene then found the disciples and gave them the great news: "I have seen the Lord!" she exclaimed. She repeated what Jesus had said to her. They had all been tearfully grieving. When she tried to tell them that Jesus was alive, and also about everything that had happened, it seemed to them just too good to be true.

After Mary Magdalene, Joanna, Mary, the mother of James, and the rest of the women had returned from the tomb, they told all this exciting news to the apostles, and to everyone they could find. Those who spoke this news to the apostles included others who had been with these same women. But the apostles didn't believe them. Their words seemed like foolish gossip.

268. Jesus Appears to Two Disciples Walking toward Emmaus - Mark 16:12-13; Luke 24:13-35

On that same day, two of his followers were walking to a village called Emmaus. It was located approximately seven miles from Jerusalem. As they were talking about all the recent events, suddenly Jesus came and began walking along with them. But by appearing in a different form, he kept them from recognizing who he was.

Jesus asked, "What have you been discussing along the way?"

They stopped as sadness showed on their faces. One of the men named Cleopas said to him, "You must be the only person visiting Jerusalem who hasn't heard about everything that has recently been happening there."

"What things?" Jesus asked.

"Everything that happened to Jesus—the man from Nazareth," they answered. "He was a great teacher and a mighty prophet who performed amazing miracles in the presence of God and all the people. The chief priests and the religious leaders handed him over to the Romans to be condemned to death and crucified.

"We were hoping he was actually the Messiah who would deliver the people of Israel. It has now been three days since all these things happened. On top of all of this, some of our women have been spreading amazing news that is very difficult to believe. They went early this morning to his tomb, but the body was missing. When they told us about this, they also claimed to have seen a vision of angels who announced that Jesus was alive. Some of our companions ran over to the tomb to see for themselves. Sure enough, his body really was gone, exactly as the women had said. They did not find Jesus."

Then Jesus spoke up and said to them, "How foolish you people are! Why are you so slow to believe everything the prophets have predicted in the Scriptures? Didn't they clearly say the Messiah would have to suffer all these things before he could enter into his glory?"

Then Jesus started with Moses, and continued discussing with them the writings of all the prophets. He explained all the things that had been written about himself in the Scriptures.

As he was finishing his teaching, they were nearing their destination, the village of Emmaus. Jesus appeared to be traveling on, but they begged him, "Please stay overnight with us, since it is already getting quite late." He agreed and went home with them.

While he was sitting at the table with them, he took some bread and thanked his Father for it. He broke it and started to share it with each one. Just as he began to do this, their eyes were suddenly opened to recognize him, but he instantly vanished from their sight. Then they asked each other, "Weren't our hearts burning within us while he was sharing the Scriptures with us as we walked along the road?"

They leapt up from the table and went back to Jerusalem. When they arrived, they found the eleven disciples meeting together, along with other followers.

Some were saying, "It's true! The Lord really has risen from the dead and he actually did appear to Simon Peter." Then the two who had invited him to stay with them, told about what had happened to them on their way. They told how they suddenly recognized Jesus while he was breaking bread with them. However, the others could not believe them either.

269. Jesus Appears to the Disciples When Thomas Is Absent - Mark 16:14; Luke 24:37-42; John 20:19-25

On Sunday evening, when the disciples were assembled with the doors locked because they feared the Jewish leaders, Jesus appeared and stood in their midst and greeted them saying, "May peace be with you!"

They were startled and afraid that he might be a ghost. Then Jesus said, "Why are you so upset and so filled with doubts? Look at me. See my hands and my feet. I am really here! Just touch me! Look—a ghost doesn't have flesh and bones like I have." Then the disciples could no longer contain their joy at seeing the Lord.

Although they were filled with excitement and amazement, they could scarcely believe their eyes. Then he asked them, "Do you have anything here for me to eat?" They brought him a piece of broiled fish, and he ate it right there in front of them all.

While they were all eating together, he scolded them for their lack of faith, and the way they had stubbornly refused to believe the witnesses who had seen him after his resurrection.

Once again, Jesus blessed them saying, "Receive my peace! Just as the Father has sent me, I am now sending you." Then he breathed upon them saying, "Receive the Holy Spirit. Whenever you forgive someone's sins, they are forgiven. If you do not forgive them, they will not be forgiven."

One of the Twelve, Thomas (also known as Didymus), was not with the other disciples when Jesus came to them. They told him, "We have seen the Lord!"

But Thomas answered, "I won't believe it unless I see the nail marks in his hands with my own eyes, and then I put my finger where the nails were, and also put my hand on the wound in his side."

270. Jesus Appears Again to the Disciples When Thomas is Present - John 20:26-29

The following week, the disciples were again together in the house. This time Thomas was there with them. Even though the doors were locked, Jesus stood among them and said, "Receive my peace!" Then he told Thomas, "Place your finger here. See my hands. Touch the wound in my side. Simply believe and stop doubting!"

"You are my Lord and my God!" Thomas exclaimed.

Jesus told him, "You are able to believe now, because of what you have seen. However, there will be many who will believe without ever having seen me. They will receive a special blessing."

271. Jesus Meets His Disciples by the Sea and Restores Peter - John 21:1-24

On another occasion, by the Sea of Galilee, Jesus appeared again to some of his disciples. This is how it happened: Simon Peter, Thomas (nicknamed the Twin), Nathanael, from the town of Cana in Galilee, James and John (the sons of Zebedee), and two other disciples were together. [Altogether, there were seven disciples by the Sea of Galilee.]

Simon Peter announced, "I'm going fishing."

They all said, "We'll come, too." So they left in the boat, but after fishing all night, they had not caught even one single fish.

At daybreak, Jesus was standing on the beach. However, from the boat the disciples could not recognize him.

Then Jesus called to them, "Fellows, did you catch anything?"

"No," they answered, "We have caught nothing."

Then he told them, "Throw the net to the right side of the boat, and you will catch some." And after they did what he told them to do, the net was so weighted down with fish, they couldn't even drag it into the boat.

Then John (the disciple Jesus loved) told Peter, "It is the Lord!" When Peter heard this, he wrapped his outer garment around himself, because he had taken off most of his cloths while he fished. Then

Peter jumped into the water, and waded toward the shore. The others followed in the boat, dragging the net filled with fish. The shore was only about a hundred yards away. When they landed, they saw a charcoal fire with fish cooking on it, and there was also some bread.

Jesus then told them, "Bring your catch of fish over here."

Peter climbed aboard and took hold of the net, then dragged it to the shore. Even though there were one hundred and fifty-three big fish, the net was not damaged.

Then Jesus invited them, saying, "Come have some breakfast."

Not one of the disciples dared ask, "Who are you?" It was obvious to them that it was the Lord.

Jesus came over, and served them some bread along with the fish. This was the third time Jesus appeared to his disciples after he had been raised from the dead.

After breakfast, Jesus asked Simon Peter, "Simon, son of John, do you love me more than these?"

"Yes, Lord." Peter said, "You know how much I love you."

Jesus replied, "Feed my lambs."

Jesus then repeated the question, "Simon, son of John, do you truly love me?"

Again, Peter answered, "Yes, Lord, you know that I love you."

"Take care of my sheep," Jesus commanded.

A third time Jesus asked, "Simon, son of John, do you love me?"

Peter felt hurt that Jesus would ask him this question three times.

"Lord, there is nothing you don't know; you surely know that I love you!"

Jesus said, "Feed my sheep. I tell you truthfully, as a young man, you did whatever you wanted to do. You could dress yourself and go wherever you wanted to go. However, when you are old, you will reach out your hands and others will dress you and take you somewhere you won't want to go." Jesus told him this to let him know how he would glorify God at the time of his death. Then Jesus said to him, "Follow me!"

Peter looked around and saw the disciple Jesus loved (John, the same one who had leaned over and asked Jesus during supper, "Lord, who will betray you?") Peter asked, "Lord, what about him?"

Jesus responded, "If I plan for him to live until I return, why does that concern you?"

Then Jesus told Peter, "You must follow me!"

This discussion started the rumor that kept spreading among the believers—that this disciple (John) was not going to die. But that's not at all what Jesus meant. He simply said, "If I want him to remain alive until I come back, what should that matter to you?"

This very disciple (John) is a witness to the events recorded in his own account. He knows that this written record is completely true and accurate.

John, who was one of the twelve disciples said: "Jesus did many other things, as well. I don't believe the whole world could contain all the books, if every one of his deeds were to be written down."

[The deeds of Jesus are continuing on in His Church through all the years since his ascension. The Holy Spirit empowers the varied and abundant work of Jesus. He still teaches through the written and spoken Word of God. He still transforms lives and performs miracles all over the World, even today.]

272. Jesus Proclaims The Great Commission in Galilee - Matt 28:16-20; Mark 16:15-18; John 20:30-31; 21:25

The eleven disciples traveled toward Galilee, and were on their way to the mountain where Jesus had told them to meet him. When they arrived and saw him, they worshiped him, but there were some that had doubts. [In addition to the eleven, there were probably other followers, among whom were doubters.]

However, Jesus assured them, "I have been given complete authority both on earth and in heaven. Therefore, you must go throughout the whole world announcing the Good News. You must encourage people in all the nations of the world to have faith in me, and to become my followers. Baptize all those who place their trust in me, in the name of the Father and the Son and the Holy Spirit. Also, teach them to carry out all the commands and instructions I have given to you.

"Each one who has faith in me and is baptized will be saved; anyone who rejects me will be condemned. Those who believe will accomplish these miraculous signs through the power of my name: some will cast out demons; some will speak new (unlearned) languages; some will be able to safely handle snakes. If they are forced to drink deadly poison, it will not harm them. When they place their hands upon those who are sick or wounded, they will be healed."

Jesus performed many other miracles that have never been recorded. If everything he did and continues doing—along with all the truth he spoke, or will inspire to be spoken—should be written down in all the world's languages, it is unlikely the world would not be able to hold all the books that would be written. However, the accounts that have been completed offer assurance that Jesus is truly the promised Messiah and the Son of God.

273. The Disciples Return to Jerusalem Where Jesus Meets Them before Ascending - Mark 16:19; Luke 24:44-53; Acts 1:3-12; 1 Cor. 15:6-8

During the forty days after his crucifixion, from time to time he appeared and gave convincing evidence to his followers that he was truly alive. On one occasion, he appeared to over five hundred of the spiritual brothers and sisters who believed in him. He also appeared to James, then later to all the apostles. During that time, he spoke to them about the Kingdom of God. Last of all, he appeared to Saul. [Saul would become known as the Apostle Paul.] He seemed like one who was born at the wrong time. [This was because he was not chosen until after Jesus ascended to the Father.]

Jesus explained to them, "During the time I physically lived among you, I told you that all the prophecies written about me in the Law of Moses and the prophets and in the Psalms, must be fulfilled."

He helped them understand the prophetic Scriptures. They had predicted that the Messiah was destined to suffer and die. Then on the third day, he would rise from the dead. He explained that the Good News of salvation, in the name of Jesus, must be proclaimed with authority to all the nations of the world, starting in Jerusalem. He also declared, "I have appointed you to be my witnesses concerning all these things."

On another occasion, while Jesus was eating with them, he explained, "Just as my Father promised, I will soon send you the Holy Spirit, and he will represent me." He also gave them this command: "You must remain right here in Jerusalem until the Holy Spirit comes and fills you with power from above."

Then they all gathered around Jesus and asked, "Lord, is this the time when you will transform Israel once again into a great Kingdom?"

Jesus answered, "You are not destined to know ahead of time the whole sequence and all the details concerning future events. The Father, in his authority, has established them all. However, when you receive the Holy Spirit, you will receive power to represent me in Jerusalem, Judea, Samaria, and to the very ends of the earth."

After leading them to a location near Bethany, he raised his hands and blessed them. As he did so, right before their eyes, he was lifted up toward heaven. A cloud covered him just as he was departing. Then he entered heaven and sat down at the right hand of God, the Father.

As he ascended, his followers kept straining their eyes toward the sky. Suddenly, two men wearing white stood right next to them.

"Men of Galilee," they said, "why are you staying here watching the sky? This same Jesus you saw rise up to heaven, will one day come back again just as you saw him go."

Then the Lord's followers left the Mount of Olives, and joyfully walked a little over a half mile back into Jerusalem. [That distance was considered to be a legitimate Sabbath Day's walk.]

They were often found in the Temple, praising God, and the Lord's disciples also went out and proclaimed the Good News everywhere. The Spirit of the Lord was present with them, confirming their message with many miraculous signs.

274. Jesus Continues to Reveal Himself - Acts 9:1-19; 22:17-21; 23:11; 26:16-18; 28:11-31; 2 Cor. 12:7-10; Gal. 1:11-12; Heb. 13:8; Rev. 22:12-20

[The Good News about Jesus, kept spreading rapidly by means of the Holy Spirit's power, working through people possessing faith in Christ. But the Jewish leaders saw this as a growing threat against their authority to lead the people.]

A certain man named Saul kept making murderous threats against the followers of the Lord. One day, as he was approaching the city of Damascus, a light suddenly flashed down from the sky, and he fell to the ground. Then he heard a voice say to him, "Saul, Saul, why are you trying to persecute me?"

Saul responded, "Lord, who are you?"

"I am Jesus," the voice replied, "and you are trying to persecute me. I have come now to appoint you to become my servant. You will become a witness of what I am now revealing to you, and what I will show you in the future. I will rescue you from your own Jewish people, and also from the Gentile people in many lands. I will send you to them that you might open their eyes to the truth. You will show them how to turn from darkness to light.

"When they trust in me, their sins will be forgiven and God's power will deliver them from Satan's traps. Then they will be welcomed into God's family. They will be among those who are dedicated to me and who have trusted me to make them holy. Now, stand up and go into the city where you will be told what to do next."

Then Saul stood up from the ground. When he tried to open his eyes, he realized that he had become blind. He could see nothing. Others came to his aid and led him into the city of Damascus. For three days, while he was still blind, he fasted both food and drink.

There was a believer named Ananias, living there in Damascus. In a vision, the Lord spoke to him, saying, "Ananias!"

"Speak Lord," he answered.

The Lord instructed him, "Go find the home of a disciple named Judas. He lives on Straight Street. Ask for a man from the city of Tarsus. His name is Saul, and he has been praying. He has seen a vision of you coming and laying your hands upon him to restore his sight. I have chosen him to become my instrument. He will announce the power of my name among the Gentile nations, and to their leaders as well. He will also be my witness to the people of Israel. I will show him that he will often suffer persecution because of his loyalty to my name."

Ananias followed the Lord's instructions. He found Saul, then placed his hands on him and blessed him. Instantly, something like scales fell from Saul's eyes and his sight was restored. Saul arose and was baptized. After eating, he began to gain back his strength.

[With the passing of time, Saul became known as the Apostle Paul. The following is the report he gave:]

"After I came back to Jerusalem, I went into the Temple to pray. There I fell into a trance and saw a vision of the Lord. He said this to me, 'Hurry! Leave Jerusalem quickly! The people here will not accept your witness about me. Go! Soon I will send you far away to announce the Good News about me to the Gentiles.'"

[On a later occasion, Paul said this to the people in Galatia], "Brothers and sisters, I want you to understand that this Good News I am bringing to you did not come from other people. No mere human taught me these things. To the contrary, Jesus Christ himself revealed this message directly to me.

"I have received tremendous revelations from God. I could have easily become conceited because of this. But the Lord gave me a thorn in my body, like a messenger from Satan. It has tormented me so much, that three times I begged the Lord to deliver me from this terrible thorn. However, the Lord's answer was, 'My merciful help is enough to see you through. My power is perfected in your weakness.' Now, for the sake of Christ, I celebrate weakness, insults, hardships, persecutions, and all kinds of difficulties. The truth is that when I know how weak I am, then his strength makes me strong."

[Later in Paul's life, when he was facing serious threats from unbelievers, he gave this account]: "The Lord stood near me and said, 'Be courageous! You testified about me faithfully in Jerusalem. Soon, you must also testify in Rome.'"

[Luke wrote what actually happened. The following is a summary of what he wrote, found in Acts 28:11-23:]

"We set out to sea in a ship from Alexandria. After spending the winter on an island, we finally reached Rome." Then Paul was permitted to live by himself with only one soldier guarding him. For two years Paul lived in his own rented house. There, he welcomed everyone who visited him. He freely announced the Kingdom of God and boldly taught people about the Lord Jesus Christ. The rest of the New Testament also contains many letters that Paul wrote to some of the early Christian churches."

[Meanwhile, after the Romans had sentenced the Apostle John to stay on the Island of Patmos, Jesus inspired him to write Revelations, the last book in the Bible. In it, Jesus declared the following:]

"Be prepared and alert. I am coming soon! I will bring my reward with me. I will reward each person based upon what they have done. I am the *Alpha* and the *Omega* [the A and the Z], the First and the Last, the Beginning and the End.

"How happy are those who wash their robes.* In this way, they prepare themselves to receive the right to enter the gates of the heavenly city where they will see the tree of life for themselves. Those left outside will include all who refuse to receive the Lord's cleansing from having engaged in occult magic, sexual immorality, murder, idolatry, and from embracing lies and all kinds of falsehood." [*Washing their robes meant turning away from ungodly living by faith, and trusting the Holy Spirit to cleanse them.]

275. God's Message Ends with a New Beginning - 2nd Peter 3:13, Revelation 20:11, 21:4-27, 22:1-21

[The passages that follow from the Book of Revelation include only some from the conclusion of that book. Every reader of the Bible should read the whole Book of Revelation at least once. The book ends with a warning to those who fail to do that.]

John then heard a shout from God's throne, saying, "God is now living with his own people! The old world order, along with its troubles and sorrows, is forever gone. Everything is completely new. I, Jesus, am the beginning and the ending of all things. I will freely give the satisfying water of life to all who are thirsty. But all evildoers and doubters who reject me are doomed to the Lake of Fire. That is the second death."

Then John was carried in the spirit to a high mountaintop where he was able to actually see the New Jerusalem. The Holy City was descending from heaven. It was shaped like a cube with a dimension of 1400 miles. This beautiful city was protected by a wall with three pearly gates on each of its four sides. An angel guarded each gate. The whole city was built out of gold and precious stones.

Jesus and the Lord God himself shine upon the holy city. There is absolutely no need for the sun or moon.

There is a beautiful, clear River of Life flowing out from God's throne. On each side of the river there are beautiful Trees of Life. They continually produce fresh fruit each month.

"I, Jesus, have sent my angel to make known to each one of you this witness that I am revealing to my churches. I am both King David's Root and his Offspring. I am the Brilliant Morning Star.

"The Holy Spirit and my Bride, who is my Church, say, 'Come!' Also, let everyone who hears this message say, 'Come!' Let every person who is thirsty for peace, come. Let all who have the desire, drink freely from the water of life."

All who receive this book's revelation of Jesus must be warned that if anyone adds to the prophetic message of this book, God will add to that person the plagues described in this book. Likewise, anyone who removes truth from this book, God will remove that person's share in the Tree of Life and in the Holy City described in this book.

Jesus, who testifies concerning all these things, has also said this:

"I am surely coming soon!"

[John responds:] "Amen. Maranatha! Even so, come, Lord Jesus!"
[*Maranatha* means "Come, Lord Jesus!" in Aramaic and Hebrew. The author of the book of Hebrews declares the following truth:] "Jesus Christ is the same yesterday and today and forever!" (Hebrews 13:8)

Compiler's Parting Note:

[The deeds of Jesus have continued through the years since his ascension. The Holy Spirit still carries on the varied and abundant works of Jesus, even to this day. He still teaches through the written and spoken Word of God, transforms lives and performs multitudes of miracles all over the World. AMEN!]

INDEX OF SECTION TITLES

Section #

37. Jesus Finds Fulfillment Ministering to the Samaritan Woman
38. Many Samaritans in Sychar Come to Faith in Jesus
39. Jesus Arrives to Minister in Galilee
40. Jesus Preaches the Message of the Kingdom of God
41. Jesus Heals a Child from Capernaum
42. The Ministry of Jesus Is Rejected in Nazareth, His Hometown
43. When Jesus Is Opposed at Nazareth, He Makes Capernaum His Headquarters
44. As a Sign of His Authority to Teach, Jesus Heals a Demon-possessed Man
45. Jesus Heals Peter's Mother-in-Law and Others
46. Jesus Tours Galilee and Judea with Simon Peter and Others
47. Jesus Calls Some Fishermen to Fish for People
48. Jesus Cleanses a Leper and Much Publicity Follows
49. Jesus Forgives and Heals a Paralyzed Man
50. Jesus Calls Matthew (also known as Levi) to Follow Him
51. Jesus Attends a Banquet at Matthew's House
52. Jesus Illustrates How Things Have Been Changed by the Arrival of the Messiah and His Kingdom
53. Jesus Heals a Lame Man on the Sabbath Day
54. The Jews Seek to Kill Jesus for Healing on the Sabbath and for Claiming God as His Father
55. Jesus Presents Evidence of His Equality with the Father
56. Jesus Answers the Criticism against His Disciples for Picking Grain on the Sabbath
57. Jesus Heals a Man's Shriveled Hand on the Sabbath
58. Jesus Withdraws to the Sea of Galilee, but a Great Multitude Follows Him
59. Jesus Appoints Twelve Apostles
60. Jesus Teaches His Followers on a Mountainside
61. Jesus Promises Happiness to the Subjects of His Kingdom, But Woes to Those Who Are Self-Sufficient
62. Jesus Announces the Responsibility of the Kingdom People: "They Are Salt and Light"
63. Jesus Explains How the Kingdom of God Relates to the Law and Righteousness
64. Jesus Teaches about Anger
65. Jesus Teaches about Reconciliation
66. Jesus Teaches about Adultery, Lust, Divorce, and Hell
67. Jesus Teaches on Keeping One's Word
68. Jesus Teaches about Merciful Behavior
69. Jesus Teaches about Love for All Persons

129. Jesus Heals a Demon-Possessed Boy, then Rebukes Those Who Lack Faith
130. Jesus Again Predicts His Suffering, Death, and Resurrection
131. Jesus Answers a Question about Paying the Temple Taxes
132. Jesus Teaches about the Unity of Those Who Trust in Him
133. Jesus Explains the Urgency of Making Peace and How to Go About Doing It
134. Jesus Tells a Story about an Unforgiving Servant
135. The Lord's Half Brothers Accuse Jesus of Lacking Boldness
136. Jesus Travels through Samaria among People Despised by the Jews
137. Jesus Requires His Followers to Be Completely Committed
138. People Have Mixed Reactions to Jesus' Teachings and Miracles at the Festival of Shelters
139. The Pharisees Fail to Arrest Jesus and Jesus Offers Living Water to All Who Believe in Him
140. Jesus Forgives a Woman Caught in Adultery
141. Jesus is Criticized for Claiming to Be the "Light of the World"
142. Jesus Calls People to Believe He Is the Christ (or Messiah)
143. Jesus Teaches Freedom through Truth, then Calls Himself the Eternal "I Am"
144. Jesus Sends Seventy-Two Followers Ahead of Him to Minister
145. Jesus Pronounces Woe upon Towns Where He Had Ministered
146. The Seventy-Two Witnesses Report Back and Jesus Rejoices
147. Jesus Tells about a Good Samaritan
148. Jesus Visits the Home of Mary and Martha
149. Jesus Teaches How to Pray and the Importance of Perseverance in prayer
150. An Accusation against Jesus of Blasphemy Leads to Teaching about Satan's Kingdom
151. The Jewish Leaders Request a Sign, but Jesus Offers Only the Sign of Jonah
152. Jesus Pronounces "Woes" upon the Pharisees While Eating with One of Them
153. Jesus Declares that Shameful Secrets Will Be Exposed, and Kingdom Secrets Must Be Proclaimed
154. Jesus Warns about Greed and Trusting in Wealth
155. Jesus Warns His Followers to Be Ready for the Coming of the Son of Man
156. Jesus Predicts Divisions as a Result of His Ministry
157. Jesus Admonishes People about the Importance of Discerning the Times

158. Jesus Teaches That Tragedy Does Not Prove Greater Guilt, but All Must Repent or Perish
159. Jesus Heals on the Sabbath, Then Teaches the Importance of Mercy
160. Jesus Heals a Man Who Had Been Born Blind
161. People React to the Healing of the Blind Man
162. The Pharisees Cross-Examine a Blind Man, then Shut Him out of the Temple
163. Jesus Makes Himself Known to the Blind Man
164. The Pharisees Blind Themselves to the Truth
165. Jesus Describes the Good Shepherd and His Sheep
166. The Jews Are Divided over the Teachings of Jesus
167. The Jews Again Attempt to Stone Jesus or at Least Arrest Him for Claiming to Be God.
168. People Follow Jesus Beyond the Jordan River
169. Jesus Responds to Questions About Salvation and Entering the Kingdom of God
170. Jesus Affirms Control over His Own Destiny and Grieves over Jerusalem
171. Jesus Heals a Man with Dropsy on the Sabbath at the Home of a Pharisee
172. Jesus Offers Examples of Humility and Honor
173. Jesus Recommends Making the Needy Your Dinner Guests and Tells about a Great Banquet
174. Jesus Urges People to Consider the Cost of True Discipleship
175. Jesus Tells Stories to Vindicate Association with Sinners
176. Jesus Tells about a Lost Sheep That Represents a Repentant Sinner
177. Jesus Tells about a Lost Coin
178. Jesus Tells about a Son Who Left Home, Then Squandered His Inheritance While His Brother Stayed
179. Jesus Tells about a Shrewd Manager
180. Jesus Warns Against Greed, Then Speaks About the Good News and the Law
181. Jesus Tells About the Rich Man Who Ignored the Beggar, Lazarus
182. Jesus Teaches About Childlikeness
183. Jesus Again Speaks of a Lost Sheep to Show the Value of a Child
184. Jesus Teaches About Persevering in Forgiveness
185. Jesus Talks About Faith and Service
186. Jesus Raises Lazarus from the Dead

187. The Jewish Sanhedrin (Council) Plans to Put Jesus to Death
188. Jesus Heals Ten Lepers, Then Answers a Question About the Kingdom of God
189. Jesus Illustrates Prayer by Telling About a Persevering Widow
190. Jesus Compares the Prayers of a Pharisee and a Tax Collector
191. The Pharisees Ask Jesus a Controversial Question About Divorce
192. Jesus Teaches That the Kingdom of God Belongs to Children and to Those Who Are Childlike
193. A Rich Ruler Chooses Earthly Wealth Over Eternal Life
194. Jesus Promises Great Rewards to Those Who Leave Everything to Follow Him
195. Jesus Tells About a Landowner Who Paid Generous Wages
196. Jesus Again Predicts His Own Resurrection from the Dead
197. Jesus Reveals the Pathway to True Greatness
198. Jesus Brings Salvation to the Household of Zacchaeus
199. Jesus Teaches the Need for Faithfulness while Waiting for the Kingdom to Arrive
200. Jesus Heals Blind Bartimaeus and His Companion
201. Jesus Arrives in Bethany
202. Mary Anoints Jesus for Burial at a Celebration in His Honor
203. Jesus Enters Jerusalem As the Triumphant Servant King
204. Jesus Weeps over a City That Is Divided Concerning Him
205. Jesus Curses a Fig Tree with Leaves but No Fruit
206. Jesus Cleanses the Temple During the Passover Season
207. Jesus Answers Some Greeks by Reminding Them of the Law of Life Springing from Death
208. Jesus Withdraws from the Crowds, Then Speaks about Faith and Unbelief
209. Jesus Uses the Withered Fig Tree to Teach About Faith
210. The Religious Leaders Challenge the Authority of Jesus
211. Jesus Illustrates Responsibility and Faithfulness
212. The Pharisees and Herodians Ask a Trap Question about Taxes
213. The Sadducees Try to Trap Jesus Concerning Eternal Life
214. An Expert in Jewish Law Asks Jesus about the Greatest Commandment
215. Jesus Challenges His Critics with a Question of His Own: "Why Does David Address the Messiah as Lord?"
216. Jesus Pronounces Woes upon the Religious Leaders
217. Jesus Expresses Compassion and Pity for Jerusalem
218. Jesus Commends a Poor Widow for Putting All She Has in the Offering

From NELLIE FENWICK

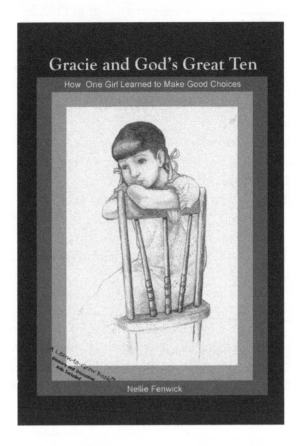

Teaching the Love of God's Word

Twelve-year-old Wilbur struggled to be the heroic "good boy" that everyone expected a pastor's son to be. Gracie, his younger sister, couldn't understand why it was so hard for her big brother to make the right choices...until she was faced with some difficult choices herself.

This delightful story, set during the Great Depression, not only teaches the virtues of God's great ten commandments, which Gracie learned to value from one challenge after another, but shows that understanding, love, family fidelity, and togetherness bring more fulfillment than the attainment of material possessions.

(A **Learn-to-Grow Book**, complete with glossary and discussion aids)

Available at Port Hole Publishing
www.PortHolePublishing.org

Inspirational Reading
From Michael MacIntosh

Falling in Love with the Bible . . .

Reveals the Bible as a personal message from God to every person, and helps create a paradigm shift in the heart from a sense of obligation to read the Bible, to a happy realization that reading God's word is an incredible privilege.

Falling in Love with Prayer . . .

Few things change a person's life like falling in love. And now, one of our nation's most dynamic pastors will help readers fall in love with prayer--and with their Creator!

Mike MacIntosh offers personal experiences . . . and powerfully directed biblical truths about the power of prayer. This book is designed to be enjoyable, informative and applicable and is a true call to intimacy with God. Be prepared to be changed forever!

Look for these and other books by Mike at
PortHolePublishing.org